Essay
Non-Fiction Reflections Upon the Self and Society

A Reader

Anna Tomasino
Hunter College

KENDALL/HUNT PUBLISHING COMPANY
4050 Westmark Drive   Dubuque, Iowa 52002

Cover photograph by Thom Taylor

TABLE OF CONTENTS

Chapter I   *Expressing the Self: Freewriting and Journaling*

Chapter II   *Reflecting upon Childhood and Children*

Chapter III   *Educating the Self*

Chapter IV   *Contemplating Career and Work*

Chapter V   *Entertaining the Self*

Chapter VI   *Connecting With Our Natural World*

Chapter VII   *Situating the Self: Society and Politics*

Preface to the Instructor

The gifted writers in <u>Essay 33: Non-Fiction Reflections Upon the Self and Society</u> share thought provoking insights and experiences of the self in relation to: self-expression, childhood, education, career, nature and society. The readings are effective in engaging the attention of students and stimulating critical thinking. The diverse selections are appropriate for all writers at any level—beginning (100), intermediate (200), and advanced (300) courses. I have found that the difference for each level (100, 200, and 300) is reflected in class discussion and more sophisticated written responses (journal entries and essays). For example, in my 120 (100 level Freshman Composition course) the students respond well to Alice Walker's "Beauty: When the Other Dancer is the Self." Usually, the students respond to the injury, the issue of self-esteem, and often compare their own experiences to that of Walker's. In my 300 level courses, more advanced students play closer attention to stylistic details—Walker's shift in tenses, concrete details, repetition, and imagery. Because it is a good essay, both my 100 and 300 classes are always engaged.

The critical thinking questions at the end of each essay encourage a close reading of the text, guiding students to think critically and analyze theme, structure, style, tone and other stylistic tools. The writing assignments are geared to lead them from critical reading to writing, from the public to the private.

Students often ask W*hat will I write about?* insisting, *I have nothing interesting to say.* So, to show by example, I have included creative writing that covers a wide range of topics—including: a notebook-"On Keeping a Notebook"/Joan Didion; a family meal-"The Art of Eating Spaghetti"/Russell Baker; bed-wetting-"An Episode of Bed-wetting"/George Orwell; a moth-"The Death of the Moth"; brown wasps-"The Brown Wasps"/Loren Eiseley; and so on. By example, the readings show students that anything—even a simple, seemingly trivial subject, such as a moth—can be an analogy to life and energy and death and defeat.

Students will see, by example, that they can write about any experience, that *yes*, it can be interesting, and that they have a unique experience *worthy* to share—an experience *worthy* of communicating in writing, *worthy* of recapturing for themselves. As Russell Baker discovers in "The Art of Eating Spaghetti": "I wanted to put it down simply for my own joy . . . It was a moment I wanted to recapture and hold for myself. I wanted to relive the pleasure of an evening at New Street."

Whether it is to re-create a moment for themselves or to understand the past, students will see the rich depository of material in the essays and by extension—in their own lives. Most importantly, through a close reading of the text they will discover the various tools writers use to create their craft. Hopefully, in the process, they will see the skill and vitality of good writing and learn not only about others, but also about themselves.

The carefully chosen 33 selections are manageable for a 32 week writing course. I have tried to compile a selective group of material that has worked for me and several of my colleagues at Hunter College, City University of New York. The essays are rich and effective for a writing course, where the focus is on writing and reading.

At the end of each selection are questions, and at the end of each chapter a section "Relating the Authors' Ideas." Here, the student will be challenged to interpret and compare the works of the respective chapter. Although the chapters are thematically organized, the writing assignments contain suggestions for essays in a variety of rhetorical modes.

At the beginning of each selection is a quotation that can serve as a freewriting exercise and/or a starting point for journal entries. Often, in class, I start the discussion with a short freewrite. I ask students to write about the quote. Frequently, students find themselves not only exploring personal thoughts, but making connections to the essay. It is an effective segue to class discussion.

Writing is an exciting communication among minds. I hope that you and your students have as much fun learning and discovering as I have with my students. Enjoy the selections!

Features

Introduction: The book begins with an introduction to the text.

Chapter Introductions: Each chapter begins with an introduction that thematically ties the selections.

Freewriting Quotations to Serve as Writing Prompts: Each of the 33 selections is preceded by quotations that are thought provoking freewriting prompts.

Selections: The selections reflect the diversity and various interests of the following writers: Joan Didion, Julia Cameron, Natalie Goldberg, Alice Walker, Scott Russell Sanders, George Orwell, Maxine Hong Kingston, Jamaica Kincaid,

Malcolm X, Rebecca Lawson, Sue Ribner, Russell Baker, William H. Honan, John Tarkov, Virginia Woolf, Bonnie Smith-Yackel, Ruth Sidel, Richard Selzer, E.B. White, Pat Mora, Elizabeth Kolbert, Stephen King, Loren Eiseley, Louise Erdrich, Annie Dillard, William F. Buckley, Jr., Lance Morrow, Edward I. Koch, Peter Tomasino, and Martin Luther King, Jr.

Biographical Information: Each selection includes brief biographical information about the author.

Questions Following Each Selection: Thinking Critically Questions to guide students to think critically by exploring theme, style, and other issues; and *Writing Assignments* designed to encourage students to explore issues in the text as well as their own personal observations, experiences, and reflections.

Relating the Authors' Ideas: At the end of each chapter, there is a series of thought-provoking questions that will lead students to compare and contrast the ideas of the respective chapter.

Index. For quick access to titles and authors.

Acknowledgments

My heart is filled with gratitude to:

Each of the writers in the text, they are the heart of the book;

Sue Saad at Kendall/Hunt who first approached me with the project and who has been consistently available for me. Her graciousness, support and accessibility are appreciated;

Colleen Zelinsky, whose tireless effort in acquiring the rights to the essays has made it possible for me to include the material;

Stefani DeMoss, whose professionalism and assistance has guided me throughout the production of the book;

Angela Shafer, who assisted me during Stefani's brief maternity leave;

Evelyn Melamed, who has been my mentor, friend and angel;

My colleagues at Hunter College, CUNY, who have throughout the years shared their successes, materials and experience;

Rebecca Lawson, my colleague and friend, whose intelligence and friendship has been a valuable asset in my life; I am grateful for her contributions to the book—her essay, "The Swimming Lesson" as well as questions for the story;

Sue Ribner, a wonderful colleague and friend. We share an office together and she has been very supportive and encouraging. I am proud to include her essay, "The Language Lesson";

Thom Taylor, for contributing his beautiful photograph to the book cover;

Lew Meyers, my mentor in English 201, his feedback truly helped me to learn the art of teaching;

Dennis Paoli, The Hunter College Writing Center, who gave me my first job as a tutor. Under his guidance, I learned many valuable skills;

Richard Barickman, the English Department Chair, Hunter College, City University of New York, who has provided me with many opportunities to teach a variety of courses;

All of my colleagues and my students; they have enriched my life and my teaching career;

Gail Giamo, who contributed questions to "Shakespeare's Sister" and "Making the Cut";

Vanessa Melchiori, who contributed questions to "The Brown Wasps";

Rita Hickey, who contributed questions to "Under the Influence" and "The Death of The Moth";

John Tomasino, a friend who has blessed my life with his presence. I am especially grateful for the biographical research he contributed on Stephen King, Martin Luther King, Jr, Malcolm X, and Pat Mora; and,

To my husband, Peter Tomasino, whose love, dedication, encouragement and support helped make this book a reality.

Introduction

Anna Tomasino

Joan Didion, Julia Cameron, Natalie Goldberg, Alice Walker, Scott Russell Sanders, George Orwell, Maxine Hong Kingston, Jamaica Kincaid, Malcolm X, Rebecca Lawson, Sue Ribner, Russell Baker, William H. Honan, John Tarkov, Virginia Woolf, Bonnie Smith-Yackel, Ruth Sidel, Richard Selzer, E.B. White, Pat Mora, Elizabeth Kolbert, Stephen King, Loren Eiseley, Louise Erdrich, Annie Dillard, William F. Buckley, Jr., Lance Morrow, Edward I. Koch, Peter Tomasino, and Martin Luther King, Jr.

The writers in Essay 33: Non-Fiction Reflections Upon the Self and Society are the heart of the book. The readings are diverse, engaging, challenging, thought-provoking, and—at times, inspiring. From freewriting to freedom, complaining to culture, beauty to a blue jay, rage to reading, and moth to men, a mosaic of topics emerges. The diversity reflects the diversity in the classroom and also proves a point: You can write about any topic, no matter how trivial it may seem. No matter who you are or where you are from, your experience is worthy of expression.

Through sharing observations during class discussion and in writing assignments, my students and I have learned new ways of seeing ourselves and the myriad relationships of the self in relation to the self as well as to the different facets of society: childhood, education, career, the natural world, entertainment, society, and politics.

It is important as you read the essays, to examine the text. First read for pleasure. As you read, note your initial reactions. Then, re-read for meaning. Why did you respond as you did? What in the text elicited the response? Also, what experiences, observations, have you had that led you to react the way you did? Don't take anything at face value. Who is saying this? What is their purpose?

We live in an ever-growing global community. Information is available everywhere. We need the power of our minds to discern what is true, false, and what is half true—of others and ourselves. Critical thinking, grounded in reflection, is a vital part of living and learning. It will help you make better decisions—it will help you make your own decisions.

But, how do we take our thoughts and place them in physical form on the page? Chapter I, Journaling and Freewriting, contains suggestions on how to put words on the page—even when inspiration is lacking.

Each of the selections begins with a quote that can be used as a freewriting prompt. In my classes, my students and I have discovered that one of the best ways to enter into a text is by warming up. We start with a short freewrite on a related quote. Then, we discuss the quote. Sometimes students offer to read their freewrites (it is not mandatory, or you wouldn't feel free). Sometimes, students choose to share the thoughts that came to mind. Either way, the freewrite invariably leads to a discussion of the text.

Be sure to arrive at class prepared. Do your homework, read the essays critically, and be prepared to listen, speak and support your point of view. Be sure to challenge your own ideas and then, be ready to defend them by using the text. Ask questions. Questions are just as important as responses.

If the text is the prism and our minds the light, then the brilliance of colors intensifies through interaction. Your point of view is vital. I care about what you think and why you think it. Your teacher cares. You'll be surprised at how much support you will get in class. Also, you'll be exhilarated by the thrill of intellectual debate. As you challenge your point of view, you may strengthen your argument, alter it, or even modify it. What is most important is to interact with an open mind—a world of possibilities awaits!

Annotated Reading

Here is an example of an annotated text. It is the first two paragraphs of "Making the Cut" by John Tarkov[*]:

THE LESSON is a hard one, and it gets no easier through repetition. I got an early dose of it in high school, when I was trying out for varsity basketball and—for reasons that must have made sense to me then—feeling confident about my chances. In the end, there was a piece of paper taped to the locker room door. On it were the names of the guys who had worn uniforms. I had to read the list more than once before I would believe it, as if my name was really up there, somewhere between the lines. After a while, I walked away.

What is the lesson?

His personal experience

I can relate

Making the cut. The phrase comes from the vocabulary of sport, but the experience extends beyond the realm of gyms and practice fields. Getting a job, starting out alone in a new city, stretching a paycheck, holding a marriage together, scavenging for status and power—whether the goal is commendable or open to question, if things work out poorly, the message a man so easily hears remains the same: *You aren't good enough.* That is the message of the cut.

The title of the essay- Definition: Yes, I've heard the phrase used in different situations. I agree with him, if things don't work out, that's what we hear

There is a gear in a man's inner workings that grinds against those words. It a man cannot—or will not—come to terms with them, they can hound him into rage or into a fixed posture of defeat.

? unclear

As you read the selections, be sure to circle words, note your responses, and list any questions. If you do not want to mark up your book, use a separate piece of paper. You can even use a pencil to lightly mark important passages. However you decide to annotate, commit to a program of close reading. Your notes will come in handy for homework assignments, class discussion, and essays.

---

[*] From *The New York Times*, September 25, 1983. Reprinted by permission.

Chapter I

Expressing the Self: Freewriting and Journaling

I

Expressing the Self:
Freewriting and Journaling

Introduction

Where do I begin? I don't know what to write about. I have writer's block.

In this chapter, Joan Didion, Julia Cameron, and Natalie Goldberg explore the value of keeping a journal or notebook. They recommend making a commitment to writing in a place where you will not be judged. Each stresses the value in getting your thoughts down on paper without judgement. Cameron states, "We are victims of our own internalized perfectionist, a nasty internal and eternal critic, the Censor."

Notebooks are valuable because they can help you discover what you think, what you feel. They are private (unless you choose to share). They provide a place for you to express your thoughts without inhibition. They belong to you and have, as Didion states, "meaning only for its maker."

Focusing on perfection can be paralyzing. Freewriting or stream-of-consciousness—writing whatever comes to mind—is an important daily practice that "frees" the writer from writer's block. Goldberg recommends timed writing to "burn through to the first thoughts, to the place where energy is unobstructed by social politeness or the internal censor, to the place where you are writing what your mind actually sees and feels, not what it thinks it *should* see or feel."

By practicing the techniques in this chapter you will never again stare at a blank page questioning where to start. Whether you time yourself as Goldberg suggests, or produce at least three pages (as Cameron recommends), the goal is the same: Commit to Writing. Don't worry about perfection.

So, what are you waiting for? Pick up your pens and paper and start writing. Keep your pen moving. Each selection begins with a quotation that you can use as a prompt for freewriting.

"So the point of keeping my notebook has never been, nor is it now, to have an accurate factual record of what I have been doing or thinking . . . . How it felt to me: that is getting closer to the truth about a notebook."

-- Joan Didion

"On Keeping a Notebook"[*]
Joan Didion

Joan Didion is a prolific essayist, novelist and screenplay writer. She has won numerous awards and nominations. She was nominated for the National Book Award in Fiction (1971) for Play It as It Lays. Her most recent book is Political Fictions (Knopf, 2001). This essay is from her bestselling book Slouching Towards Bethlehem.[†]

" 'THAT WOMAN ESTELLE,' " the note reads, " 'is partly the reason why George Sharp and I are separated today.' *Dirty crepe-de-Chine wrapper, hotel bar, Wilmington RR, 9:45 a.m. August Monday morning.*"

Since the note is in my notebook, it presumably has some meaning to me. I study it for a long while. At first I have only the most general notion of what I was doing on an August Monday morning in the bar of the hotel across from the Pennsylvania Railroad station in Wilmington, Delaware (waiting for a train? missing one? 1960? 1961? why Wilmington?), but I do remember being there. The woman in the dirty crepe-de-Chine wrapper had come down from her room for a beer, and the bartender had heard before the reason why George Sharp and she were separated today. "Sure," he said, and went on mopping the floor. "You

[*in margin: ? ° recalls but unclear*]

---

[*] Reprinted by permission of Farrar, Straus and Giroux, LLC: "On Keeping a Notebook" from *Slouching Towards Bethlehem* by Joan Didion. Copyright © 1966, 1968, renewed 1996 by Joan Didion.

[†] "Joan Didion," *Contemporary Authors Online.* The Gale Group, 2001. 4 April 2001. January 26, 2002 < http://www.galenet.com/servlet/LitRC?c=1&ai=24249&ste=6&docNum= H1000 0254 98 &bConts=16303&tab=1&vrsn=3&ca=1&tbst=arp&ST=Didion%2C+Joan&srchtp=athr&n=10 &locID=nypl&OP=contains>.

told me." At the other end of the bar is a girl. She is talking, pointedly, not to the man beside her but to a cat lying in the triangle of sunlight cast through the open door. She is wearing a plaid silk dress from Peck & Peck, and the hem is coming down.

Here is what it is: the girl has been on the Eastern Shore, and now she is going back to the city, leaving the man beside her, and all she can see ahead are the viscous summer sidewalks and the 3 a.m. long-distance calls that will make her lie awake and then sleep drugged through all the steaming mornings left in August (1960? 1961?). Because she must go directly from the train to lunch in New York, she wishes that she had a safety pin for the hem of the plaid silk dress, and she also wishes that she could forget about the hem and the lunch and stay in the cool bar that smells of disinfectant and malt and make friends with the woman in the crepe-de-Chine wrapper. She is afflicted by a little self-pity, and she wants to compare Estelles. That is what that was all about. →what?

Why did I write it down? In order to remember, of course, but exactly what was it I wanted to remember? How much of it actually happened? Did any of it? Why do I keep a notebook at all? It is easy to deceive oneself on all those scores. The impulse to write things down is a peculiarly compulsive one, inexplicable to those who do not share it, useful only accidentally, only secondarily, in the way that any compulsion tries to justify itself. I suppose that it begins or does not begin in the cradle. Although I have felt compelled to write things down since I was five years old, I doubt that my daughter ever will, for she is a singularly blessed and accepting child, delighted with life exactly as life presents itself to her, unafraid to go to sleep and unafraid to wake up. Keepers of private notebooks are a different breed altogether, lonely and resistant rearrangers of things, anxious malcontents, children afflicted apparently at birth with some presentiment of loss. I disagree

My first notebook was a Big Five tablet, given to me by my mother with the sensible suggestion that I stop whining and learn to amuse myself by writing down my thoughts. She returned the tablet to me a few years ago; the first entry is an account of a woman who believed herself to be freezing to death in the Arctic night, only to find, when day broke, that she had stumbled onto the Sahara Desert, where she would die of the heat before lunch. I have no idea what turn of a five-year-old's mind could have prompted so insistently "ironic" and exotic a story, but it does reveal a certain predilection for the extreme which has dogged me into adult life; perhaps if I were analytically inclined I would find it a truer story than any I might have told about Donald Johnson's birthday party or the day my cousin Brenda put Kitty Litter in the aquarium.

So the point of my keeping a notebook has never been, nor is it now, to have an accurate factual record of what I have been doing or thinking. That would be a different impulse entirely, an instinct for reality which I sometimes envy but do not possess. At no point have I ever been able successfully to keep a diary; my approach to daily life ranges from the grossly negligent to the merely absent, and on those few occasions when I have tried dutifully to record a day's events, boredom has so overcome me that the results are mysterious at best. What is this business about "shopping, typing piece, dinner with E, depressed?" Shopping for what? Typing what piece? Who is E? Was this "E" depressed, or was I depressed? Who cares?

In fact I have abandoned altogether that kind of pointless entry; instead I tell what some would call lies. "That's simply not true," the members of my family frequently tell me when they come up against my memory of a shared event. "The party was *not* for you, the spider was *not* a black widow, *it wasn't that way at all*." Very likely they are right, for not only have I always had trouble distinguishing between what happened and what merely might have happened, but I remain unconvinced that the distinction, for my purposes, matters. The cracked crab that I recall having for lunch the day my father came home from Detroit in 1945 must certainly be embroidery, worked into the day's pattern to lend verisimilitude; I was ten years old and would not now remember the cracked crab. The day's events did not turn on cracked crab. And yet it is precisely that fictitious crab that makes me see the afternoon all over again, a home movie run all too often, the father bearing gifts, the child weeping, an exercise in family love and guilt. Or that is what it was to me. Similarly, perhaps it never did snow that August in Vermont; perhaps there never were flurries in the night wind, and maybe no one else felt the ground hardening and summer already dead even as we pretended to bask in it, but that was how it felt to me, and it might as well have snowed, could have snowed, did snow.

How it felt to me: that is getting closer to the truth about a notebook. I sometimes delude myself about why I keep a notebook, imagine that some thrifty virtue derives from preserving everything observed. See enough and write it down, I tell myself, and then some morning when the world seems drained of wonder, some day when I am only going through the motions of doing what I am supposed to do, which is write—on that bankrupt morning I will simply open my notebook and there it will all be, a forgotten account with accumulated interest, paid passage back to the world out there: dialogue overheard in hotels and elevators and at the hat check counter in Pavillion (one middle-aged man shows his hat check to another and says, "That's my old football number"); impressions of Bettina Aptheker and Benjamin Sonnenberg and Teddy ("Mr. Acapulco") Stauffer; careful *aperçus* about tennis bums and failed fashion models and Greek shipping heiresses, one of whom taught me a significant lesson (a lesson I could have learned from F. Scott Fitzgerald, but perhaps we all must meet the very rich for ourselves) by asking, when I arrived to interview her in her orchid-filled sitting room on the second day of a paralyzing New York blizzard, whether it was snowing outside.

I imagine, in other words, that the notebook is about other people. But of course it is not. I have no real business with what one stranger said to another at the hat check counter in Pavillion; in fact I suspect that the line "That's my old football number" touched not my own imagination at all, but merely some memory of something once read, probably "The Eighty-Yard Run." Nor is my concern with a woman in a dirty crepe-de-Chine wrapper in a Wilmington bar. My stake is always, of course, in the unmentioned girl in the plaid silk dress. *Remember what it was to be me*: that is always the point.   *Wonder why she wrote it down*

It is a difficult point to admit. We are brought up in the ethic that others, any others, all others, are by definition more interesting than ourselves; taught to be diffident, just this side of self-effacing. ("You're the least important person in the room and don't forget it," Jessica Mitford's governess would hiss in her ear on the advent of any social occasion; I copied that into my notebook because it is only recently that I have been able to enter a room without hearing some such phrase in my inner ear.) Only the very young and the very old may recount their dreams at breakfast, dwell upon self, interrupt with memories of beach picnics and favorite Liberty lawn dresses and the rainbow trout in a creek near Colorado Springs. The rest of us are expected, rightly, to affect absorption in other people's favorite dresses, other people's trout.

And so we do. But our notebooks give us away, for however dutifully we record what we see around us, the common denominator of all we see is always, transparently, shamelessly, the implacable "I." We are not talking here about the kind of notebook that is patently for public consumption, a structural conceit for binding together a series of graceful *pensées*; we are talking about something private, about bits of the mind's string too short to use, an indiscriminate and erratic assemblage with meaning only for its maker. → *only the person writing it know what they write*

And sometimes even the maker has difficulty with the meaning. There does not seem to be, for example, any point in my knowing for the rest of my life that, during 1964, 720 tons of soot fell on every square mile of New York City, yet there it is in my notebook, labeled "FACT." Nor do I really need to remember that Ambrose Bierce liked to spell Leland Stanford's name "£eland $tanford" or that "smart women almost always wear black in Cuba," a fashion hint without much potential for practical application. And does not the relevance of these notes seem marginal at best?:

> In the basement museum of the Inyo County Courthouse in Independence, California, sign pinned to a mandarin coat: "This MANDARIN COAT was often worn by Mrs. Minnie S. Brooks when giving lectures on her TEAPOT COLLECTION."

> Redhead getting out of car in front of Beverly Wilshire Hotel, chinchilla stole, Vuitton bags with tags reading:
>
> MRS LOU FOX
> HOTEL SAHARA
> VEGAS

Well, perhaps not entirely marginal. As a matter of fact, Mrs. Minnie S. Brooks and her MANDARIN COAT pull me back into my own childhood, for although I never knew Mrs. Brooks and did not visit Inyo County until I was thirty, I grew up in just such a world, in houses cluttered with Indian relics and bits of gold ore and ambergris and the souvenirs my Aunt Mercy Farnsworth brought back from the Orient. It is a long way from that world to Mrs. Lou Fox's world, where we all live now, and is it not just as well to remember that? Might not Mrs. Minnie S. Brooks help me to remember what I am? Might not Mrs. Lou Fox help me to remember what I am not?

But sometimes the point is harder to discern. What exactly did I have in mind when I noted down that it cost the father of someone I know $650 a month to light the place on the Hudson in which he lived before the Crash? What use was I planning to make of this line by Jimmy Hoffa: "I may have my faults, but being wrong ain't one of them?" And although I think it interesting to know where the girls who travel with the Syndicate have their hair done when they find themselves on the West Coast, will I ever make suitable use of it? Might I not be better off just passing it on to John O'Hara? What is a recipe for sauerkraut doing in my notebook? What kind of magpie keeps this notebook? *"He was born the night the Titanic went down."* That seems a nice enough line, and I even recall who said it, but is it not really a better line in life than it could ever be in fiction?

But of course that is exactly it: not that I should ever use the line, but that I should remember the woman who said it and the afternoon I heard it. We were on her terrace by the sea, and we were finishing the wine left from lunch, trying to get what sun there was, a California winter sun. The woman whose husband was born the night the *Titanic* went down wanted to rent her house, wanted to go back to her children in Paris. I remember wishing that I could afford the house, which cost $1,000 a month. "Someday you will," she said lazily. "Someday it all comes." There in the sun on her terrace it seemed easy to believe in someday, but later I had a low-grade afternoon hangover and ran over a black snake on the way to the supermarket and was flooded with inexplicable fear when I heard the checkout clerk explaining to the man ahead of me why she was finally divorcing her husband. "He left me no choice," she said over and over as she punched the register. "He has a little seven-month-old baby by her, he left me no choice." I would like to believe that my dread then was for the human condition, but of course it was for me, because I wanted a baby and did not then have one and because I wanted to own the house that cost $1,000 a month to rent and because I had a hangover. Author wished to have a baby & money

It all comes back. Perhaps it is difficult to see the value in having one's self back in that kind of mood, but I do see it; I think we are well advised to keep on nodding terms with the people we used to be, whether we find them attractive company or not. Otherwise they turn up unannounced and surprise us, come hammering on the mind's door at 4 a.m. of a bad night and demand to know who deserted them, who betrayed them, who is going to make amends. We forget all too soon the things we thought we could never forget. We forget the loves and the betrayals alike, forget what we whispered and what we screamed, forget who we were. I have already lost touch with a couple of people I used to be; one of them, a seventeen-year-old, presents little threat, although it would be of some interest to me to know again what it feels like to sit on a river levee drinking vodka-and-orange-juice and listening to Les Paul and Mary Ford and their echoes sing "How High the Moon" on the car radio. (You see I still have the scenes, but I no longer perceive myself among those present, no longer could even improvise the dialogue.) The other one, a twenty-three-year-old, bothers me more. She was always a good deal of trouble, and I suspect she will reappear when I least want to see her, skirts too long, shy to the point of aggravation, always the injured party, full of recriminations and little hurts and stories I do not want to hear again, at once saddening me and angering me with her vulnerability and ignorance, an apparition all the more insistent for being so long banished.

It is a good idea, then, to keep in touch, and I suppose that keeping in touch is what notebooks are all about. And we are all on our own when it comes to keeping those lines open to ourselves: your notebook will never help me, nor mine you. *So what's new in the whiskey business?* What could that possibly mean to you? To me it means a blonde in a Pucci bathing suit sitting with a couple of fat men by the pool at the Beverly Hills Hotel. Another man approaches, and they all regard one another in silence for a while. "So what's new in the whiskey business?" one of the fat men finally says by way of welcome, and the blonde stands up, arches one foot and dips it in the pool, looking all the while at the cabaña where Baby Pignatari is talking on the telephone. That is all there is to that, except that several years later I saw the blonde coming out of Saks Fifth Avenue in New York with her California complexion and a voluminous mink coat. In the harsh wind that day she looked old and irrevocably tired to me, and even the skins in the mink coat were not worked the way they were doing them that year, not the way she would have wanted them done, and there is the point of the story. For a while after that I did not like to look in the mirror, and my eyes would skim the newspapers and pick out only the deaths, the cancer victims, the premature coronaries, the suicides, and I stopped riding the Lexington Avenue IRT because I noticed for the first time that all the strangers I had seen for years—the man with the seeing-eye dog, the spinster who read the classified pages every day, the fat girl who always got off with me at Grand Central— looked older than they once had.

It all comes back. Even that recipe for sauerkraut: even that brings it back. I was on Fire Island when I first made that sauerkraut, and it was raining, and we drank a lot of bourbon and ate the sauerkraut and went to bed at ten, and I listened to the rain and the Atlantic and felt safe. I made the sauerkraut again last night and it did not make me feel any safer, but that is, as they say, another story.

What she once wrote in a notebook meant something but now its a totally new story. But wishes to remember what it meant back when she wrote it & why she wrote it.

Critical Thinking

1.   What reasons does Didion give for abandoning "diary" entries and keeping a notebook instead? What does she mean by "I tell what some would call lies"?

2.   Locate in the text references to memory, remembering, and forgetting. Why does she use parenthetical information, such as "(1960? 1961?)"? What point is she trying to make?

3.   Why does she believe it is vital to "keep on nodding terms with the people we used to be"?

Writing Assignments

1.   Describe the difference between a journal entry and a diary entry. Which do you prefer?

2.   Start a journal. Be diligent. Write in it at least once a day for a week. After a week, review your entries. Are they useful? Explain why or why not?

3.   In the essay, Didion discusses how memories of a shared event differ. Write about a time when you and your family (or friends) reminisced about an event. Did each of you have different versions of the story? Explain.

"The [morning] pages are a pathway to a strong and clear sense of self. They are a trail that we follow into our own interior, where we meet both our own creativity and our creator."

-- Julia Cameron

"The Morning Pages"*
Julia Cameron

Poet, essayist, journalist and writer Julia Cameron is well known for her popular workshops on creativity. Her bestselling books include <u>The Artist's Way</u> and <u>The Right to Write</u>. The following excerpt is from her book <u>The Artist's Way</u>.†

In order to retrieve your creativity, you need to find it. I ask you to do this by an apparently pointless process I call *the morning pages*. You will do the pages daily through all the weeks of the course and, I hope, much longer. I have been doing them for a decade now. I have students who have worked with them nearly that long and who would no more abandon them than breathing.

Ginny, a writer-producer, credits the morning pages with inspiration for her recent screenplays and clarity in planning her network specials. "I'm superstitious about them by now," she says. "When I was editing my last special, I would get up at 5:00 A.M. to get them done before I went in to work."

What are morning pages? Put simply, the morning pages are three pages of longhand writing, strictly stream-of-consciousness: "Oh, god, another morning. I have NOTHING to say. I need to wash the curtains. Did I get my laundry yesterday? Blah, blah, blah . . ." They might also, more ingloriously, be called *brain drain*, since that is one of their main functions.

---

† "Julia Cameron." <u>Penguin Putnam Biography For Author: Julia Cameron, website</u>. January 26, 2002 <http://www.penguinputnam.com/Author/AuthorFrame/ 0,1018,,00.html?0CS^0000031275>.

There is no wrong way to do morning pages. These daily morning meanderings are not meant to be *art*. Or even *writing*. I stress that point to reassure the nonwriters working with this book. Writing is simply one of the tools. Pages are meant to be, simply, the act of moving the hand across the page and writing down *whatever* comes to mind. Nothing is too petty, too silly, too stupid, or too weird to be included.

The morning pages are not supposed to sound smart—although sometimes they might. Most times they won't, and nobody will ever know except you. Nobody is allowed to read your morning pages except you. And you shouldn't even read them yourself for the first eight weeks or so. Just write three pages, and stick them into an envelope. Or write three pages in a spiral notebook and don't leaf back through. *Just write three pages . . .* and write three more pages the next day.

> September 30, 1991 . . . Over the weekend, for Domenica's biology project, she and I went bug hunting on the Rio Grande and Pott Creek. We collected water crawlies and butterflies. I made a crimson homemade butterfly net that was quite functional although dragonflies eluded us to our dismay. We did not catch the tarantula strolling down the dirt road near our house. We just enjoyed spotting it.

Although occasionally colorful, the morning pages are often negative, frequently fragmented, often self-pitying, repetitive, stilted or babyish, angry or bland—even silly sounding. Good!

> Oct. 2, 1991 . . . I am up and have had a headache and have taken aspirin and feel a little better although still shaky. I may have that flu after all. I am getting to the bottom of a lot of unpacking and still no teapot from Laura whom I am sorely missing. What a heartbreak . . .

All that angry, whiny, petty stuff that you write down in the morning stands between you and your creativity. Worrying about the job, the laundry, the funny knock in the car, the weird look in your lover's eye—this stuff eddies through our subconscious and muddles our days. Get it on the page.

The morning pages are the primary tool of creative recovery. As blocked artists, we tend to criticize ourselves mercilessly. Even if we look like functioning artists to the world, we feel we never do enough and what we do isn't right. We are victims of our own internalized perfectionist, a nasty internal and eternal critic, the Censor, who resides in our (left) brain and keeps up a constant stream of subversive remarks that are often disguised as the truth. The Censor says wonderful things like: "You call that writing? What a joke. You can't even punctuate. If you haven't done it by now you never will. You can't even spell. What makes you think you can be creative?" And on and on.

Make this a rule: always remember that your Censor's negative opinions are not the truth. This takes practice. By spilling out of bed and straight onto the page every morning, you learn to evade the Censor. Because there is no wrong way to write the morning pages, the Censor's opinion doesn't count. Let your Censor rattle on. (And it will.) Just keep your hand moving across the page. Write down the Censor's thoughts if you want to. Note how it loves to aim for your creative jugular. Makes no mistake: the Censor is out to get you. It's a cunning foe. Every time you get smarter, so does it. So you wrote one good play? The Censor tells you that's all there is. So you drew your first sketch? The Censor says, "It's not Picasso."

Think of your Censor as a cartoon serpent, slithering around your creative Eden, hissing vile things to keep you off guard. If a serpent doesn't appeal to you, you might want to find a good cartoon image of your Censor, maybe the shark from *Jaws*, and put an X through it. Post it where you tend to write or on the inside cover of your notebook. Just making the Censor into the nasty, clever little character that it is begins to pry loose some of its power over you and your creativity.

More than one student has tacked up an unflattering picture of the parent responsible for the Censor's installation in his or her psyche and called that his or her Censor. The point is to stop taking the Censor as the voice of reason and learn to hear it for the blocking device that it is. Morning pages will help you to do this.

Morning pages are nonnegotiable. Never skip or skimp on morning pages. Your mood doesn't matter. The rotten thing your Censor says doesn't matter. We have this idea that we need to be in the mood to write. We don't.

Morning pages will teach you that your mood doesn't really matter. Some of the best creative work gets done on the days when you feel that everything you're doing is just plain junk. The morning pages will teach you to stop judging and just let yourself write. So what if you're tired, crabby, distracted, stressed? Your artist is a child and it needs to be fed. Morning pages feed your artist child. So write your morning pages.

Three pages of whatever crosses your mind—that's all there is to it. If you can't think of anything to write, then write, "I can't think of anything to write. . . ." Do this until you have filled three pages. *Do anything until you have filled three pages.*

When people ask, "Why do we write morning pages?" I joke, "To get to the other side." They think I am kidding, but I'm not. Morning pages do get us to the other side: the other side of our fear, of our negativity, of our moods. Above all, they get us beyond our Censor. Beyond the reach of the Censor's babble we find our own quiet center, the place where we hear the still, small voice that is at once our creator's and our own.

A word is in order here about logic brain and artist brain. *Logic brain* is our brain of choice in the Western Hemisphere. It is the categorical brain. It thinks in a neat, linear fashion. As a rule, logic brain perceives the world according to known categories. A horse is a certain combination of animal parts that make up a horse. A fall forest is viewed as a series of colors that add up to "fall forest." It looks at a fall forest and notes: red, orange, yellow, green, gold.

Logic brain was and is our survival brain. It works on known principles. Anything unknown is perceived as wrong and possibly dangerous. Logic brain likes things to be neat little soldiers marching in a straight line. Logic brain is the brain we usually listen to, especially when we are telling ourselves to be sensible.

Logic brain is our Censor, our second (and third and fourth) thoughts. Faced with an original sentence, phrase, paint squiggle, it says, "What the hell is that? That's not right!"

Artist brain is our inventor, our child, and our very own personal absent-minded professor. Artist brain says, "Hey! That is so neat!" It puts odd things together (boat equals wave and walker). It likes calling a speeding GTO a wild animal: "The black howling wolf pulled into the drive-in . . ."

Artist brain is our creative, holistic brain. It thinks in patterns and shadings. It sees a fall forest and thinks: Wow! Leaf bouquet! Pretty! Gold-gilt-shimmery-earthskin-king's carpet! Artist brain is associative and freewheeling. It makes new connections, yoking together images to invoke meaning: like the Norse myths calling a boat "wave-horse." In *Star Wars*, the name Skywalker is a lovely artist-brain flash.

Why all this logic-brain/artist-brain talk? Because the morning pages teach logic brain to stand aside and let artist brain play.

The Censor is part of our leftover survival brain. It was the part in charge of deciding whether it was safe for us to leave the forest and go out into the meadow. Our Censor scans our creative meadow for any dangerous beasties. Any original thought can look pretty dangerous to our Censor.

The only sentences/paintings/sculptures/photographs it likes are ones that it has seen many times before. Safe sentences. Safe paintings. Not exploratory blurts, squiggles, or jottings. Listen to your Censor and it will tell you that everything original is wrong/dangerous/rotten.

Who wouldn't be blocked if every time you tiptoed into the open somebody (your Censor) made fun of you? The morning pages will teach you to stop listening to that ridicule. They will allow you to detach from your negative Censor.

It may be useful for you to think of the morning pages as meditation. It may not be the practice of meditation you are accustomed to. You may, in fact, not be accustomed to meditating at all. The pages may not seem spiritual or even meditative—more like negative and materialistic, actually—but they are a valid form of meditation that gives us insight and helps us effect change in our lives.

Let's take a look at what we stand to gain by meditating. There are many ways of thinking about meditation. Scientists speak of it in terms of brain hemispheres and shunting techniques. We move from logic brain to artist brain and from fast to slow, shallow to deep. Management consultants, in pursuit of corporate physical health, have learned to think of meditation primarily as a stress-management technique. Spiritual seekers choose to view the process as a gateway to God. Artists and creativity mavens approve of it as a conduit for higher creative insights.

All of these notions are true—as far as they go. They do not go far enough. Yes, we will alter our brain hemisphere, lower our stress, discover an inner contact with a creative source, and have many creative insights. Yes, for any one of these reasons, the pursuit is a worthy one. Even taken in combination, however, they are still intellectual constructs for what is primarily an experience of wholeness, rightness, and power.

We meditate to discover our own identity, our right place in the scheme of the universe. Through meditation, we acquire and eventually acknowledge our connection to an inner power source that has the ability to transform our outer world. In other words, meditation gives us not only the light of insight but also the power for expansive change.

Insight in and of itself is an intellectual comfort. Power in and of itself is a blind force that can destroy as easily as build. It is only when we consciously learn to link power and light that we begin to feel our rightful identities as creative beings. The morning pages allow us to forge this link. They provide us with a spiritual ham-radio set to contact the Creator Within. For this reason, the morning pages are a spiritual practice.

It is impossible to write morning pages for any extended period of time without coming into contact with an unexpected inner power. Although I used them for many years before I realized this, the pages are a pathway to a strong and clear sense of self. They are a trail that we follow into our own interior, where we meet both our own creativity and our creator.

Morning pages map our own interior. Without them, our dreams may remain terra incognita. I know mine did. Using them, the light of insight is coupled with the power for expansive change. It is very difficult to complain about a situation morning after morning, month after month, without being moved to constructive action. The pages lead us out of despair and into undreamed-of solutions.

The first time I did morning pages, I was living in Taos, New Mexico. I had gone there to sort myself out—into what, I didn't know. For the third time in a row, I'd had a film scuttled due to studio politics. Such disasters are routine to screenwriters, but to me they felt like miscarriages. Cumulatively, they were disastrous. I wanted to give the movies up. Movies had broken my heart. I didn't want any more brainchildren to meet untimely deaths. I'd gone to New Mexico to mend my heart and see what else, if anything, I might want to do.

Living in a small adobe house that looked north to Taos Mountain, I began a practice of writing morning pages. Nobody told me to do them. I had never heard of anybody doing them. I just got the insistent, inner sense that I should do them and so I did. I sat at a wooden table looking north to Taos Mountain and I wrote.

The morning pages were my pastime, something to do instead of staring at the mountain all the time. The mountain, a humpbacked marvel different in every weather, raised more questions than I did. Wrapped in clouds one day, dark and wet the next, that mountain dominated my view and my morning pages as well. What did it—or anything—mean? I asked page after page, morning after morning. No answer.

And then, one wet morning, a character named Johnny came strolling into my pages. Without planning to, I was writing a novel. The morning pages had shown me a way.

Anyone who faithfully writes morning pages will be led to a connection with a source of wisdom within. When I am stuck with a painful situation or problem that I don't think I know how to handle, I will go to the pages and ask for guidance. To do this, I write "LJ" as a shorthand for me, "Little Julie," and then I ask my question.

LJ: What should I tell them about this inner wisdom? (Then I listen for the reply and write that down, too.)

ANSWER: You should tell them everyone has a direct dial to God. No one needs to go through an operator. Tell them to try this technique with a problem of their own. They will.

Sometimes, as above, the answer may seem flippant or too simple. I have come to believe that *seem* is the operative word. Very often, when I act on the advice I have been given, it is exactly right—far more right than something more complicated would have been. And so, for the record, I want to say: pages are my way of meditating; I do them because they work.

A final assurance: the morning pages will work for painters, for sculptors, for poets, for actors, for lawyers, for housewives—for anyone who wants to try anything creative. Don't think they are a tool for writers only. Hooey. These pages are not intended for writers only. Lawyers who use them swear they make them more effective in court. Dancers claim their balance improves—and not just emotionally. If anything, writers, who have a regrettable desire to *write* morning pages instead of just do them, may have the hardest time seeing their impact. What they're likely to see is that their other writing seems to suddenly be far more free and expansive and somehow easy to do. In short, no matter what your reservation or your occupation, morning pages will function for you.

Timothy, a buttoned-down, buttoned-lip curmudgeon millionaire, began writing morning pages with a skeptic's scorn. He didn't want to do them without some proof that they would work. The damn pages had no label, no Dun and Bradstreet rating. They just sounded silly, and Timothy hated silly.

Timothy was, in street parlance, a serious player. His poker face was so straight it looked more like a fireplace poker than a mere cardsharp's defense. Practiced for years in the corporate board room, Timothy's invincible facade was as dark, shiny, and expensive as mahogany. No emotions scratched the surface of this man's calm. He was a one-man monument to the Masculine Mystique.

"Oh, all right. . ." Timothy agreed to the pages, but only because he had paid good money to be told to do them. Within three weeks, straightlaced, pin-striped Timothy became a morning pages advocate. The results of his work with them convinced him. He started—heaven forbid—to have a little creative fun. "I bought guitar strings for this old guitar I had lying around," he reported one week. And then, "I rewired my stereo. I bought some wonderful Italian recordings." Although he hesitated to acknowledge it, even to himself, Timothy's writer's block was melting. Up at dawn, Gregorian chants on the stereo, he was writing freely.

Not everyone undertakes the morning pages with such obvious antagonism. Phyllis, a leggy, racehorse socialite who for years had hidden her brains behind her beauty and her life behind her man's, tried the morning pages with a great deal of surface cheer—and an inner conviction they would never work for her. It had been ten years since she had allowed herself to write anything other than letters and bread-and-butter lists. About a month into morning pages, seemingly out of nowhere, Phyllis got her first poem. In the three years she has used pages since, she has written poems, speeches, radio shows, and a nonfiction book.

Anton, grumpy but graceful in his use of the pages, accomplished unblocking as an actor. Laura, talented but blocked as a writer, painter, and musician found that the morning pages moved her to her piano, typewriter, and paint supplies.

While you may undertake this course with an agenda as to what you want unblocked, the tools may free creative areas you have long ignored or even been blind to. Ingeborg, using the pages to unblock her creative writer, moved from being one of Germany's top music critics to composing for the first time in twenty years. She was stunned and made several ecstatic transatlantic calls to share her good news.

Often, the students most resistant to morning pages come to love them the best. In fact, hating the morning pages is a very good sign. Loving them is a good sign, too, if you keep writing even when you suddenly don't. A neutral attitude is the third position, but it's really just a defensive strategy that may mask boredom.

Boredom is just "What's the use?" in disguise. And "What's the use?" is fear, and fear means you are secretly in despair. So put your fears on the page. Put anything on the page. Put three pages of it on the page.

Critical Thinking

1.   What are "The Morning Pages"? What examples does she use to illustrate the effectiveness of the pages?

2.   Describe the "internal critic" as presented by Cameron?

3.   What are the distinguishing characteristics of the "logic brain" and the "artist brain"?

Writing Assignments

1.   Describe your own internal critic. What does your "internal critic" tell you? Explain how you respond.

2.   Start doing morning pages now. After a week, write a one page letter to Julia Cameron about your experience.

3.   Are you skeptical of Cameron's ideas? Write an essay responding to the main points she makes. Which ideas do you agree with? Which ideas do you disagree with? Explain with support from the text and from your own experience.

"First thoughts are unencumbered by ego . . . . So if you express something egoless, it is [ ] full of energy because it is expressing the truth of the way things are."
-- Natalie Goldberg

"First Thoughts"*
Natalie Goldberg

Natalie Goldberg is a teacher and is well known for her writing workshops. She has written numerous books. The following excerpt is from her bestselling book, <u>Writing Down the Bones</u>.[†]

The basic unit of writing practice is the timed exercise. You may time yourself for ten minutes, twenty minutes, or an hour. It's up to you. At the beginning you may want to start small and after a week increase your time, or you may want to dive in for an hour the first time. It doesn't matter. What does matter is that whatever amount of time you choose for that session, you must commit yourself to it for that full period:

1. *Keep your hand moving.* (Don't pause to reread the line you have just written. That's stalling and trying to get control of what you're saying.)

2. *Don't cross out.* (That is editing as you write. Even if you write something you didn't mean to write, leave it.)

3. *Don't worry about spelling, punctuation, grammar.* (Don't even care about staying within the margins and lines on the page.)

4. *Lose control.*

5. *Don't think. Don't get logical.*

6. *Go for the jugular.* (If something comes up in your writing that is scary or naked, dive right into it. It probably has lots of energy.)

[*] From *Writing Down the Bones* by Natalie Goldberg. © 1986 by Natalie Goldberg. Reprinted by arrangement with Shambhala Publications, Inc., Boston, www.shambhala.com
[†] "Natalie Goldberg," *Contemporary Authors Online*. The Gale Group, 2001. 29 August 2001. January 26, 2002 < http://www.galenet.com/servlet/LitRC?c=1&ai=108822&ste=6&docNum=H10 00122 346&bConts=2191&tab=1&vrsn=3&ca=1&tbst=arp&ST=Goldberg%2C+Natalie&srchtp=athr &n=10&locID=nypl&OP=contains >.

These are the rules. It is important to adhere to them because the aim is to burn through to first thoughts, to the place where energy is unobstructed by social politeness or the internal censor, to the place where you are writing what your mind actually sees and feels, not what it *thinks* it should see or feel. It's a great opportunity to capture the oddities of your mind. Explore the rugged edge of thought. Like grating a carrot, give the paper the colorful coleslaw of your consciousness.

First thoughts have tremendous energy. It is the way the mind first flashes on something. The internal censor usually squelches them, so we live in the realm of second and third thoughts, thoughts on thought, twice and three times removed from the direct connection of the first fresh flash. For instance, the phrase, "I cut the daisy from my throat" shot through my mind. Now my second thought, carefully tutored in 1 + 1 = 2 logic, in politeness, fear, and embarrassment at the natural, would say, "That's ridiculous. You sound suicidal. Don't show yourself cutting your throat. Someone will think you are crazy." And instead, if we give the censor its way, we write, "My throat was a little sore, so I didn't say anything." Proper and boring.

First thoughts are also unencumbered by ego, by that mechanism in us that tries to be in control, tries to prove the world is permanent and solid, enduring and logical. The world is not permanent, is ever-changing and full of human suffering. So if you express something egoless, it is also full of energy because it is expressing the truth of the way things are. You are not carrying the burden of ego in your expression, but are riding for moments the waves of human consciousness and using your personal details to express the ride.

In Zen meditation you sit on a cushion called a zafu with your legs crossed, back straight, hands at your knees or in front of you in a gesture called a mudra. You face a white wall and watch your breath. No matter what you feel—great tornadoes of anger and resistance, thunderstorms of joy and grief—you continue to sit, back straight, legs crossed, facing the wall. You learn to not be tossed away no matter how great the thought or emotion. That is the discipline: to continue to sit.

The same is true in writing. You must be a great warrior when you contact first thoughts and write from them. Especially at the beginning you may feel great emotions and energy that will sweep you away, but you don't stop writing. You continue to use your pen and record the details of your life and penetrate into the heart of them. Often in a beginning class students break down crying when they read pieces they have written. That is okay. Often as they write they cry, too. However,

I encourage them to continue reading or writing right through the tears so they may come out the other side and not be thrown off by the emotion. Don't stop at the tears; go through to truth. This is the discipline.

Why else are first thoughts so energizing? Because they have to do with freshness and inspiration. Inspiration means "breathing in." Breathing in God. You actually become larger than yourself, and first thoughts are present. They are not a cover-up of what is actually happening or being felt. The present is imbued with tremendous energy. It is what is. My friend who is a Buddhist said once after coming our of a meditation retreat, "The colors were so much more vibrant afterward." Her meditation teacher said, "When you are present, the world is truly alive."

Critical Thinking

1.   According to Goldberg, what are first thoughts?

2.   In what order does she present her rules?

3.   What analogies does Goldberg make to zen meditation? Are they effective? Explain why or why not?

Writing Assignments

1.   Follow her instructions. Write a timed freewrite. After you complete the freewrite, record your experience. Is it a valuable technique you plan on using? Why or why not?

2.   Try expanding her list of six instructions. Add at least three more.

3.   Write a piece of similar length about writer's block.

RELATING THE AUTHORS' IDEAS

1. How do we retrieve creativity? Compare and contrast the methods discussed by Didion, Cameron, and Goldberg. In what ways are the methods similar? In what ways do they differ?

2. Compare and contrast how any two or three of the authors use their notebooks. What does Didion think about her notebook, why does she find it useful? Compare to the reasons why Cameron keeps a notebook and why she finds it useful.

3. In what context do Goldberg and Cameron discuss meditation?

4. Cameron and Goldberg each describe the "Internal Censor." Compare and contrast their views. You may also want to discuss your own experience with your internal censor.

Chapter II

Reflecting upon Childhood and Children

II

Reflecting upon Childhood and Children

Introduction

In <u>Letters to A Young Poet</u>, Rainer Maria Rilke reminds a young poet of the "treasure house of memories" to be found in "childhood." He encourages the young poet: "Try to raise up the sunken feelings of this enormous past."

As writers, let us journey inward and reflect upon childhood experiences. The joyful memories are naturally more pleasurable to reminisce. However, as we will see in this unit, there are also treasures to be found in painful memories. Scott Russell Sanders digs, delves back in time, he says, "to drag into the light what eats at me—the fear, the guilt, the shame-so that my own children may be spared." Although his father has passed away, Sanders remains "Under the Influence" of his father's alcoholism: "The story continues for my brother, my sister, my mother, and me, and will continue so long as memory holds."

Scott Russell Sanders, George Orwell, Alice Walker, and Maxine Hong Kingston reflect upon their individual "treasure house of memories" and share their childhood experiences and lessons. Maxine Hong Kingston recollects the storytelling tradition in her family: "Night after night my mother would talk-story until we fell asleep. I couldn't tell where the stories left off and the dreams began, her voice and the voice of heroines in my sleep."

When we look at our past with fresh eyes and begin with a "fresh" page, we may not know where the story is going, or how much of it we will remember. Reflective writing, grounded in reflective time, is valuable. An undiscovered world encompassing a myriad of emotions surfaces. The word essay is from the French, *essai*—attempt. Each of these writers of the personal essay is attempting with words to capture, understand, and relive moments. In "An Episode of Bed-wetting" George Orwell reflects upon his painful childhood experience at St. Cyprian's. In the essay he makes an important point about memory. Perhaps, Orwell states, "one's memories of any period must necessarily weaken as one moves away from it . . . But it can also happen that one's memories grow sharper after a long lapse of time, because one is looking at the past with fresh eyes."

In "Beauty: When the Other Dancer Is The Self" Alice Walker describes the self-loathing she experienced after her childhood injury: "That night, as I do almost every night, I abuse my eye. I rant and rave at it, in front of the mirror. I plead with it to clear up before morning. I tell it I hate and despise it. I do not pray for sight. I pray for beauty." Later, however, she experiences an epiphany: "*But I might have missed seeing the desert*! The shock of that possibility—and gratitude for over twenty-five years of sight—sends me literally to my knees."

As writers, let us explore the stories in our life—joyful and painful. "Perhaps," as Rilke posits "all the dragons in our lives are princesses."

"The worst loneliness is not to be comfortable with yourself."
-- Mark Twain

"Beauty: When the Other Dancer is the Self"[*]
Alice Walker

Bestselling author Alice Walker is the recipient of numerous nominations and awards. In 1983 she received the Pulitzer Prize and American Book Award for The Color Purple*. This essay is from her book* In Search of our Mothers' Gardens: Womanist Prose*.[†]*

It is a bright summer day in 1947. My father, a fat, funny man with beautiful eyes and a subversive wit, is trying to decide which of his eight children he will take with him to the county fair. My mother, of course, will not go. She is knocked out from getting most of us ready: I hold my neck stiff against the pressure of her knuckles as she hastily completes the braiding and then beribboning of my hair.

My father is the driver for the rich old white lady up the road. Her name is Miss Mey. She owns all the land for miles around, as well as the house in which we live. All I remember about her is that she once offered to pay my mother thirty-five cents for cleaning her house, raking up piles of her magnolia leaves, and washing her family's clothes, and that my mother—she of no money, eight children, and a chronic earache—refused it. But I do not think of this in 1947. 1 am two and a half years old. I want to go everywhere my daddy goes. I am excited at the prospect of riding in a car. Someone has told me fairs are fun. That there is room in the car for only three of us doesn't faze me at all. Whirling happily in my starchy frock, showing off my biscuit-polished patent-leather shoes and lavender socks, tossing my head in a way that makes my ribbons bounce, I stand, hands on hips, before my father. "Take me, Daddy," I say with assurance; "I'm the prettiest!"

[†] "Alice (Malsenior) Walker" *Contemporary Authors Online*. The Gale Group, 2001. 24 October 2001. January 26, 2002 <http://www.galenet.com/servlet/LitRC?c=1&ai=91747&ste=6&doc Num=H1000102701&bConts=16303&tab=1&vrsn=3&ca=2&tbst=arp&ST=Walker%2C+Alice+ %28Malsenior%29&srchtp=athr&n=10&locID=nypl&OP=contains>.

Later, it does not surprise me to find myself in Miss Mey's shiny black car, sharing the back seat with the other lucky ones. Does not surprise me that I thoroughly enjoy the fair. At home that night I tell the unlucky ones all I can remember about the merry-go-round, the man who eats live chickens, and the teddy bears, until they say: that's enough, baby Alice. Shut up now, and go to sleep.

It is Easter Sunday, 1950. 1 am dressed in a green, flocked, scalloped-hem dress (handmade by my adoring sister, Ruth) that has its own smooth satin petticoat and tiny hot-pink roses tucked into each scallop. My shoes, new T-strap patent-leather, again highly biscuit-polished. I am six years old and have learned one of the longest Easter speeches to be heard that day, totally unlike the speech I said when I was two: "Easter lilies / pure and white / blossom in / the morning light." When I rise to give my speech I do so on a great wave of love and pride and expectation. People in the church stop rustling their new crinolines. They seem to hold their breath. I can tell they admire my dress, but it is my spirit, bordering on sassiness (womanishness), they secretly applaud.

"That girl's a little *mess*," they whisper to each other, pleased.

Naturally I say my speech without stammer or pause, unlike those who stutter, stammer, or, worst of all, forget. This is before the word "beautiful" exists in people's vocabulary, but "Oh, isn't she the *cutest* thing!" frequently floats my way. "And got so much sense!" they gratefully add . . . for which thoughtful addition I thank them to this day.

It was great fun being cute. But then, one day, it ended.

I am eight years old and a tomboy. I have a cowboy hat, cowboy boots, checkered shirt and pants, all red. My playmates are my brothers, two and four years older than I. Their colors are black and green, the only difference in the way we are dressed. On Saturday nights we all go to the picture show, even my mother; Westerns are her favorite kind of movie. Back home, "on the ranch," we pretend we are Tom Mix, Hopalong Cassidy, Lash LaRue (we've even named one of our dogs Lash LaRue); we chase each other for hours rustling cattle, being outlaws, delivering damsels from distress. Then my parents decide to buy my brothers guns. These are not "real" guns. They shoot "BBs," copper pellets my brothers say will kill birds. Because I am a girl, I do not get a gun. Instantly I am relegated to the position of Indian. Now there appears a great distance between us. They shoot and shoot at everything with their new guns. I try to keep up with my bow and arrows.

One day while I am standing on top of our makeshift "garage"—pieces of tin nailed across some poles—holding my bow and arrow and looking out toward the fields, I feel an incredible blow in my right eye. I look down just in time to see my brother lower his gun.

Both brothers rush to my side. My eye stings, and I cover it with my hand. "If you tell," they say, "we will get a whipping. You don't want that to happen, do you?" I do not. "Here is a piece of, wire," says the older brother, picking it up from the roof; "say you stepped on one end of it and the other flew up and hit you." The pain is beginning to start. "Yes," I say. "Yes, I will say that is what happened." If I do not say this is what happened, I know my brothers will find ways to make me wish I had. But now I will say anything that gets me to my mother.

Confronted by our parents we stick to the lie agreed upon. They place me on a bench on the porch and I close my left eye while they examine the right. There is a tree growing from underneath the porch that climbs past the railing to the roof. It is the last thing my right eye sees. I watch as its trunk, its branches, and then its leaves are blotted out by the rising blood.

I am in shock. First there is intense fever, which my father tries to break using lily leaves bound around my head. Then there are chills: my mother tries to get me to eat soup. Eventually, I do not know how, my parents learn what has happened. A week after the "accident" they take me to see a doctor. "Why did you wait so long to come?" he asks, looking into my eye and shaking his head. "Eyes are sympathetic," he says. "If one is blind, the other will likely become blind too."

This comment of the doctor's terrifies me. But it is really how I look that bothers me most. Where the BB pellet struck there is a glob of whitish scar tissue, a hideous cataract, on my eye. Now when I stare at people—a favorite pastime, up to now—they will stare back. Not at the "cute" little girl, but at her scar. For six years I do not stare at anyone, because I do not raise my head.

Years later, in the throes of a mid-life crisis, I ask my mother and sister whether I changed after the "accident." "No," they say, puzzled. "What do you mean?"

What do I mean?

I am eight, and, for the first time, doing poorly in school, where I have been something of a whiz since I was four. We have just moved to the place where the "accident" occurred. We do not know any of the people around us because this is a different county. The only time I see the friends I knew is when we go back to our old church. The new school is the former state penitentiary. It is a large stone building, cold and drafty, crammed to overflowing with boisterous, ill-disciplined children. On the third floor there is a huge circular imprint of some partition that has been torn out.

"What used to be here?" I ask a sullen girl next to me on our way past it to lunch.

"The electric chair," says she.

At night I have nightmares about the electric chair, and about all the people reputedly "fried" in it. I am afraid of the school, where all the students seem to be budding criminals.

"What's the matter with your eye?" they ask, critically.

When I don't answer (I cannot decide whether it was an "accident" or not), they shove me, insist on a fight.

My brother, the one who created the story about the wire, comes to my rescue. But then brags so much about "protecting" me, I become sick.

After months of torture at the school, my parents decide to send me back to our old community, to my old school. I live with my grandparents and the teacher they board. But there is no room for Phoebe, my cat. By the time my grandparents decide there *is* room, and I ask for my cat, she cannot be found. Miss Yarborough, the boarding teacher, takes me under her wing, and begins to teach me to play the piano. But soon she marries an African—a "prince," she says—and is whisked away to his continent.

At my old school there is at least one teacher who loves me. She is the teacher who "knew me before I was born" and bought my first baby clothes. It is she who makes life bearable. It is her presence that finally helps me turn on the one child at the school who continually calls me "one-eyed bitch." One day I simply grab him by his coat and beat him until I am satisfied. It is my teacher who tells me my mother is ill.

My mother is lying in bed in the middle of the day, something I have never seen. She is in too much pain to speak. She has an abscess in her ear. I stand looking down on her, knowing that if she dies, I cannot live. She is being treated with warm oils and hot bricks held against her cheek. Finally a doctor comes. But I must go back to my grandparents' house. The weeks pass but I am hardly aware of it. All I know is that my mother might die, my father is not so jolly, my brothers still have their guns, and I am the one sent away from home.

"You did not change," they say.

Did I imagine the anguish of never looking up?

I am twelve. When relatives come to visit I hide in my room. My cousin Brenda, just my age, whose father works in the post office and whose mother is a nurse, comes to find me. "Hello," she says. And then she asks, looking at my recent school picture, which I did not want taken, and on which the "glob," as I think of it, is clearly visible, "You still can't see out of that eye?"

"No," I say, and flop back on the bed over my book.

That night, as I do almost every night, I abuse my eye. I rant and rave at it, in front of the mirror. I plead with it to clear up before morning. I tell it I hate and despise it. I do not pray for sight. I pray for beauty.

"You did not change," they say.

I am fourteen and baby-sitting for my brother Bill, who lives in Boston. He is my favorite brother and there is a strong bond between us. Understanding my feelings of shame and ugliness he and his wife take me to a local hospital, where the "glob" is removed by a doctor named O. Henry. There is still a small bluish crater where the scar tissue was, but the ugly white stuff is gone. Almost immediately I become a different person from the girl who does not raise her head. Or so I think. Now that I've raised my head I win the boyfriend of my dreams. Now that I've raised my head I have plenty of friends. Now that I've raised my head classwork comes from my lips as faultlessly as Easter speeches did, and I leave high school as valedictorian, most popular student, and *queen*, hardly believing my luck. Ironically, the girl who was voted most beautiful in our class (and was) was later shot twice through the chest by a male companion, using a "real" gun, while she was pregnant. But that's another story in itself. Or is it?

"You did not change," they say.

It is now thirty years since the "accident." A beautiful journalist comes to visit and to interview me. She is going to write a cover story for her magazine that focuses on my latest book. "Decide how you want to look on the cover," she says. "Glamorous, or whatever."

Never mind "glamorous," it is the "whatever" that I hear. Suddenly all I can think of is whether I will get enough sleep the night before the photography session: if I don't, my eye will be tired and wander, as blind eyes will.

At night in bed with my lover I think up reasons why I should not appear on the cover of a magazine. "My meanest critics will say I've sold out," I say. "My family will now realize I write scandalous books."

"But what's the real reason you don't want to do this?" he asks.

"Because in all probability," I say in a rush, "my eye won't be straight."

"It will be straight enough," he says. Then, "Besides, thought you'd made your peace with that."

And I suddenly remember that I have.

I remember:

I am talking to my brother Jimmy, asking if he remembers anything unusual about the day I was shot. He does not know I consider that day the last time my father, with his sweet home remedy of cool lily leaves, chose me, and that I suffered and raged inside because of this. "Well," he says, "all I remember is standing by the side of the highway with Daddy, trying to flag down a car. A white man stopped, but when Daddy said be needed somebody to take his little girl to the doctor, he drove off."

I remember:

I am in the desert for the first time. I fall totally in love with it. I am so overwhelmed by its beauty, I confront for the first time, consciously, the meaning of the doctor's words years ago: "Eyes are sympathetic. If one is blind, the other will likely become blind too." I realize I have dashed about the world madly, looking at this, looking at that, storing up images against the fading of the light. *But I might have missed seeing the desert*! The shock of that possibility—and gratitude for over twenty-five years of sight—sends me literally to my knees. Poem after poem comes—which is perhaps how poets pray.

ON SIGHT

I am so thankful I have seen
The Desert
And the creatures in the desert
And the desert Itself.

The desert has its own moon
Which I have seen
With my own eye.

There is no flag on it.

Trees of the desert have arms
All of which are always up
That is because the moon is up
The sun is up
Also the sky
The stars
Clouds
None with flags.

If there were flags, I doubt
the trees would point.
Would you?

But mostly, I remember this:

I am twenty-seven, and my baby daughter is almost three. Since her birth I have worried about her discovery that her mother's eyes are different from other people's. Will she be embarrassed? I think. What will she say? Every day she watches a television program called "Big Blue Marble." It begins with a picture of the earth as it appears from the moon. It is bluish, a little battered-looking, but full of light, with whitish clouds swirling around it. Every time I see it I weep with love, as if it is a picture of Grandma's house. One day when I am putting Rebecca down for her nap, she suddenly focuses on my eye. Something inside me cringes, gets ready to try to protect myself. All children are cruel about physical differences, I know from experience, and that they don't always mean to be is another matter. I assume Rebecca will be the same.

But no-o-o-o. She studies my face intently as we stand, her inside and me outside her crib. She even holds my face maternally between her dimpled little hands. Then, looking every bit as serious and lawyerlike as her father, she says, as if it may just possibly have slipped my attention: "Mommy, there's a *world* in your eye." (As in, "Don't be alarmed, or do anything crazy.") And then, gently, but with great interest: "Mommy, where did you *get* that world in your eye?"

For the most part, the pain left then. (So what, if my brothers grew up to buy even more powerful pellet guns for their sons and to carry real guns themselves. So what, if a young "Morehouse man" once nearly fell off the steps of Trevor Arnett Library because he thought my eyes were blue.) Crying and laughing I ran to the bathroom, while Rebecca mumbled and sang herself off to sleep. Yes indeed, I realized, looking into the mirror. There *was* a world in my eye. And I saw that it was possible to love it: that in fact, for all it had taught me of shame and anger and inner vision, I *did* love it. Even to see it drifting out of orbit in boredom, or rolling up out of fatigue, not to mention floating back at attention in excitement (bearing witness, a friend has called it), deeply suitable to my personality, and even characteristic of me.

That night I dream I am dancing to Stevie Wonder's song "Always" (the name of the song is really "As," but I hear it as "Always"). As I dance, whirling and joyous, happier than I've ever been in my life, another bright-faced dancer joins me. We dance and kiss each other and hold each other through the night. The other dancer has obviously come through all right, as I have done. She is beautiful, whole and free. And she is also me.

[1983]

Critical Thinking

1.   Why the title "Beauty: When the Other Dancer is the Self"?

2.   Where does Walker use repetition? For what purpose?

3.   Describe in detail Walker's insight(s).

Writing Assignments

1. How closely is your self-esteem tied to your appearance? Write an essay about a time in your life when your self-esteem was injured. (Alternately, you can write about how a friend or family member changed his or her behavior as a result of an injury.) How did you (or a friend or family member) regain your self-esteem? Or is it still damaged?

2. Write a stylistic analysis essay. Analyze Walker's use of stylistic detail and show how it relates to the theme. For example, where does she use repetition? For what purpose? How does the repetition tie in to the theme? What effect does the repetition have on the reader?

3. Walker was shot in the eye by a BB pellet. She mentions a classmate who received two gunshot wounds by a man. What issues are raised by the references to males and guns?

> *"All happy families resemble one another, but each unhappy family is unhappy in its own way."*
> *-- Leo Tolstoy*

"Under the Influence"[*]
Scott Russell Sanders

Born in 1945, award winning essayist Scott Russell Sanders has written numerous essays for magazines, newspapers and books. This essay originally appeared in Harper's *magazine.[†]*

MY FATHER DRANK. HE DRANK AS A GUT-PUNCHED boxer gasps for breath, as a starving dog gobbles food—compulsively, secretly, in pain and trembling. I use the past tense not because he ever quit drinking but because he quit living. That is how the story ends for my father, age sixty-four, heart bursting, body cooling and forsaken on the linoleum of my brother's trailer. The story continues for my brother, my sister, my mother, and me, and will continue so long as memory holds.

In the perennial present of memory, I slip into the garage or barn to see my father tipping back the flat green bottles of wine, the brown cylinders of whiskey, the cans of beer disguised in paper bags. His Adam's apple bobs, the liquid gurgles, he wipes the sandy-haired back of a hand over his lips, and then, his bloodshot gaze bumping into me, he stashes the bottle or can inside his jacket, under the workbench, between two bales of hay, and we both pretend the moment has not occurred.

"What's up, buddy?" he says, thick-tongued and edgy.

"Sky's up," I answer, playing along.

"And don't forget prices," he grumbles. "Prices are always up. And taxes."

[†] "Scott Russell Sanders," *Contemporary Authors Online.* The Gale Group, 2001. 11 December 2001. January 26, 2002 <http://www.galenet.com/servlet/LitRC?c=1&ai=77902 &ste=6&docNum=H1000086895&bConts=2191&tab=1&vrsn=3&ca=1&tbst=arp&ST=Sanders%2C+scott+russell&srchtp=athr&n=10&locID=nypl&OP=contains>.

In memory, his white 1951 Pontiac with the stripes down the hood and the Indian head on the snout jounces to a stop in the driveway; or it is the 1956 Ford station wagon, or the 1963 Rambler shaped like a toad, or the sleek 1969 Bonneville that will do 120 miles per hour on straightaways; or it is the robin's-egg blue pickup, new in 1980, battered in 1981, the year of his death. He climbs out, grinning dangerously, unsteady on his legs, and we children interrupt our game of catch, our building of snow forts, our picking of plums, to watch in silence as he weaves past into the house, where he slumps into his overstuffed chair and falls asleep. Shaking her head, our mother stubs out the cigarette he has left smoldering in the ashtray. All evening, until our bedtimes, we tiptoe past him, as past a snoring dragon. Then we curl in our fearful sheets, listening. Eventually he wakes with a grunt, Mother slings accusations at him, he snarls back, she yells, he growls, their voices clashing. Before long, she retreats to their bedroom, sobbing—not from the blows of fists, for he never strikes her, but from the force of words.

Left alone, our father prowls the house, thumping into furniture, rummaging in the kitchen, slamming doors, turning the pages of the newspaper with a savage crackle, muttering back at the late-night drivel from television. The roof might fly off, the walls might buckle from the pressure of his rage. Whatever my brother and sister and mother may be thinking on their own rumpled pillows, I lie there hating him, loving him, fearing him, knowing I have failed him. I tell myself he drinks to ease an ache that gnaws at his belly, an ache I must have caused by disappointing him somehow, a murderous ache I should be able to relieve by doing all my chores, earning A's in school, winning baseball games, fixing the broken washer and the burst pipes, bringing in money to fill his empty wallet. He would not hide the green bottles in his tool box, would not sneak off to the barn with a lump under his coat, would not fall asleep in the daylight, would not roar and fume, would not drink himself to death, if only I were perfect.

I am forty-two as I write these words, and I know full well now that my father was an alcoholic, a man consumed by disease rather than by disappointment. What had seemed to me a private grief is in fact a public scourge. In the United States alone some ten or fifteen million people share his ailment, and behind the doors they slam in fury or disgrace, countless other children tremble. I comfort myself with such knowledge, holding it against the throb of memory like an ice pack against a bruise. There are keener sources of grief: poverty, racism, rape, war.   I do not wish to compete for a trophy in suffering.   I am only trying to understand the corrosive mixture of helplessness, responsibility, and shame that I learned to feel as the son of an alcoholic.   I realize now that I did not cause my father's illness, nor could I have cured it.   Yet for all this grown-up knowledge, I am still ten years old, my own son's age, and as that boy I struggle in guilt and confusion to save my father from pain.

CONSIDER A FEW of our synonyms for *drunk*:   tipsy, tight, pickled, soused, and plowed; stoned and stewed, lubricated and inebriated, juiced and sluiced; three sheets to the wind, in your cups, out of your mind, under the table; lit up, tanked up, wiped out; besotted, blotto, bombed, and buzzed; plastered, polluted, putrefied; loaded or looped, boozy, woozy, fuddled, or smashed; crocked and shit-faced, corked and pissed, snockered and sloshed.

It is a mostly humorous lexicon, as the lore that deals with drunks—in jokes and cartoons, in plays, films, and television skits—is largely comic.   Aunt Matilda nips elderberry wine from the sideboard and burps politely during supper. Uncle Fred slouches to the table glassy-eyed, wearing a lamp shade for a hat and murmuring, "Candy is dandy but liquor is quicker."   Inspired by cocktails, Mrs. Somebody recounts the events of her day in a fuzzy dialect, while Mr. Somebody nibbles her ear and croons a bawdy song.   On the sofa with Boyfriend, Daughter giggles, licking gin from her lips, and loosens the bows in her hair.   Junior knocks back some brews with his chums at the Leopard Lounge and stumbles home to the wrong house, wonders foggily why he cannot locate his pajamas, and crawls naked into bed with the ugliest girl in school.   The family dog slurps from a neglected martini and wobbles to the nursery, where he vomits in Baby's shoe.

It is all great fun.   But if in the audience you notice a few laughing faces turn grim when the drunk lurches on stage, don't be surprised, for these are the children of alcoholics.   Over the grinning mask of Dionysus, the leering mask of Bacchus, these children cannot help seeing the bloated features of their own parents.   Instead of laughing, they wince, they mourn.   Instead of celebrating the drunk as one freed from constraints, they pity him as one enslaved.   They refuse to believe *in vino veritas*, having seen their befuddled parents skid away from truth toward folly and oblivion.   And so these children bite their lips until the lush staggers into the wings.

My father, when drunk, was neither funny nor honest; he was pathetic, frightening, deceitful. There seemed to be a leak in him somewhere, and he poured in booze to keep from draining dry. Like a torture victim who refuses to squeal, he would never admit that he had touched a drop, not even in his last year, when he seemed to be dissolving in alcohol before our very eyes. I never knew him to lie about anything, ever, except about this one ruinous fact. Drowsy, clumsy, unable to fix a bicycle tire, throw a baseball, balance a grocery sack, or walk across the room, he was stripped of his true self by drink. In a matter of minutes, the contents of a bottle could transform a brave man into a coward, a buddy into a bully, a gifted athlete and skilled carpenter and shrewd businessman into a bumbler. No dictionary of synonyms for *drunk* would soften the anguish of watching our prince turn into a frog.

FATHER'S DRINKING became the family secret. While growing up, we children never breathed a word of it beyond the four walls of our house. To this day, my brother and sister rarely mention it, and then only when I press them. I did not confess the ugly, bewildering fact to my wife until his wavering walk and slurred speech forced me to. Recently, on the seventh anniversary of my father's death, I asked my mother if she ever spoke of his drinking to friends. "No, no, never," she replied hastily. "I couldn't bear for anyone to know."

The secret bores under the skin, gets in the blood, into the bone, and stays there. Long after you have supposedly been cured of malaria, the fever can flare up, the tremors can shake you. So it is with the fevers of shame. You swallow the bitter quinine of knowledge, and you learn to feel pity and compassion toward the drinker. Yet the shame lingers in your marrow, and, because of the shame, anger.

FOR A LONG STRETCH of my childhood we lived on a military reservation in Ohio, an arsenal where bombs were stored underground in bunkers, vintage airplanes burst into flames, and unstable artillery shells boomed nightly at the dump. We had the feeling, as children, that we played in a mine field, where a heedless footfall could trigger an explosion. When Father was drinking, the house, too, became a mine field. The least bump could set off either parent.

The more he drank, the more obsessed Mother became with stopping him. She hunted for bottles, counted the cash in his wallet, sniffed at his breath. Without meaning to snoop, we children blundered left and right into damning evidence.   On afternoons when he came home from work sober, we flung ourselves at him for hugs, and felt against our ribs the telltale lump in his coat. In the barn we tumbled on the hay and heard beneath our sneakers the crunch of buried glass.   We tugged open a drawer in his workbench, looking for screwdrivers or crescent wrenches, and spied a gleaming six-pack among the tools. Playing tag, we darted around the house just in time to see him sway on the rear stoop and heave a finished bottle into the woods. In his good night kiss we smelled the cloying sweetness of Clorets, the mints he chewed to camouflage his dragon's breath.

I can summon up that kiss right now by recalling Theodore Roethke's lines about his own father in "My Papa's Waltz":

> The whiskey on your breath
> Could make a small boy dizzy;
> But I hung on like death:
> Such waltzing was not easy.

Such waltzing was hard, terribly hard, for with a boy's scrawny arms I was trying to hold my tipsy father upright.

For years, the chief source of those incriminating bottles and cans was a grimy store a mile from us, a cinder block place called Sly's, with two gas pumps outside and a moth-eaten dog asleep in the window. A strip of flypaper, speckled the year round with black bodies, coiled in the doorway. Inside, on rusty metal shelves or in wheezing coolers, you could find pop and Popsicles, cigarettes, potato chips, canned soup, raunchy postcards, fishing gear, Twinkies, wine, and beer. When Father drove anywhere on errands, Mother would send us kids along as guards, warning us not to let him out of our sight. And so with one or more of us on board, Father would cruise up to Sly's, pump a dollar's worth of gas or plump the tires with air, and then, telling us to wait in the car, he would head for that fly-spangled door way.

Dutiful and panicky, we cried, "Let us go in with you!"

"No," he answered. "I'll be back in two shakes."

"Please!"

"No!" he roared. "Don't you budge, or I'll jerk a knot in your tails!"

So we stayed put, kicking the seats, while he ducked inside. Often, when he had parked the car at a careless angle, we gazed in through the window and saw Mr. Sly fetching down from a shelf behind the cash register two green pints of Gallo wine. Father swigged one of them right there at the counter, stuffed the other in his pocket, and then out he came, a bulge in his coat, a flustered look on his red face.

Because the Mom and Pop who ran the dump were neighbors of ours, living just down the tar-blistered road, I hated them all the more for poisoning my father. I wanted to sneak in their store and smash the bottles and set fire to the place. I also hated the Gallo brothers, Ernest and Julio, whose jovial faces shone from the labels of their wine, labels I would find, torn and curled, when I burned the trash. I noted the Gallo brothers' address, in California, and I studied the road atlas to see how far that was from Ohio, because I meant to go out there and tell Ernest and Julio what they were doing to my father, and then, if they showed no mercy, I would kill them.

WHILE GROWING UP on the back roads and in the country schools and cramped Methodist churches of Ohio and Tennessee, I never heard the word *alcoholism*, never happened across it in books or magazines. In the nearby towns, there were no addiction treatment programs, no community mental health centers, no Alcoholics Anonymous chapters, no therapists. Left alone with our grievous secret, we had no way of understanding Father's drinking except as an act of will, a deliberate folly or cruelty, a moral weakness, a sin. He drank because he chose to, pure and simple. Why our father, so playful and competent and kind when sober, would choose to ruin himself and punish his family, we could not fathom.

Our neighborhood was high on the Bible, and the Bible was hard on drunkards. "Woe to those who are heroes at drinking wine, and valiant men in mixing strong drink," wrote Isaiah. "The priest and the prophet reel with strong drink, they are confused with wine, they err in vision, they stumble in giving judgment. For all tables are full of vomit, no place is without filthiness." We children had seen those fouled tables at the local truck stop where the notorious boozers hung out, our father occasionally among them. "Wine and new wine take away the understanding," declared the prophet Hosea. We had also seen evidence of that in our father, who could multiply seven-digit numbers in his head when sober, but when drunk could not help us with fourth-grade math. Proverbs warned: "Do not look at wine when it is red, when it sparkles in the cup and goes down smoothly. At the last it bites like a serpent, and stings like an adder. Your eyes will see strange things, and your mind utter perverse things." Woe, woe.

Dismayingly often, these biblical drunkards stirred up trouble for their own kids. Noah made fresh wine after the flood, drank too much of it, fell asleep without any clothes on, and was glimpsed in the buff by his son Ham, whom Noah promptly cursed. In one passage—it was so shocking we had to read it under our blankets with flashlights—the patriarch Lot fell down drunk and slept with his daughters. The sins of the fathers set their children's teeth on edge.

Our ministers were fond of quoting St. Paul's pronouncement that drunkards would not inherit the kingdom of God. These grave preachers assured us that the wine referred to during the Last Supper was in fact grape juice. Bible and sermons and hymns combined to give us the impression that Moses should have brought down from the mountain another stone tablet, bearing the Eleventh Commandment: Thou shalt not drink.

The scariest and most illuminating Bible story apropos of drunkards was the one about the lunatic and the swine. Matthew, Mark, and Luke each told a version of the tale. We knew it by heart: When Jesus climbed out of his boat one day, this lunatic came charging up from the graveyard, stark naked and filthy, frothing at the mouth, so violent that he broke the strongest chains. Nobody would go near him. Night and day for years this madman had been wailing among the tombs and bruising himself with stones. Jesus took one look at him and said, "Come out of the man, you unclean spirits!" for he could see that the lunatic was possessed by demons. Meanwhile, some hogs were conveniently rooting nearby. "If we have to come out," begged the demons, "at least let us go into those swine." Jesus agreed. The unclean spirits entered the hogs, and the hogs rushed straight off a cliff and plunged into a lake. Hearing the story in Sunday school, my friends thought mainly of the pigs. (How big a splash did they make? Who paid for the lost pork?) But I thought of the redeemed lunatic, who bathed himself and put on clothes and calmly sat at the feet of Jesus, restored—so the Bible said—to "his right mind."

When drunk, our father was clearly in his wrong mind. He became a stranger, as fearful to us as any graveyard lunatic, not quite frothing at the mouth but fierce enough, quick-tempered, explosive; or else he grew maudlin and weepy, which frightened us nearly as much. In my boyhood despair, I reasoned that maybe he wasn't to blame for turning into an ogre. Maybe, like the lunatic, he was possessed by demons. I found support for my theory when I heard liquor referred to as "spirits," when the newspapers reported that somebody had been arrested for "driving under the influence," and when church ladies railed against that "demon drink."

If my father was indeed possessed, who would exorcise him? If he was a sinner, who would save him? If he was ill, who would cure him? If he suffered, who would ease his pain? Not ministers or doctors, for we could not bring ourselves to confide in them; not the neighbors, for we pretended they had never seen him drunk; not Mother, who fussed and pleaded but could not budge him; not my brother and sister, who were only kids. That left me. It did not matter that I, too, was only a child, and a bewildered one at that. I could not excuse myself.

ON FIRST READING a description of delirium tremens—in a book on alcoholism I smuggled from the library—I thought immediately of the frothing lunatic and the frenzied swine. When I read stories or watched films about grisly metamorphoses—Dr. Jekyll becoming Mr. Hyde, the mild husband changing into a werewolf, the kindly neighbor taken over by a brutal alien—I could not help seeing my own father's mutation from sober to drunk. Even today, knowing better, I am attracted by the demonic theory of drink, for when I recall my father's transformation, the emergence of his ugly second self, I find it easy to believe in possession by unclean spirits. We never knew which version of Father would come home from work, the true or the tainted, nor could we guess how far down the slope toward cruelty he would slide.

How far a man *could* slide we gauged by observing our back-road neighbors—the out-of-work miners who had dragged their families to our corner of Ohio from the desolate hollows of Appalachia, the tightfisted farmers, the surly mechanics, the balked and broken men. There was, for example, whiskey-soaked Mr. Jenkins, who beat his wife and kids so hard we could hear their screams from the road. There was Mr. Lavo the wino, who fell asleep smoking time and again, until one night his disgusted wife bundled up the children and went outside and left him in his easy chair to burn; he awoke on his own, staggered out coughing into the yard, and pounded her flat while the children looked on and the shack turned to ash. There was the truck driver, Mr. Sampson, who tripped over his son's tricycle one night while drunk and got so mad that he jumped into his semi and drove away, shifting through the dozen gears, and never came back. We saw the bruised children of these fathers clump onto our school bus, we saw the abandoned children huddle in the pews at church, we saw the stunned and battered mothers begging for help at our doors.

Our own father never beat us, and I don't think he ever beat Mother, but he threatened often. The Old Testament Yahweh was not more terrible in his wrath. Eyes blazing, voice booming, Father would pull out his belt and swear to give us a whipping, but he never followed through, never needed to, because we could imagine it so vividly. He shoved us, pawed us with the back of his hand, as an irked bear might smack a cub, not to injure, just to clear a space. I can see him grabbing Mother by the hair as she cowers on a chair during a nightly quarrel. He twists her neck back until she gapes up at him, and then he lifts over her skull a glass quart bottle of milk, the milk running down his forearm, and he yells at her, "Say just one more word, one goddamn word, and I'll shut you up!" I fear she will prick him with her sharp tongue, but she is terrified into silence, and so am I, and the leaking bottle quivers in the air, and milk slithers through the red hair of my father's uplifted arm, and the entire scene is there to this moment, the head jerked back, the club raised.

When the drink made him weepy, Father would pack a bag and kiss each of us children on the head, and announce from the front door that he was moving out. "Where to?" we demanded, fearful each time that he would leave for good, as Mr. Sampson had roared away for good in his diesel truck. "Someplace where I won't get hounded every minute," Father would answer, his jaw quivering. He stabbed a look at Mother, who might say, "Don't run into the ditch before you get there," or, "Good riddance," and then he would slink away. Mother watched him go with arms crossed over her chest, her face closed like the lid on a box of snakes. We children bawled. Where could he go? To the truck stop, that den of iniquity? To one of those dark, ratty flophouses in town? Would he wind up sleeping under a railroad bridge or on a park bench or in a cardboard box, mummied in rags, like the bums we had seen on our trips to Cleveland and Chicago? We bawled and bawled, wondering if he would ever come back.

He always did come back, a day or a week later, but each time there was a sliver less of him.

IN KAFKA'S *The Metamorphosis*, which opens famously with Gregor Samsa waking up from uneasy dreams to find himself transformed into an insect, Gregor's family keep reassuring themselves that things will be just fine again, "When he comes back to us." Each time alcohol transformed our father, we held out the same hope, that he would really and truly come back to us, our authentic father, the tender and playful and competent man, and then all things would be fine. We had grounds for such hope. After his weepy departures and chapfallen returns, he would sometimes go weeks, even months without drinking. Those were glad times. Joy banged inside my ribs. Every day without the furtive glint of bottles, every meal without a fight, every bedtime without sobs encouraged us to believe that such bliss might go on forever.

Mother was fooled by just such a hope all during the forty-odd years she knew this Greeley Ray Sanders. Soon after she met him in a Chicago delicatessen on the eve of World War II, and fell for his butter-melting Mississippi drawl and his wavy red hair, she learned that he drank heavily. But then so did a lot of men. She would soon coax or scold him into breaking the nasty habit. She would point out to him how ugly and foolish it was, this bleary drinking, and then he would quit. He refused to quit during their engagement, however, still refused during the first years of marriage, refused until my sister came along. The shock of fatherhood sobered him, and he remained sober through my birth at the end of the war and right on through until we moved in 1951 to the Ohio arsenal, that paradise of bombs. Like all places that make a business of death, the arsenal had more than its share of alcoholics and drug addicts and other varieties of escape artists. There I turned six and started school and woke into a child's flickering awareness, just in time to see my father begin sneaking swigs in the garage.

He sobered up again for most of a year at the height of the Korean War, to celebrate the birth of my brother. But aside from that dry spell, his only breaks from drinking before I graduated from high school were just long enough to raise and then dash our hopes. Then during the fall of my senior year—the time of the

Cuban missile crisis, when it seemed that the nightly explosions at the munitions dump and the nightly rages in our household might spread to engulf the globe— Father collapsed. His liver, kidneys, and heart all conked out. The doctors saved him, but only by a hair. He stayed in the hospital for weeks, going through a withdrawal so terrible that Mother would not let us visit him. If he wanted to kill himself, the doctors solemnly warned him, all he had to do was hit the bottle again. One binge would finish him.

Father must have believed them, for he stayed dry the next fifteen years. It was an answer to prayer, Mother said, it was a miracle. I believe it was a reflex of fear, which he sustained over the years through courage and pride. He knew a man could die from drink, for his brother Roscoe had. We children never laid eyes on doomed Uncle Roscoe, but in the stories Mother told us he became a fairy-tale figure, like a boy who took the wrong turning in the woods and was gobbled up by the wolf.

The fifteen-year dry spell came to an end with Father's retirement in the spring of 1978. Like many men, he gave up his identity along with his job. One day he was a boss at the factory, with a brass plate on his door and a reputation to uphold; the next day he was a nobody at home. He and Mother were leaving Ontario, the last of the many places to which his job had carried them, and they were moving to a new house in Mississippi, his childhood stomping grounds. As a boy in Mississippi, Father sold Coca-Cola during dances while the moonshiners peddled their brew in the parking lot; as a young blade, he fought in bars and in the ring, seeking a state Golden Gloves championship; he gambled at poker, hunted pheasants, raced motorcycles and cars, played semiprofessional baseball, and, along with all his buddies—in the Black Cat Saloon, behind the cotton gin, in the woods—he drank. It was a perilous youth to dream of recovering.

After his final day of work, Mother drove on ahead with a car full of begonias and violets, while Father stayed behind to oversee the packing. When the van was loaded, the sweaty movers broke open a six-pack and offered him a beer.

"Let's drink to retirement!" they crowed. "Let's drink to freedom! to fishing! hunting! loafing! Let's drink to a guy who's going home!"

At least I imagine some such words, for that is all I can do, imagine, and I see Father's hand trembling in midair as he thinks about the fifteen sober years and about the doctors' warning, and he tells himself *Goddamnit, I am a free man,* and *Why can't a free man drink one beer after a lifetime of hard work?* and I see his arm reaching, his fingers closing, the can tilting to his lips. I even supply a label for the beer, a swaggering brand that promises on television to deliver the essence of life. I watch the amber liquid pour down his throat, the alcohol steal into his blood, the key turn in his brain.

SOON AFTER MY PARENTS moved back to Father's treacherous stomping ground, my wife and I visited them in Mississippi with our five-year-old daughter. Mother had been too distraught to warn me about the return of the demons. So when I climbed out of the car that bright July morning and saw my father napping in the hammock, I felt uneasy, for in all his sober years I had never known him to sleep in daylight. Then he lurched upright, blinked his bloodshot eyes, and greeted us in a syrupy voice. I was hurled back helpless into childhood.

"What's the matter with Papaw?" our daughter asked.

"Nothing," I said. "Nothing!"

Like a child again, I pretended not to see him in his stupor, and behind my phony smile I grieved. On that visit and on the few that remained before his death, once again I found bottles in the workbench, bottles in the woods. Again his hands shook too much for him to run a saw, to make his precious miniature furniture, to drive straight down back roads. Again he wound up in the ditch, in the hospital, in jail, in treatment centers. Again he shouted and wept. Again he lied. "I never touched a drop," he swore. "Your mother's making it up."

I no longer fancied I could reason with the men whose names I found on the bottles—Jim Beam, Jack Daniel's—nor did I hope to save my father by burning down a store. I was able now to press the cold statistics about alcoholism against the ache of memory: ten million victims, fifteen million, twenty. And yet, in spite of my age, I reacted in the same blind way as I had in childhood, ignoring biology, forgetting numbers, vainly seeking to erase through my efforts whatever drove him to drink. I worked on their place twelve and sixteen hours a day, in the swelter of Mississippi summers, digging ditches, running electrical wires, planting trees, mowing grass, building sheds, as though what nagged at him was some list of chores, as though by taking his worries on my shoulders I could redeem him.   I was flung back into boyhood, acting as though my father would not drink himself to death if only I were perfect.

I failed of perfection; he succeeded in dying. To the end, he considered himself not sick but sinful. "Do you want to kill yourself?" I asked him. "Why not?" he answered. "Why the hell not? What's there to save?" To the end, he would not speak about his feelings, would not or could not give a name to the beast that was devouring him.

In silence, he went rushing off the cliff.   Unlike the biblical swine, however, he left behind a few of the demons to haunt his children. Life with him and the loss of him twisted us into shapes that will be familiar to other sons and daughters of alcoholics. My brother became a rebel, my sister retreated into shyness, I played the stalwart and dutiful son who would hold the family together. If my father was unstable, I would be a rock. If he squandered money on drink, I would pinch every penny. If he wept when drunk—and only when drunk—I would not let myself weep at all. If he roared at the Little League umpire for calling my pitches balls, I would throw nothing but strikes. Watching him flounder and rage, I came to dread the loss of control. I would go through life without making anyone mad. I vowed never to put in my mouth or veins any chemical that would banish my everyday self. I would never make a scene, never lash out at the ones I loved, never hurt a soul. Through hard work, relentless work, I would achieve something dazzling—in the classroom, on the basketball floor, in the science lab, in the pages of books—and my achievement would distract the world's eyes from his humiliation.   I would become a worthy sacrifice, and the smoke of my burning would please God.

It is far easier to recognize these twists in my character than to undo them. Work has become an addiction for me, as drink was an addiction for my father. Knowing this, my daughter gave me a placard for the wall: WORKAHOLIC. The labor is endless and futile, for I can no more redeem myself through work than I could redeem my father. I still panic in the face of other people's anger, because his drunken temper was so terrible.   I shrink from causing sadness or disappointment even to strangers, as though I were still concealing the family shame. I still notice every twitch of emotion in the faces around me, having learned as a child to read the weather in faces, and I blame myself for their least pang of unhappiness or anger. In certain moods I blame myself for everything. Guilt burns like acid in my veins.

I AM MOVED TO WRITE these pages now because my own son, at the age of ten, is taking on himself the griefs of the world, and in particular the griefs of his father. He tells me that when I am gripped by sadness he feels responsible; he feels there must be something he can do to spring me from depression, to fix my life. And that crushing sense of responsibility is exactly what I felt at the age of ten in the face of my father's drinking. My son wonders if I, too, am possessed. I write, therefore, to drag into the light what eats at me—the fear, the guilt, the shame—so that my own children may be spared.

I still shy away from nightclubs, from bars, from parties where the solvent is alcohol. My friends puzzle over this, but it is no more peculiar than for a man to shy away from the lions' den after seeing his father torn apart. I took my own first drink at the age of twenty-one, half a glass of burgundy. I knew the odds of my becoming an alcoholic were four times higher than for the sons of nonalcoholic fathers. So I sipped warily.

I still do——once a week, perhaps, a glass of wine, a can of beer, nothing stronger, nothing more. I listen for the turning of a key in my brain.

Critical Thinking

1.   Who is "Under the Influence"? Be specific.

2.   How does Sanders illustrate his father's transformation?

3.   Sanders reveals a variety of conflicting emotions. What are they? How does he convey the burden he lives with as a grown man with a family of his own?

Writing Assignments

1.   Sanders tells how his life revolved around his father's alcoholism. The entire family was affected by the father's addiction. Write an essay in which you compare and/or contrast your experience or observation of addiction to Sanders' experience of growing up with alcoholism.

2.   Write a stylistic analysis essay. Select two or three stylistic tools—repetition, dialogue, figurative language, literary allusions. Where does he use them? How do they relate to the theme(s)?

3.   Sanders writes about how he lived "under the influence" of his father. Write a personal essay about an adult who influenced your childhood (either positively or negatively).

In general, one's memories of any period must necessarily weaken as one moves away from it . . . But it can also happen that one's memories grow sharper after a long lapse of time, because one is looking at the past with fresh eyes." - George Orwell

"An Episode of Bedwetting"[*]
George Orwell

Born in 1903, essayist and political writer George Orwell was best known for <u>Animal Farm</u> (1945) and <u>Nineteen Eighty-Four</u> (1949) This excerpt is from his posthumously published <u>Such, Such Were the Joys</u>.[†]

SOON AFTER I ARRIVED AT CROSSGATES (NOT IMMEDIATELY, BUT a week or two, just when I seemed to be settling into the routine of school life) I began wetting my bed. I was now aged eight, so that this was a reversion to a habit which I must have grown out of at least four years earlier.

Nowadays, I believe, bed-wetting in such circumstances is taken for granted. It is a normal reaction in children who have been removed from their homes to a strange place. In those days, however, it was looked on as a disgusting crime which the child committed on purpose and for which the proper cure was a beating. For my part I did not need to be told it was a crime. Night after night I prayed, with a fervour never previously attained in my prayers, "Please God, do not let me wet my bed! Oh, please God, do not let me wet my bed!" but it made remarkably little difference. Some nights the thing happened, others not. There was no volition about it, no consciousness. You did not

[†] "George Orwell," *Contemporary Authors Online.* The Gale Group, 2001. January 26, 2002 <http://www.galenet.com/servlet/LitRC?c=1&ai=10159&ste=6&docNum=H1200003418&bConts =16303&tab=1&vrsn=3&ca=1&tbst=arp&ST=Orwell%2C+George&srchtp=athr&n=10&locID=n ypl&OP=contains>.

properly speaking *do* the deed: you merely woke up in the morning and found that the sheets were wringing wet.

After the second or third offence I was warned that I should be beaten next time, but I received the warning in a curiously roundabout way. One afternoon, as we were filing out from tea, Mrs. Simpson, the headmaster's wife, was sitting at the head of one of the tables, chatting with a lady of whom I know nothing, except that she was on an afternoon's visit to the school. She was an intimidating, masculine-looking person wearing a riding habit, or something that I took to be a riding-habit. I was just leaving the room when Mrs. Simpson called me back, as though to introduce me to the visitor.

Mrs. Simpson was nicknamed Bingo, and I shall call her by that name for I seldom think of her by any other. (Officially, however, she was addressed as Mum, probably a corruption of' the "Ma'am" used by pubic schoolboys to their housemasters' wives.) She was a stocky square-built woman with hard red checks, a flat top to her head, prominent brows and deepset, suspicious eyes. Although a great deal of the time she was full of false heartiness, jollying one along with mannish slang ("*Buck* up, old chap!" and so forth), and even using one's Christian name, her eyes never lost their anxious, accusing look. It was very difficult to look her in the face without feeling guilty, even at moments when one was not guilty of anything in particular.

"Here is a little boy," said Bingo, indicating me to the strange lady, "who wets his bed every night. Do you know what I am going to do if you wet your bed again?" she added, turning to me. "I am going to get the Sixth Form to beat you."

The strange lady put on an air of being inexpressibly shocked, and exclaimed "I-should-think-so!" And here occurred one of those wild, almost lunatic misunderstandings which are part of the daily experience of childhood. The Sixth Form was a group of older boys who were selected as having "character" and were empowered to beat smaller boys. I had not yet learned of their existence, and I mis-heard the phrase "the Sixth Form" as "Mrs. Form." I took it as referring to the strange lady—I thought, that is, that her name was Mrs. Form. It was an improbable name, but a child has no judgment in such matters. I imagined, therefore, that it was *she* who was to be deputed to beat me. It did not strike me as strange that this job should be turned over to a casual visitor in no way connected with the school. I merely assumed that "Mrs. Form" was a stern disciplinarian who enjoyed beating people (somehow her appearance seemed to bear this out) and I had an immediate terrifying vision of her arriving for the occasion in full riding kit and armed with a hunting whip. To this day I can feel myself almost swooning with shame as I stood, a very small, round-faced boy in short corduroy knickers, before the two women. I could not speak. I felt that I should die if "Mrs. Form" were to beat me. But my dominant feeling was not fear or even resentment: it was simply shame because one more person, and that a woman, had been told of my disgusting offence.

A little later, I forget how, I learned that it was not after all "Mrs. Form" who would do the beating. I cannot remember whether it was that very night that I wetted my bed again, but at any rate I did wet it again quite soon. Oh, the despair, the feeling of cruel injustice, after all my prayers and resolutions, at once again waking between the clammy sheets! There was no chance of hiding what I had done. The grim statuesque matron, Daphne by name, arrived in the dormitory specially to inspect my bed. She pulled back the clothes, then drew herself up, and the dreaded words seemed to come rolling out of her like a peal of thunder:

"REPORT YOURSELF to the headmaster after breakfast!"

I do not know how many times I heard that phrase during my early years at Crossgates. It was only very rarely that it did not mean a beating. The words always had a portentous sound in my ears, like muffled drums or the words of the death sentence.

When I arrived to report myself, Bingo was doing something or other at the long shiny table in the ante-room to the study. Her uneasy eyes searched me as I went past. In the study Mr. Simpson, nicknamed Sim, was waiting. Sim was a round-shouldered, curiously oafish-looking man, not large but shambling in gait, with a chubby face which was like that of an overgrown baby, and which was capable of good humour. He knew, of course, why I had been sent to him, and had already taken a bone-handled riding crop out of the cupboard, but it was part of the punishment of reporting yourself that you had to proclaim your offence with your own lips. When I had said my say, he read me a short but pompous lecture, then seized me by the scruff of the neck, twisted me over and began beating me with the riding crop. He had a habit of continuing his lecture while he flogged you, and I remember the words "you dir-ty lit-tle boy" keeping time with the blows. The beating did not hurt (perhaps as it was the first time, he was not hitting me very hard), and I walked out feeling very much better. The fact that the beating had not hurt was a sort of victory and partially wiped out the shame of the bed-wetting. I was even incautious enough to wear a grin on my face. Some small boys were hanging about in the passage outside the door of the ante-room.

"D'you get the cane?"

"It didn't hurt," I said proudly.

Bingo had heard everything. Instantly her voice came screaming after me:

"Come here! Come here this instant! What was that you said?"

"I said it didn't hurt," I faltered out.

"How dare you say a thing like that? Do you think that is a proper thing to say? Go in and REPORT YOURSELF AGAIN!"

This time Sim laid on in real earnest. He continued for a length of time that frightened and astonished me—about five minutes, it seemed—ending up by breaking the riding crop. The bone handle went flying across the room.

"Look what you've made me do!" he said furiously, holding up the broken crop.

I had fallen into a chair, weakly snivelling. I remember that this was the only time throughout my boyhood when a beating actually reduced me to tears, and curiously enough I was not even now crying because of the pain. The second beating had not hurt very much either. Fright and shame seemed to have anaesthetised me. I was crying partly because I felt that this was expected of me, partly from genuine repentance, but partly also because of a deeper grief which is peculiar to childhood and not easy to convey: a sense of desolate loneliness and helplessness, of being locked up not only in a hostile world but in a world of good and evil where the rules were such that it was actually not possible for me to keep them.

I knew that bed-wetting was (a) wicked and (b) outside my control. The second fact I was personally aware of, and the first I did not question. It was possible, therefore, to commit a sin without knowing that you committed it, without wanting to commit it, and without being able to avoid it. Sin was not necessarily something that you did: it might be something that happened to you. I do not want to claim that this idea flashed into my mind as a complete novelty at this very moment, under the blows of Sim's cane: I must have had glimpses of it even before I left home, for my early childhood had not been altogether happy.

But at any rate this was the great, abiding lesson of my boyhood: that I was in a world where it was *not possible* for me to be good. And the double beating was a turning-point, for it brought home to me for the first time the harshness of the environment into which I had been flung. Life was more terrible, and I was more wicked, than I had imagined. At any rate, as I sat on the edge of a chair in Sim's study, with not even the self-possession to stand up while he stormed at me, I had a conviction of sin and folly and weakness, such as I do not remember to have felt before.

In general, one's memories of any period must necessarily weaken as one moves away from it. One is constantly learning new facts, and old ones have to drop out to make way for them. At twenty I could have written the history of my schooldays with an accuracy which would be quite impossible now. But it can also happen that one's memories grow sharper after a long lapse of time, because one is looking at the past with fresh eyes and can isolate and, as it were, notice facts which previously existed undifferentiated among a mass of others. Here are two things which in a sense I remembered, but which did not strike me as strange or interesting until quite recently. One is that the second beating seemed to me a just and reasonable punishment. To get one beating, and then to get another and far fiercer one on top of it, for being so unwise as to show that the first had not hurt—that was quite natural. The gods are jealous, and when you have good fortune you should conceal it. The other is that I accepted the broken riding crop as my own crime. I can still recall my feeling as I saw the handle lying on carpet—the feeling of having done an ill-bred, clumsy thing, and ruined an expensive object. *I* had broken it: so Sim told me, and so I believed. This acceptance of guilt lay unnoticed in my memory for twenty or thirty years.

So much for the episode of the bed-wetting. But there is one more thing to be remarked. This is that I did not wet my bed again—at least, I did wet it once again, and received another beating, after which the trouble stopped. So perhaps this barbarous remedy does work; though at a heavy price, I have no doubt.

Critical Thinking

1. What roles does memory play in the essay? Where in the text are there references to memory and what point is Orwell trying make about the reliability of memory?

2.   Orwell states, "Sin was not necessarily something you did; it might be something that happened to you." Explain.

3.   Examine Orwell's use of word choice. For example, what effect do the words "crime," "death sentence," "beating," "guilty," and "offense" have on the reader?

Writing Assignments

1.   Do you think that the punishment was "barbaric"? Explain why or why not.

2.   Orwell is very careful in writing about his moments of insight: "I do not want to claim that this idea flashed in my mind as a complete novelty at this very moment, under the blows of Sim's cane." What are insights and how do we receive them?

3.   What is the difference between committing a sin with intent and committing a sin without intent?

"Stories set the inner life into motion." –

Clarissa Pinkola Estés

"White Tigers"[*]
Maxine Hong Kingston

Essayist and novelist Maxine (Ting Ting) Hong Kingston has received numerous awards, including the National Book Critics Circle Award (1976) for The Woman Warrior: Memoirs of a Girlhood Among Ghosts—the following is an excerpt from this highly acclaimed bestselling book.[†]

When we Chinese girls listened to the adults talk-story, we learned that we failed if we grew up to be but wives or slaves. We could be heroines, swordswomen. Even if she had to rage across all China, a swordswoman got even with anybody who hurt her family. Perhaps women were once so dangerous that they had to have their feet bound. It was a woman who invented white crane boxing only two hundred years ago. She was already an expert pole fighter, daughter of a teacher trained at the Shao-lin temple, where there lived an order of fighting monks. She was combing her hair one morning when a white crane alighted outside her window. She teased it with her pole, which it pushed aside with a soft brush of its wing. Amazed, she dashed outside and tried to knock the crane off its perch. It snapped her pole in two. Recognizing the presence of great power, she asked the spirit of the white crane if it would teach her to fight. It answered with a cry that white crane boxers imitate today. Later the bird returned

[*] From *The Woman Warrior* by Maxine Hong Kingston, copyright © 1975, 1976 by Maxine Hong Kingston. Used by permission of Alfred A. Knopf, a division of Random House, Inc.
[†] "Maxine (Ting Ting) Hong Kingston" *Contemporary Authors Online*. The Gale Group, 2001. 3 March 2001. January 26, 2002. <http://www.galenet.com/servlet/LitRC?c=1&ai=49432&ste =6&docNum=H1000054308&bConts=16047&tab=1&vrsn=3&ca=1&tbst=arp&ST=Kingston%2 C+Maxine%28Ting+Ting%29&srchtp=athr&n=10&locID=nypl&OP=contains>.

as an old man, and he guided her boxing for many years. Thus she gave the world a new martial art.

This was one of the tamer, more modern stories, mere introduction. My mother told others that followed swordswomen through woods and palaces for years. Night after night my mother would talk-story until we fell asleep. I couldn't tell where the stories left off and the dreams began, her voice the voice of the heroines in my sleep. And on Sundays, from noon to midnight, we went to the movies at the Confucius Church. We saw swordswomen jump over houses from a standstill; they didn't even need a running start.

At last I saw that I too had been in the presence of great power, my mother talking-story. After I grew up, I heard the chant of Fa Mu Lan, the girl who took her father's place in battle. Instantly I remembered that as a child I had followed my mother about the house, the two of us singing about how Fa Mu Lan fought gloriously and returned alive from war to settle in the village. I had forgotten this chant that was once mine, given me by my mother, who may not have known its power to remind. She said I would grow up a wife and a slave, but she taught me the song of the warrior woman, Fa Mu Lan. I would have to grow up a warrior woman. —> She did not do what her mom said . . .

The call would come from a bird that flew over our roof. In the brush drawings it looks like the ideograph for "human," two black wings. The bird would cross the sun and lift into the mountains (which look like the ideograph "mountain"), there parting the mist briefly that swirled opaque again. I would be a little girl of seven the day I followed the bird away into the mountains. The brambles would tear off my shoes and the rocks cut my feet and fingers, but I would keep climbing, eyes upward to follow the bird. We would go around and around the tallest mountain, climbing ever upward. I would drink from the river, which I would meet again and again. We would go so high the plants would change, and the river that flows past the village would become a waterfall. At the height where the bird used to disappear, the clouds would gray the world like an ink wash.

Even when I got used to that gray, I would only see peaks as if shaded in pencil, rocks like charcoal rubbings, everything so murky. There would be just two black strokes—the bird. Inside the clouds—inside the dragon's breath—I would not know how many hours or days passed. Suddenly, without noise, I would break clear into a yellow, warm world. New trees would lean toward me at mountain angles, but when I looked for the village, it would have vanished under the clouds.

The bird, now gold so close to the sun, would come to rest on the thatch of a hut, which, until the bird's two feet touched it, was camouflaged as part of the mountainside . . . .

My American life has been such a disappointment.

"I got straight A's, Mama."

"Let me tell you a true story about a girl who saved her village."

I could not figure out what was my village. And it was important that I do something big and fine, or else my parents would sell me when we made our way back to China. In China there were solutions for what to do with little girls who ate up food and threw tantrums. You can't eat straight A's.

When one of my parents or the emigrant villagers said, " 'Feeding girls is feeding cowbirds,' " I would thrash on the floor and scream so hard I couldn't talk. I couldn't stop.

"What's the matter with her?"

"I don't know. Bad, I guess. You know how girls are. 'There's no profit in raising girls. Better to raise geese than girls.' "

"I would hit her if she were mine. But then there's no use wasting all that discipline on a girl. 'When you raise girls, you're raising children for strangers.' "

"Stop that crying!" my mother would yell. "I'm going to hit you if you don't stop. Bad girl! Stop!" I'm going to remember never to hit or to scold my children for crying, I thought, because then they will only cry more.

"I'm not a bad girl," I would scream. "I'm not a bad girl. I'm not a bad girl." I might as well have said, "I'm not a girl."

"When you were little, all you had to say was 'I'm not a bad girl,' and you could make yourself cry," my mother says, talking-story about my childhood.

I minded that the emigrant villagers shook their heads at my sister and me. "One girl—and another girl," they said, and made our parents ashamed to take us out together. The good part about my brothers being born was that people stopped saying, "All girls," but I learned new grievances. "Did you roll an egg on *my* face like that when *I* was born?" "Did you have a full-month party for *me*?" "Did you turn on all the lights?" "Did you send my picture to Grandmother?" "Why not? Because I'm a girl? Is that why not?" "Why didn't you teach me English?" "You like having me beaten up at school, don't you?"

"She is very mean, isn't she?" the emigrant villagers would say.

"Come, children. Hurry. Hurry. Who wants to go out with Great-Uncle?" On Saturday mornings my great-uncle, the ex-river pirate, did the shopping. "Get your coats, whoever's coming."

"I'm coming. I'm coming. Wait for me."

When he heard girls' voices, he turned on us and roared, "No girls!" and left my sisters and me hanging our coats back up, not looking at one another. The boys came back with candy and new toys. When they walked through Chinatown, the people must have said, "A boy—and another boy—and another boy!" At my great-uncle's funeral I secretly tested out feeling glad that he was dead—the six-foot bearish masculinity of him. → she held a grudge against him

I went away to college—Berkeley in the sixties—and I studied, and I marched to change the world, but I did not turn into a boy. I would have liked to bring myself back as a boy for my parents to welcome with chickens and pigs. That was for my brother, who returned alive from Vietnam.

→ If I went to Vietnam, I would not come back; females desert families. It was said, "There is an outward tendency in females," which meant that I was getting straight A's for the good of my future husband's family, not my own. I did not plan ever to have a husband. I would show my mother and father and the nosey emigrant villagers that girls have no outward tendency. I stopped getting straight A's.

And all the time I was having to turn myself American-feminine, or no dates.

There is a Chinese word for the female *I*—which is "slave." Break the women with their own tongues!

I refused to cook. When I had to wash dishes, I would crack one or two. "Bad girl," my mother yelled, and sometimes that made me gloat rather than cry. Isn't a bad girl almost a boy?

"What do you want to be when you grow up, little girl?"

"A lumberjack in Oregon."

Even now, unless I'm happy, I burn the food when I cook. I do not feed people. I let the dirty dishes rot. I eat at other people's tables but won't invite them to mine, where the dishes are rotting.

If I could not eat, perhaps I could make myself a warrior like the swordswoman who drives me. I will—I must—rise and plow the fields as soon as the baby comes out.

Once I get outside the house, what bird might call me; on what horse could I ride away? Marriage and childbirth strengthen the swordswoman, who is not a maid like Joan of Arc. Do the women's work; then do more work, which will become ours too. No husband of mine will say, "I could have been a drummer, but I had to think about the wife and kids. You know how it is." Nobody supports me at the expense of his own adventure. Then I get bitter: no one supports me; I am not loved enough to be supported. That I am not a burden has to compensate for the sad envy when I look at women loved enough to be supported. Even now China wraps double binds around my feet.

Women don't have the freedom

Critical Thinking

1.   Why do you think the mother would "talkstory" night after night? What stories did she tell?

2.   Compare the attitudes revealed towards girls—both in reality and in the stories.

3.   Respond to the last line, "Even now China wraps double binds around my feet."

Writing Assignments

1.   Write an essay about stories you were told as a child. What impact did they have on you? Why do parents tell children stories?

2.   Although this story is specific to Chinese culture, in what ways is it universal?

3.   "There's no profit in raising girls." Use this sentence as a freewriting prompt. After your freewrite, review your responses. How did you react to the statement. Compare your answers with other classmates.

RELATING THE AUTHORS' IDEAS

1. What is shame? Sanders writes about the shame he experienced as a result of concealing his father's addiction. Likewise, Walker describes how she would hide in her room whenever relatives arrived for a visit. Compare and contrast Sanders' experience of shame to Walker's.

2. Both Walker and Orwell experience moments of insight. Compare and contrast the insights gained.

3. Orwell says, "I was in a world where it was not *possible* to be good." Likewise, Kingston was living in a world where it was not possible for her to valued as much as the boys in her culture. Did you ever experience a time when you felt defeated—not because of anything you voluntarily did, but because of who you were? Explain.

4. In each of the stories, the writers re-create the myriad of emotions experienced in childhood–for example, love, fear, hate. Select any two or three writers and compare and/or contrast how each writer re-creates the experience so that we, the reader, feel the emotion.

Chapter III

Educating the Self

III

Educating the Self

Introduction

From childhood into adulthood, we receive various forms of education: social, from our parents and other family members; academic, from schools and universities; and self, from our own proactive inquiries. The selections by Jamaica Kincaid, Malcolm X, Rebecca Lawson, Sue Ribner, Russell Baker, and William H. Honan explore the complexities involved in educating the self: at home, in school, and, for a lifetime.

In Jamaica Kincaid's "Girl," the young girl receives a social education. The girl's mother gives her a series of repetitive "how-to" instructions on a variety of activities: washing clothes, cooking, eating, walking, sewing, ironing, setting a table, loving, etc. The repetitive instructions separated by semicolons continue for over a page. As young adults, many of us have experienced (and continue to experience) similar indoctrination by parents and other figures of authority. Unlike the aggressive mother in "Girl," the mother in "The Swimming Lesson", by Rebecca Lawson, is passive. Lawson observes that parents uncomfortable making "tough or unpleasant decisions" often "respond to their fears by paradoxically treating their children as peers—seeking their input on every little decision." Which parenting style do you prefer? Which is more effective?

Ideally, children are expected to receive an equal education in school. What happens when a student is deprived of an education while in school, merely because she is a girl? In "The Language Lesson" Sue Ribner writes about her experience as a young girl in Hebrew school. Although she tries to participate in the learning process, she is dismissed, ignored, relegated to a post in the back—expected not to learn, encouraged to remain silent.

Russell Baker, in contrast, had a teacher who encouraged him. In "The Art of Eating Spaghetti," Baker relives the "pure ecstasy" he experienced in high school when he first discovered his calling as a writer, that his "words had the power to make people laugh." His support opened new doors for him. For the first time, he sensed a possibility. He discovered he had a talent. Malcolm X, on the other hand, was inspired to learn how to read by a fellow inmate Bimbi. Driven by curiosity and sustained by discipline, Malcolm X taught himself how to read while in prison. In "Learning To Read," he says, "I have often reflected upon the new vistas that reading opened to me. I knew right there in prison that reading had changed forever the course of my life. As I see it today, the ability to read awoke inside me some long dormant craving to be mentally alive." During his prison stay he was disciplined and focused. He states, "Prison enabled me to study far more intensively than I would have if my life had gone differently and I had attended some college. I imagine that one of the biggest troubles with colleges is there are too many distractions, too much panty-raiding fraternities, and boola-boola and all of that." Are there too many distractions in college? What are the benefits of pursuing your own studies? Are there any drawbacks?

In fact, what is the value of attending a university with a set curriculum? In "Curriculum and Culture: New Round is Opened in A Scholarly Fistfight" William H. Honan explores the heated debate over what should be at the center of studies in a college curriculum. The debate is not new, as Honan observes: "Through the centuries, classicists and modernists have clashed over how to best educate the young."

Introspection is an important tool in understanding the roots of our education. Just as it is vital to reflect upon who influenced us at home and in school, it is just as vital to understand what motivates us to learn now. May curiosity continually propel us forward on our quest to educate the self for a lifetime.

"Women are traditionally trained to place others' needs first . . . their satisfaction to be in making it possible for others to use their abilities."
--Tillie Olsen <u>Silences</u> (1978)

"Girl"[*]
Jamaica Kincaid

Jamaica Kincaid is writer, essayist, and novelist. She is the recipient of numerous nominations and awards. Her books include, <u>At the Bottom of the River</u>, <u>The Autobiography of My Mother</u> and <u>My Brother</u>. The excerpt is from her book <u>At the Bottom of the River</u>.[†]

Wash the white clothes on Monday and put them on the stone heap; wash the color clothes on Tuesday and put them on the clothesline to dry; don't walk barehead in the hot sun; cook pumpkin fritters in very hot sweet oil; soak your little clothes right after you take them off; when buying cotton to make yourself a nice blouse, be sure that it doesn't have gum on it, because that way it won't hold up well after a wash; soak salt fish overnight before you cook it; is it true that you sing *benna* in Sunday school?; always eat your food in such a way that it won't turn someone else's stomach; on Sundays try to walk like a lady and not like the slut you are so bent on becoming; don't sing *benna* in Sunday school; you mustn't speak to wharf-rat boys, not even to give directions; don't eat fruits on the street—flies will follow you; *but I don't sing benna on Sundays at all and never in Sunday school*; this is how to sew on a button; this is how to make a buttonhole for the button you have just sewed on; this is how to hem a dress when you see the hem coming down and so to prevent yourself from looking like the slut I know you are so bent on becoming; this is how you iron your father's khaki shirt

---

[†] "Jamaica Kincaid," *Contemporary Authors Online*. The Gale Group, 2001. 10 October, 2001. January 26, 2002 <http://www.galenet.com/servlet/LitRC?c=1&ai=49245&ste= 6&docNum =H10 00054093&bConts=16303&tab=1&vrsn=3&ca=1&tbst=arp&ST=Kincaid%2C+Jamaica&srchtp= athr&n=10&locID=nypl&OP=contains>.

so that it doesn't have a crease; this is how you iron your father's khaki pants so that they don't have a crease; this is how you grow okra—far from the house, because okra tree harbors red ants; when you are growing dasheen, make sure it gets plenty of water or else it makes your throat itch when you are eating it; this is how you sweep a corner; this is how you sweep a whole house; this is how you sweep a yard; this is how you smile to someone you don't like too much; this is how you smile to someone you don't like at all; this is how you smile to someone you like completely; this is how you set a table for tea; this is how you set a table for dinner; this is how you set a table for dinner with an important guest; this is how you set a table for lunch; this is how you set a table for breakfast; this is how to behave in the presence of men who don't know you very well, and this way they won't recognize immediately the slut I have warned you against becoming; be sure to wash every day, even if it is with your own spit; don't squat down to play marbles—you are not a boy, you know; don't pick people's flowers—you might catch something; don't throw stones at blackbirds, because it might not be a blackbird at all; this is how to make a bread pudding; this is how to make *doukona*; this is how to make pepper pot; this is how to make a good medicine for a cold; this is how to make a good medicine to throw away a child before it even becomes a child; this is how to catch a fish; this is how to throw back a fish you don't like, and that way something bad won't fall on you; this is how to bully a man; this is how a man bullies you; this is how to love a man, and if this doesn't work there are other ways, and if they don't work don't feel too bad about giving up; this is how to spit up in the air if you feel like it, and this is how to move quick so that it doesn't fall on you; this is how to make ends meet; always squeeze bread to make sure it's fresh; *but what if the baker won't let me feel the bread?*; you mean to say that after all you are really going to be the kind of woman who the baker won't let near the bread?

Critical Thinking

1.   Who is speaking?

2.   Examine the sentence structure. Why does Kincaid use so many semi-colons?

3.   What phrases and words are repeated? What purpose do you think they serve? Are they effective? Why or why not?

Writing Assignments

1. Respond to the mother. Write a page of similar length in which you imagine the conversation from the daughter's point of view.

2. Parents often give advice to their children. What advice did you receive and in what manner?

3. What is a social education? Explain.

> *"How many a man has dated a new era in his life from the reading of a book"*
> — Thoreau, "Reading," <u>Walden</u>

"Learning to Read"[*]
Malcolm X

Born Malcolm Little, civil rights activist Malcolm X changed his surname to "X" in 1952 "to signify his lost tribal name." He "considered Little a slave name." [†] *In this excerpt from <u>The Autobiography of Malcolm X</u> (with Alex Haley) he describes how he acquired his "homemade education" during a prison sentence for burglary (1946-53). As he mentions in the text, he converted to Muslim while in prison. Malcolm X was assassinated in 1965.*

start off

It was because of my letters that I happened to stumble upon starting to acquire some kind of a homemade education.

I became increasingly frustrated at not being able to express what I wanted to convey in letters that I wrote, especially those to Mr. Elijah Muhammed. In the street, I had been the most articulate hustler out there—I had commanded attention when I said something. But now, trying to write simple English, I not only wasn't articulate, I wasn't even functional. How would I sound writing in slang, the way I would *say* it, something such as "Look, daddy, let me pull your coat about a cat, Elijah Muhammed—"

Many who today hear me somewhere in person, or on television, or those who read something I've said, will think I went to school far beyond the eighth grade. This impression is due entirely to my prison studies.

It had really begun back in the Charlestown Prison, when Bimbi first made me feel envy of his stock of knowledge. Bimbi had always taken charge of any conversation he was in, and I had tried to emulate him. But every book I picked

---

[*] From *The Autobiography of Malcolm X* by Malcolm X and Alex Haley, copyright © 1964 by Alex Haley and Malcolm X Copyright © 1965 by Alex Haley and Betty Shabazz. Used by permission of Random House, Inc.
[†] "Malcolm X," *Estate of Malcolm X Website,* © *2001.* January 20, 2001. <www.cmgww.com /historic/malcolm/bio.html>.

up had few sentences which didn't contain anywhere from one to nearly all of the words that might as well have been in Chinese. When I just skipped those words, of course, I really ended up with little idea of what the book said. So I had come to the Norfolk Prison Colony still going through only book-reading motions. Pretty soon, I would have quit even these motions, unless I had received the motivation that I did.

I saw that the best thing I could do was get hold of a dictionary—to study, to learn some words. I was lucky enough to reason also that I should try to improve my penmanship. It was sad. I couldn't even write in a straight line. It was both ideas together that moved me to request a dictionary along with some tablets and pencils from the Norfolk Prison Colony school.

I spent two days just riffling uncertainly through the dictionary's pages. I'd never realized so many words existed! I didn't know *which* words I needed to learn. Finally, just to start some kind of action, I began copying.

In my slow, painstaking, ragged handwriting, I copied into my tablet everything printed on that first page, down to the punctuation marks.

I believe it took me a day. Then, aloud, I read back, to myself, everything I'd written on the tablet. Over and over aloud, to myself, I read my own handwriting.

I woke up the next morning, thinking about those words—immensely proud to realize that not only had I written so much at one time, but I'd written words that I never knew were in the world. Moreover, with a little effort, I also could remember what many of these words meant. I reviewed the words whose meanings I didn't remember. Funny thing, from the dictionary first page right now, that "aardvark" springs to my mind. The dictionary had a picture of it, a long-tailed, long-eared, burrowing African mammal, which lives off termites caught by sticking out its tongue as an anteater does for ants.

I was so fascinated that I went on—I copied the dictionary's next page. And the same experience came when I studied that. With every succeeding page, I also learned of people and places and events from history. Actually the dictionary is like a miniature encyclopedia. Finally the dictionary's A section had filled a whole tablet—and I went on into the B's. That was the way I started copying what eventually became the entire dictionary. It went a lot faster after so much practice helped me to pick up handwriting speed. Between what I wrote in my tablet, and writing letters, during the rest of my time in prison I would guess I wrote a million words.

I suppose it was inevitable that as my word-base broadened, I could for the first time pick up a book and read and now begin to understand what the book was saying. Anyone who has read a great deal can imagine the new world that opened. Let me tell you something: from then until I left that prison, in every free moment I had, if I was not reading in the library, I was reading on my bunk. You couldn't have gotten me out of books with a wedge. Between Mr. Muhammed's teachings, my correspondence, my visitors—usually Ella and Reginald—and my reading of books, months passed without my even thinking about being imprisoned. In fact, up to then, I never had been so truly free in my life.

The Norfolk Prison Colony's library was in the school building. A variety of classes was taught there by instructors who came from such places as Harvard and Boston universities. The weekly debates between inmate teams were also held in the school building. You would be astonished to know how worked up convict debaters and audiences would get over subjects like "Should Babies Be Fed Milk?"

Available on the prison library's shelves were books on just about every general subject. Much of the big private collection that Parkhurst had willed to the prison was still in crates and boxes in the back of the library—thousands of old books. Some of them looked ancient: covers faded, old-time parchment-looking binding. Parkhurst, I've mentioned, seemed to have been principally interested in history and religion. He had the money and the special interest to have a lot of books that you wouldn't have in general circulation. Any college library would have been lucky to get that collection.

As you can imagine, especially in a prison where there was heavy emphasis on rehabilitation, an inmate was smiled upon if he demonstrated an unusually intense interest in books. There was a sizable number of well-read inmates, especially the popular debaters. Some were said by many to be practically walking encyclopedias. They were almost celebrities. No university would ask any student to devour literature as I did when this new world opened to me, of being able to read and *understand*.

I read more in my room than in the library itself. An inmate who was known to read a lot could check out more than the permitted maximum number of books. I preferred reading in the total isolation of my own room.

When I had progressed to really serious reading, every night at about ten p.m., I would be outraged with the "lights out." It always seemed to catch me right in the middle of something engrossing.

Fortunately, right outside my door was a corridor light that cast a glow into my room. The glow was enough to read by, once my eyes adjusted to it. So when "lights out" came, I would sit on the floor where I could continue reading in that glow.

At one-hour intervals the night guards paced past every room. Each time I heard the approaching footsteps, I jumped into bed and feigned sleep. And as soon as the guard passed, I got back out of bed onto the floor area of that light-glow, where I would read for another fifty-eight minutes—until the guard approached again. That went on until three or four every morning. Three or four hours of sleep a night was enough for me. Often in the years in the streets I had slept less than that.

The teachings of Mr. Muhammed stressed how history had been "whitened"—when white men had written history books, the black man simply had been left out. Mr. Muhammed couldn't have said anything that would have struck me much harder. I had never forgotten how when my class, me and all of those whites, had studied seventh-grade United States history back in Mason, the history of the Negro had been covered in one paragraph, and the teacher had gotten a big laugh with his joke, "Negroes' feet are so big that when they walk, they leave a hole in the ground."

This is one reason why Mr. Muhammed's teachings spread so swiftly all over the United States, among *all* Negroes, whether or not they became followers of Mr. Muhammed. The teachings ring true—to every Negro. You can hardly show me a black adult in America—or a white one, for that matter—who knows from the history books anything like the truth about the black man's role. In my own case, once I heard of the "glorious history of the black man," I took special pains to hunt in the library for books that would inform me on details about black history.

I can remember accurately the very first set of books that really impressed me. I have since bought that set of books and have it at home for my children to read as they grow up. It's called *Wonders of the World*. It's full of pictures of archeological finds, statues that depict, usually, non-European people.

I found books like Will Durant's *Story of Civilization*. I read H. G. Wells' *Outline of History*. *Souls of Black Folk* by W. E. B. Du Bois gave me a glimpse into the black people's history before they came to this country. Carter G. Woodson's *Negro History* opened my eyes about black empires before the black slave was brought to the United States, and the early Negro struggles for freedom.

J. A. Rogers' three volumes of *Sex and Race* told about race-mixing before Christ's time; about Aesop being a black man who told fables; about Egypt's Pharaohs; about the great Coptic Christian Empires; about Ethiopia, the earth's oldest continuous black civilization, as China is the oldest continuous civilization.

Mr. Muhammad's teaching about how the white man had been created led me to *Findings In Genetics* by Gregor Mendel. (The dictionary's G section was where I had learned what "genetics" meant.) I really studied this book by the Austrian monk. Reading it over and over, especially certain sections, helped me to understand that if you started with a black man, a white man could be produced; but starting with a white man, you never could produce a black man—because the white gene is recessive. And since no one disputes that there was but one Original Man, the conclusion is clear.

During the last year or so, in the *New York Times*, Arnold Toynbee used the word "bleached" in describing the white man. (His words were: "White (i.e. bleached) human beings of North European origin . . . ") Toynbee also referred to the European geographic area as only a peninsula of Asia. He said there is no such thing as Europe. And if you look at the globe, you will see for yourself that America is only an extension of Asia. (But at the same time Toynbee is among those who have helped to bleach history. He has written that Africa was the only continent that produced no history. He won't write that again. Every day now, the truth is coming to light.)

I never will forget how shocked I was when I began reading about slavery's total horror. It made such an impact upon me that it later became one of my favorite subjects when I became a minister of Mr. Muhammad's. The world's most monstrous crime, the sin and the blood on the white man's hands, are almost impossible to believe. Books like the one by Frederick Olmstead opened my eyes to the horrors suffered when the slave was landed in the United States. The European woman, Fannie Kimball, who had married a Southern white slaveowner, described how human beings were degraded. Of course I read *Uncle* ⌐

Tom's Cabin. In fact, I believe that's the only novel I have ever read since I started serious reading.

Parkhurst's collection also contained some bound pamphlets of the Abolitionist Anti-Slavery Society of New England. I read descriptions of atrocities, saw those illustrations of black slave women tied up and flogged with whips; of black mothers watching their babies being dragged off, never to be seen by their mothers again; of dogs after slaves, and of the fugitive slave catchers, evil white men with whips and clubs and chains and guns. I read about the slave preacher Nat Turner, who put the fear of God into the white slavemaster. Nat Turner wasn't going around preaching pie-in-the-sky and "non-violent" freedom for the black man. There in Virginia one night in 1831, Nat and seven other slaves started out at his master's home and through the night they went from one plantation "big house" to the next, killing, until by the next morning 57 white people were dead and Nat had about 70 slaves following him. White people, terrified for their lives, fled from their homes, locked themselves up in public buildings, hid in the woods, and some even left the state. A small army of soldiers took two months to catch and hang Nat Turner. Somewhere I have read where Nat Turner's example is said to have inspired John Brown to invade Virginia and attack Harper's Ferry nearly thirty years later, with thirteen white men and five Negroes.

I read Herodotus, "the father of History," or, rather, I read about him. And I read the histories of various nations, which opened my eyes gradually, then wider and wider, to how the whole world's white men had indeed acted like devils, pillaging and raping and bleeding and draining the whole world's non-white people. I remember, for instance, books such as Will Durant's story of Oriental civilization, and Mahatma Gandhi's accounts of the struggle to drive the British out of India.

Book after book showed me how the white man had brought upon the world's black, brown, red, and yellow peoples every variety of the sufferings of exploitation. I saw how since the sixteenth century, the so-called "Christian trader" white man began to ply the seas in his lust for Asian and African empires, and plunder, and power. I read, I saw, how the white man never has gone among the non-white peoples bearing the Cross in the true manner and spirit of Christ's teachings—meek, humble, and Christ-like.

I perceived, as I read, how the collective white man had been actually nothing but a piratical opportunist who used Faustian machinations to make his own Christianity his initial wedge in criminal conquests.   First, always "religiously," he branded "heathen" and "pagan" labels upon ancient non-white cultures and civilizations.   The stage thus set, he then turned upon his non-white victims his weapons of war.

I read how, entering India—half a *billion* deeply religious brown people— the British white man, by 1759, through promises, trickery and manipulations, controlled much of India through Great Britain's East India Company.   The parasitical British administration kept tentacling out to half of the sub-continent. In 1857, some of the desperate people of India finally mutinied—and, excepting the African slave trade, nowhere has history recorded any more unnecessary bestial and ruthless human carnage than the British suppression of the non-white Indian people.

Over 115 million African blacks—close to the 1930's population of the United States—were murdered or enslaved during the slave trade. And I read how when the slave market was glutted, the cannibalistic white powers of Europe next carved up, as their colonies, the richest areas of the black continent.   And Europe's chancelleries for the next century played a chess game of naked exploitation and power from Cape Horn to Cairo.

Ten guards and the warden couldn't have torn me out of those books. Not even Elijah Muhammad could have been more eloquent than those books were in providing indisputable proof that the collective white man had acted like a devil in virtually every contact he had with the world's collective non-white man. I listen today to the radio, and watch television, and read the headlines about the collective white man's fear and tension concerning China. When the white man professes ignorance about why the Chinese hate him so, my mind can't help flashing back to what I read, there in prison, about how the blood forebears of this same white man raped China at a time when China was trusting and helpless. Those original white "Christian traders" sent into China millions of pounds of opium. By 1839, so many of the Chinese were addicts that China's desperate government destroyed twenty thousand chests of opium. The first Opium War was promptly declared by the white man. Imagine! Declaring *war* upon someone who objects to being narcotized! The Chinese were severely beaten, with Chinese-invented gunpowder.

The Treaty of Nanking made China pay the British white man for the destroyed opium; forced open China's major ports to British trade; forced China to abandon Hong Kong; fixed China's import tariffs so low that cheap British articles soon flooded in, maiming China's industrial development.

After a second Opium War, the Tientsin Treaties legalized the ravaging opium trade, legalized a British-French-American control of China's customs. China tried delaying that Treaty's ratification; Peking was looted and burned.

"Kill the foreign white devils!" was the 1901 Chinese war cry in the Boxer Rebellion.   Losing again, this time the Chinese were driven from Peking's choicest areas.   The vicious, arrogant white man put up the famous signs, "Chinese and dogs not allowed."

Red China after World War II closed its doors to the Western white world. Massive Chinese agricultural, scientific, and industrial efforts are described in a book that *Life* magazine recently published.   Some observers inside Red China have reported that the world never has known such a hate-white campaign as is now going on in this non-white country where, present birth-rates continuing, in fifty more years Chinese will be half the earth's population.   And it seems that some Chinese chickens will soon come home to roost, with China's recent successful nuclear tests.

Let us face reality.   We can see in the United Nations a new world order being shaped, along color lines—an alliance among the non-white nations. America's U.N. Ambassador Adlai Stevenson complained not long ago that in the United Nations "a skin game" was being played.   He was right.   He was facing reality.   A "skin game" *is* being played.   But Ambassador Stevenson sounded like Jesse James accusing the marshal of carrying a gun.   Because who in the world's history ever has played a worse "skin game" than the white man?

Mr. Muhammad, to whom I was writing daily, had no idea of what a new world had opened up to me through my efforts to document his teachings in books.

When I discovered philosophy, I tried to touch all the landmarks of philosophical development.   Gradually, I read most of the old philosophers, Occidental and Oriental.   The Oriental philosophers were the ones I came to prefer; finally, my impression was that most Occidental philosophy had largely been borrowed from the Oriental thinkers.   Socrates, for instance, traveled in Egypt.   Some sources even say that Socrates was initiated into some of the

Egyptian mysteries. Obviously Socrates got some of his wisdom among the East's wise men.

I have often reflected upon the new vistas that reading opened to me. I knew right there in prison that reading had changed forever the course of my life. As I see it today, the ability to read awoke inside me some long dormant craving to be mentally alive. I certainly wasn't seeking any degree, the way a college confers a status symbol upon its students. My homemade education gave me, with every additional book that I read, a little bit more sensitivity to the deafness, dumbness, and blindness that was afflicting the black race in America. Not long ago, an English writer telephoned me from London, asking questions. One was, "What's your alma mater?" I told him, "Books." You will never catch me with a free fifteen minutes in which I'm not studying something I feel might be able to help the black man.

Yesterday I spoke in London, and both ways on the plane across the Atlantic I was studying a document about how the United Nations proposes to ensure the human rights of the oppressed minorities of the world. The American black man is the world's most shameful case of minority oppression. What makes the black man think of himself as only an internal United States issue is just a catch-phrase, two words, "civil rights." How is the black man going to get "civil rights" before first he wins his *human* rights? If the American black man will start thinking about his *human* rights, and then start thinking of himself as part of one of the world's great peoples, he will see he has a case for the United Nations.

I can't think of a better case! Four hundred years of black blood and sweat invested here in America, and the white man still has the black man begging for what every immigrant fresh off the ship can take for granted the minute he walks down the gangplank.

But I'm digressing. I told the Englishman that my alma mater was books, a good library. Every time I catch a plane, I have with me a book that I want to read—and that's a lot of books these days. If I weren't out here every day battling the white man, I could spend the rest of my life reading, just satisfying my curiosity—because you can hardly mention anything I'm not curious about. I don't think anybody ever got more out of going to prison than I did. In fact, prison enabled me to study far more intensively than I would have if my life had gone differently and I had attended some college. I imagine that one of the biggest troubles with colleges is there are too many distractions, too much panty-raiding, fraternities, and boola-boola and all of that. Where else but in a prison could I have attacked my ignorance by being able to study intensely sometimes as much as fifteen hours a day?

Critical Thinking

1.   Describe Malcolm X's "homemade education."

2.   What is a "word base"?

3.   What insights did Malcolm X gain from his studies?

Writing Assignments

1.   Make a list of several of the books on your bookshelf (or of the last ten books you borrowed from the library). Which have you read and which do you plan on reading? What interests does the content of your bookshelf reflect?

2.   Malcolm X states, "No university would ask any student to devour literature as I did when this new world opened to me, of being able to read and *understand*." Consider whether or not you think there are any drawbacks to a "homemade education." Explain. You may want to consider his statement that *Uncle Tom's Cabin* was the only novel he read since he began "serious reading."

3.   Write about a time when you read a book that opened your eyes and made you gain new insights into yourself, or your culture.

Parenthood is an endless series of small events, periodic conflicts, and sudden crises which call for a response. The response is not without consequence: it affects personality for better or worse."
—Haim G. Ginott, <u>Between Parent & Teenager</u> (1969)

"Learning to Swim"[*]
Rebecca Lawson

Rebecca Lawson teaches writing and literature at John Jay and Hunter colleges in New York City. She's been a contributor to several online publications. An earlier version of this essay appeared in the webzine, "Off-the-lip.com."

Recently I was sitting by the pool at a friend's house as her eight-year old daughter, Maggie, was having a swimming lesson. The lesson was about breathing techniques. I watched as the instructor gently floated Maggie around the pool on her stomach and, in her most soothing yogi tone, tried to coax her to put her head under water. But Maggie would have none of it. She winced, gurgled and eventually worked herself into near hysteria. My friend was quick to intercede. "Don't push her," she told the instructor. "I don't want her to be afraid of the water."

"Too late," I wanted to say. "She's already afraid. And you've given her eight years to think about it."

But I held my tongue. Instead, I nodded in false sympathy, while my friend rocked her child and attempted to explain to her (for what I could only imagine was the fiftieth time) that if she wanted to learn to swim, she had to put her head under the water. It wasn't at all clear to me that the girl *did* want to learn to swim, or was old enough to have any idea why it mattered more than her fear. At eight, the only thing I *knew* I wanted---the only thing that seemed truly relevant to my life---was a Malibu Barbie and her Dreamhouse.

---

[*] Reprinted by permission of Rebecca Lawson.

My friend's behavior is not unlike that of many modern parents I know, who make teaching a child to swim, or even the simplest life lessons, an overly complicated matter. They ease their children into such activities gingerly, with a caution formerly reserved for the crises of, say, divorce or a debilitating chronic illness. Their children aren't pushed to do anything until they're "ready." And if they're never ready, well, that's just fine too.

It strikes me that many parents today are terrified of their responsibilities, terrified of making tough or unpleasant decisions as parents. They're afraid of being disliked by their kids. But they also seem to see every interaction between themselves and their children as fraught with potential psychological damage. They respond to their fears by paradoxically treating their children as peers--- seeking their input on every little decision---while simultaneously attempting to shelter them (and themselves) from discomfort whenever possible. These parents fail to recognize the logical notion that an older person with greater wisdom and life experience is generally in a better position to make certain decisions. And while it's natural for parents to want to protect their kids, I can't help but wonder whether sheltering a child from every unpleasant circumstance prepares them for a world that is often filled with pain and adversity equal to joy and comfort.

After watching my friend with her daughter, I thought about my own, very different, childhood experience. I grew up in a much more practical era, when parents tended not to overthink things. If you wanted to teach a puppy to swim, you grabbed it by the scruff of the neck, carried it to the end of the dock, and threw it in. Children were treated much the same way. At about four years old, my father decided I'd waded in the shallow waters of my grandfather's lake long enough. Since I was a skinny kid and didn't have much of a scruff, he picked me up under both arms, carried me to the end of the dock, and unceremoniously threw me in. Whoever said necessity is the mother of invention was right. After a few gulps of water, and before I had time to think, I found myself instinctively dog paddling toward shore. Initially, I was a little upset, but by the end of the week, I was confidently throwing myself off the dock, thrilled to be swimming with the big kids.

My parents did other things in teaching me how to swim that would make today's parents cringe. When my father was trying to increase my endurance, we used to play a game. He would stand in the middle of the pool and I would swim to him. As I approached, he would move a few steps back, forcing me to go a little farther with each attempt. When I finally figured out what was going on, I was pretty mad about being duped, but by then, I could already swim the length of the pool.

At age seven, there were also my dreaded swimming lessons. For an entire summer, despite much protesting and whining, my sister and I were roused at 7:00 a.m. and dragged through the early morning fog to the outdoor pool, where we spent a teeth-chattering hour practicing laps of freestyle, breast, and sidestroke. Had my parents been more sensitive and asked us what we wanted, we'd have eagerly told them that we wanted to wake up at 10:00 and spend the rest of the morning watching cartoons. But to their Old School thinking, a little cold water and exercise wouldn't hurt us. More important, it never occurred to them that at seven and eight, my sister and I could possibly know what would be best for us down the road.

Does all this sound appalling? I have a feeling my friend would think so. And sometimes I think so too. But other times, I'm not so sure. While I'm not arguing for insensitivity towards children, my heart occasionally yearns for what I sense as the wisdom of simpler times. Of course, who knows the psychological ramifications of those so-called simpler times. Perhaps I will spend years in therapy examining the various laws of trust and respect violated by my practical, but well-meaning, parents. Then again, perhaps some degree of psychological trauma is the inevitable price we pay for coming of age and surviving in a complex, difficult world. And perhaps there are worse things than minor discomfort and pain, such as *not* learning to swim.

I can't deny that my parents could have found a happier medium between their Old School practicality and a more sensitive method of parenting. They could have been more concerned about their children's feelings, perhaps asked for our input a little more. But intuitively they seemed focused on a bigger picture. They loved us and kept us safe, but didn't try to shelter us from what they saw as routine discomfort. In fact, as with swimming, they often pushed us to confront difficult situations. Their goal was not to keep us comfortable, but to make us self-reliant. So if, as a child, I was sometimes forced to confront and transcend discomfort, as an adult, it's comforting to know that if I'm ever shipwrecked, I can swim like a fish.

Critical Thinking

1. Lawson begins with an anecdote about a swimming lesson. What happens in the lesson, and what does it illustrate about the mother's attitude toward parenting?

2. What does Lawson identify as some of the problems with current attitudes toward parenting? How do they contrast with the "Old School" practicality she experienced growing up?

3. What is the significance of the title? When Lawson refers to the importance of learning to swim, is she being literal?

Writing Assignments

1. Lawson suggests that teaching a child to be self-sufficient and to confront challenges is an important goal of parenting and should sometimes outweigh other concerns, such as physical or emotional comfort. What do you feel are the most important characteristics and goals of good parenting? In answering the question, you might want to consider the attitudes toward parenting in your household, and which you feel are positive and which are negative? Be sure to refer to both Lawson's ideas and personal experience to support your position.

2. Write an essay about a time when someone taught you how to do something. Were they effective? Why or why not?

3. Recall a time when you observed someone teaching someone else how to do something. Write an essay, of similar length to Lawson's, about your observations.

"I never again shall tell you what I think. / I shall be sweet and crafty, soft and sly; / You will not catch me reading any more:"
- Edna St. Vincent Millay
(1892-1950)

"The Language Lesson"[*]
Sue Ribner

Sue Ribner teaches writing at Hunter College in New York City. She has published numerous articles on women's history, the martial arts, children's literature, and human rights. She has co-authored several books.

From the back row, I hear Rabbi Fried's squeaky voice as I watch his black-robed arm swing back and forth like a large bat wing, and I wonder how the strange marks he scratches on the board have anything to do with making language. Yet the boys in the front row, the obedient brood, nod their dark heads toward the winged one and make odd huffy sounds in the back of their throats. The proud Rabbi grins, exposing his small, pointy teeth.

I know these symbols on the board have names, but I recognize only two: the "Mem," which resembles a fat English M with a tail added, and the "Shin," shaped like a Viking ship with three prongs in the air--the high-curved prow and stern and the tall mast in the middle. It's where I'd like to be now, sailing out of this temple cave, off into the wind, led by a bold, blond, wooden mermaid, carved on the prow, as we crash through the waves toward the bright green trees and sunny beaches of Non-Jewish Land, where I'll understand the language and won't feel stupid.

But here I am at Reform Sunday School in the dank, windowless classroom of the temple basement, slouched in the back row, where the girls congregate, squeezed between Judy Greenbaum and Sarah Kaplan. We're supposed to be learning this Hebrew although the Bat-Rabbi never calls on us and doesn't seem to care whether we get it or not.

---

[*] Reprinted by permission of Sue Ribner.

To be honest, we're not entirely without voice here in the girls' row--in Girl Land, you could say. We scribble hasty notes in English about movie dates, doodle hearts and arrows in our book margins, and whisper about our crushes on the new boy Stevie Savitt. But the Hebrew letters are a mystery and serve only as the substance of our favorite joke. Under our breath, we chant the alphabet as it sounds to us: "Aleph, Beth, Veis, Gimme a Dollar, . . . "He, Waw, Zayin, Yuff, Huff, Puff and I'll blow your house down."

We crumple forward and slap our hands to our mouths to stifle the laughter. Tears drip down our flushed cheeks. We've flown out of the cave for a moment.

The Bat-Rabbi bangs his chalk on the old wooden desk, peering at us with his close-set eyes.

"Girls!" he yells. "Girls!"

We're back in our seats, silenced.

Only once do I speak out to the whole class, trying to break through that invisible partition of Girl Land. It's about the title of our new history textbook, When the Jewish People Was Young. I'm troubled by this incredible subject-verb agreement mistake and excited that no one else has discovered it yet. At home I sit on my bed and run my fingers across the title on this blue cover, saying over and over to myself, "People was?" "People was?" I prepare a small speech on grammar for the class.

The next Sunday, with unusual bravado, I flash my hand in the air, startling the Rabbi with my unexpected efforts. "Our new book has a mistake in the title," is what I say.

He's not impressed. "You're wrong," he says, swirling in his blackness, returning to his Hebrew lesson. And the discussion ends.

I do not speak publicly again until our Confirmation three months later. For this show I'm placed in the front row on the stage before our audience of parents, and I watch as cute Stevie Savitt and the rest of the boy brood, disguised now in dark blue suits and yamulkes, take turns reading from the Torah, miraculously blending those Hebrew letters and making words that smoothly roll and huff out of their mouths. We girls have been handed typed speeches, in English, pasted on cardboard and covered in plastic, yellowed with age. These are the words I will mouth as I stand at the podium in my white organdy dress with the bulbous, white chrysanthemum corsage almost blocking my vision.

Dutifully, I follow the written directions. "Today (look left) we are gathered together (look center) to celebrate (look right)...."

This too is a language with no meaning.

When Sarah, the last reader, has finished, I know we're almost free. But the Bat-Rabbi, in an unrehearsed move, asks each of us to stand with him, one by one, at the back of the stage, before the open Ark. Those of us still seated can't see what is happening behind us, can't make out the Rabbi's words. On my turn, I step to the back and face him. He lifts his huge wings and places his long, skinny fingers on my hair

"I want you to make three promises," he says, squinting at me and pressing down hard on my skull.

Right now, while I'm in his clutches, close enough to see the pores in his nose, before the entire standing congregation, before the God I don't believe in but think just might be watching in that brightly lit Ark, in that velvet and golden place filled with light where the Torah is kept, the Rabbi, after all this time, wants to have a talk. He craves my words, my blood.

I'm ambushed, blind-sided by this Bat-Rabbi. My throat closes up, my sinuses hurt, my legs shake.

Will I keep the Jewish faith forever, he asks. Will I raise my children as Jews? And finally, the clincher, will I promise never to marry a Christian? I'm stunned he could ask this of me, a 13-year-old, without warning, in a place where I cannot refuse. Secretly I cross the fingers of my right hand, and through clenched teeth, three times, mutter "Yes."

I escape home with my parents and shed my white dress. With it I throw off the creepy Rabbi, Judaism, prepared speeches, Hebrew and all foreign alphabets. I pull on my bright pink shorts and blue tank top, grab the Sunday paper, and run out barefoot into the light-green of the back yard's early summer trees and grass. I lie back in the yellow hammock, which is stretched between our two tallest trees, and sway back and forth, as if on a ship, feeling the breeze, the warmth. I find the best part of the paper, the comics, the only newsprint with color, the only section with few words, with simple language—a place where I'm happy to be and think I want to stay.

Critical Thinking

1. What is the main idea?

2. Examine Ribner's use of the bat metaphor.

3. What do you make of the conclusion? Why does she retreat into the comics?

Writing Assignments

1. Describe a time when you challenged an authority figure. If you have never challenged an authority figure, describe why you did not.

2. Are girls treated differently from boys? Write an essay about different attitudes you have encountered. Use examples from your experience and observations.

3. Write a comparison/contrast essay. Compare and contrast your experience of learning in school to Ribner's.

"The Art of Eating Spaghetti"[*]
Russell Baker

Humorist, journalist, and author Russell (Wayne) Baker has published numerous articles, essays, and books. He is well known for his "Observer" column for the <u>New York Times</u> and as host for the PBS Television series "Masterpiece Theatre." This excerpt is from his award winning autobiography <u>Growing Up</u>.[†]

The notion of becoming a writer had flickered off and on in my head since the Belleville days, but it wasn't until my third year in high school that the possibility took hold. Until then I'd been bored by everything associated with English courses. I found English grammar dull and baffling. I hated the assignments to turn out "compositions," and went at them like heavy labor, turning out leaden, lackluster paragraphs that were agonies for teachers to read and for me to write. The classics thrust on me to read seemed as deadening as chloroform.

When our class was assigned to Mr. Fleagle for third-year English I anticipated another grim year in that dreariest of subjects. Mr. Fleagle was notorious among city students for dullness and inability to inspire. He was said to be stuffy, dull, and hopelessly out of date. To me he looked to be sixty or seventy and prim to a fault. He wore primly severe eyeglasses, his wavy hair was primly cut and primly combed. He wore prim vested suits with neckties blocked primly against the collar buttons of his primly starched white shirts. He had a primly pointed jaw, a primly straight nose, and a prim manner of speaking that was so correct, so gentlemanly, that he seemed a comic antique.

I anticipated a listless, unfruitful year with Mr. Fleagle and for a long time was not disappointed. We read *Macbeth*. Mr. Fleagle loved *Macbeth* and wanted us to love it too, but he lacked the gift of infecting others with his own passion. He tried to convey the murderous ferocity of Lady Macbeth one day by reading aloud the passage that concludes.

> . . . I have given suck, and know
> How tender 'tis to love the babe that milks me.
> I would, while it was smiling in my face,
> Have plucked my nipple from his boneless gums . . . .

The idea of prim Mr. Fleagle plucking his nipple from boneless gums was too much for the class. We burst into gasps of irrepressible snickering. Mr. Fleagle stopped.

"There is nothing funny, boys, about giving suck to a babe. It is the—the very essence of motherhood, don't you see."

He constantly sprinkled his sentences with "don't you see." It wasn't a question but an exclamation of mild surprise at our ignorance. "Your pronoun needs an antecedent, don't you see," he would say, very primly. "The purpose of the Porter's scene, boys, is to provide comic relief from the horror, don't you see."

Late in the year we tackled the informal essay. "The essay, don't you see, is the . . ." My mind went numb. Of all forms of writing, none seemed so boring as the essay. Naturally we would have to write informal essays. Mr. Fleagle distributed a homework sheet offering us a choice of topics. None was quite so simpleminded as "What I Did on My Summer Vacation," but most seemed to be almost as dull. I took the list home and dawdled until the night before the essay was due. Sprawled on the sofa, I finally faced up to the grim task, took the list out of my notebook, and scanned it. The topic on which my eye stopped was "The Art of Eating Spaghetti."

This title produced an extraordinary sequence of mental images. Surging up out of the depths of memory came a vivid recollection of a night in Belleville when all of us were seated around the supper table—Uncle Allen, my mother, Uncle Charlie, Doris, Uncle Hal—and Aunt Pat served spaghetti for supper. Spaghetti was an exotic treat in those days. Neither Doris nor I had ever eaten spaghetti, and none of the adults had enough experience to be good at it. All the good humor of Uncle Allen's house reawoke in my mind as I recalled the laughing arguments we had that night about the socially respectable method for moving spaghetti from plate to mouth.

Suddenly I wanted to write about that, about the warmth and good feeling of it, but I wanted to put it down simply for my own joy, not for Mr. Fleagle. It was a moment I wanted to recapture and hold for myself. I wanted to relive the pleasure of an evening at New Street. To write it as I wanted, however, would violate all the rules of formal composition I'd learned in school, and Mr. Fleagle would surely give it a failing grade. Never mind. I would write something else for Mr. Fleagle after I had written this thing for myself.

When I finished it the night was half gone and there was no time left to compose a proper, respectable essay for Mr. Fleagle. There was no choice next morning but to turn in my private reminiscence of Belleville. Two days passed before Mr. Fleagle returned the graded papers, and he returned everyone's but mine. I was bracing myself for a command to report to Mr. Fleagle immediately after school for discipline when I saw him lift my paper from his desk and rap for the class's attention.

"Now, boys," he said, "I want to read you an essay. This is titled 'The Art of Eating Spaghetti.' "

And he started to read. My words! He was reading *my words* out loud to the entire class. What's more, the entire class was listening. Listening attentively. Then somebody laughed, then the entire class was laughing, and not in contempt and ridicule, but with openhearted enjoyment. Even Mr. Fleagle stopped two or three times to repress a small prim smile.

I did my best to avoid showing pleasure, but what I was feeling was pure ecstasy at this startling demonstration that my words had the power to make people laugh. In the eleventh grade, at the eleventh hour as it were, I had discovered a calling. It was the happiest moment of my entire school career. When Mr. Fleagle finished he put the final seal on my happiness by saying, "Now that, boys, is an essay, don't you see. It's—don't you see—it's of the very essence of the essay, don't you see. Congratulations, Mr. Baker."

For the first time, light shone on a possibility. It wasn't a very heartening possibility, to be sure. Writing couldn't lead to a job after high school, and it was hardly honest work, but Mr. Fleagle had opened a door for me. After that I ranked Mr. Fleagle among the finest teachers in the school.

Critical Thinking

1. What is your first impression of Mr. Fleagle?

2. Why did the young Russell Baker write "The Art of Eating Spaghetti"?

3. What did he discover as a result of the assignment?

Writing Assignments

1. Write an essay about the first time you discovered you were good at something. Use details. How did you discover your talent? Did anyone encourage you?

2. Compare and contrast your own attitudes towards writing assignments, particularly essays, to Baker's.

3. For your own pleasure, write an essay about a moment you would like to recapture. Follow Baker's lead, write the story for yourself.

*"There is only one subject-matter
for education, and that is Life in
all its manifestations."*
*--Alfred North Whitehead, The
Aims of Education*

"Curriculum and Culture: New Round Is Opened in a Scholarly Fistfight"[*]
William H. Honan

*Journalist William H(olmes) Honan has written numerous articles
for various publication, including the New Yorker, Newsweek,
Time magazine, and The New York Times. The article appeared in
The New York Times, August 21, 1996.[†]*

In 1987, Allan Bloom, then an obscure translator of Plato and Rousseau, touched a raw nerve when he argued in his book *The Closing of the American Mind* that the surrender of college and university administrations and faculties to the demands of student, feminist and Black Power movements in the 1960s and 1970s had fatally compromised American higher education.

Writing with zest and hyperbole, the political philosopher compared radical feminism to the Reign of Terror in the French Revolution, dismissed the anthropologist Margaret Mead as a "sexual adventurer," likened the Woodstock gathering to Hitler's Nuremberg rallies and denounced "cultural relativism," which treats all cultures as equals. Professor Bloom called this "the suicide of science." He also argued that efforts to include non-Western cultures in the curriculum were displacing what he regarded as the more valuable teaching of the Western canon.

The book appeared on *The New York Times* best-seller list for 10 weeks, sold more than a million copies and made Professor Bloom, who died in 1992,

[*] From 8/21/1996 *The New York Times*. Reprinted by permission.
[†] "William H. Honan," *Contemporary Authors Online*. The Gale Group, 2001. 20 August 2001. January 26, 2002 <http://www.galenet.com/servlet/LitRC?c=1&ai=49245&ste=6&docNum=H100 0054093&bConts=16303&tab=1&vrsn=3&ca=1&tbst=arp&ST=Honan%2C+Honan &srchtp=athr&n=10&locID=nypl&OP=contains>.

one of the most widely quoted and criticized authors. While Professor Bloom has his followers, many liberal-minded scholars are now saying he has finally met his match. Even before its official publication date on Sept. 3, *The Opening of the American Mind* (Beacon Press, $20), by Lawrence W. Levine, a longtime professor of cultural history at the University of California at Berkeley, is being both hailed and denounced with unusual fervor.

Professor Levine's book is a defense of all that Professor Bloom held unholy. The debate centers on how open or closed society should be to many cultures. The enemy to Professor Bloom was cultural relativism and the lack of restraint that came with it. Professor Levine, on the other hand, champions multiculturalism, which he sees as the inevitable, and praiseworthy, product of constitutional democracy. "Multiculturalism," Professor Levine said in an interview, "means that in order to understand the nature and complexities of American culture, it is crucial to study and comprehend the widest possible array of the contributing cultures and their interaction with one another." Among the major points made in his book are these:

*Conservative critics like Professor Bloom, who blame the fragmentation of American society on the university, do not realize that it has been "endemic in the United States from the outset."

*The college curriculum is not immutable, as Professor Bloom said, but has steadily evolved over the last 200 years.

*The prospect for the future is "increasing openness, greater inclusiveness, expanded choice, the study of the modern as well as of the ancient, a concentration on American, African and Asian as well as European culture."

Professor Levine is also critical of higher education. He calls for more courses that "build on one another," minimizing jargon, better communication with colleagues in other disciplines and a renewed emphasis on teaching ability.

Throughout the summer, as the book became available, scholars began to take sides. "This is the book we've been waiting for," said Stanley N. Katz, president of the American Council of Learned Societies. "It should put an end to the 'culture war' talk." Lynne Cheney, who served as chairwoman of the National Endowment for the Humanities under Presidents Reagan and Bush, and who is criticized in the book, disagreed. "It's the same-old, same-old," she said. "It's the Left deliberately misconstruing the arguments of its opponents while offering no substantive evidence for its own."

A MacArthur fellow, Professor Levine is the former president of the Organization of American Historians. After spending 32 years at Berkeley, he joined the faculty of George Mason University in Fairfax, Va., where he now teaches history. "What I tried to show in this book," he said, "is that the genius of America has been its ability to renew its essential spirit by admitting a constant infusion of different peoples who demand that the ideals and principles embodied in the Constitution be put into practice. The result has been to open America to great diversity, and colleges and universities are beginning to reflect this heterogeneity. It has not led to repression as Bloom argued, but to the very opposite -- a flowering of ideas and scholarly innovation unmatched in our history."

Professor Bloom's book, he said was a reaction to this. "He and the people who agreed with him could not accept the expansion of interests, the less parochial world view, and the more comprehensive view of what was important to teach and to learn."

Over the years, many authors have written intellectual sequels to Professor Bloom's book -- including William Bennett, Dinesh D'Souza, Roger Kimball and John Searle. And not a few authors also have attacked Professor Bloom -- among them Michael Berube, Henry Louis Gates Jr., Gerald Graff, Francis Oakley, Peter N. Stearns and W. B. Carnochan.

The battle of the books did not originate with Allan Bloom; it can be traced back at least to 1762 when Rousseau argued in "Emile" that it was more important for students to read a commercial novel like "Robinson Crusoe" than to read Aristotle.

Through the centuries, classicists and modernists have clashed over how best to educate the young. Fundamentally, the issue was whether to stuff them or stretch them -- stuff them with the classics or stretch them with contemporary issues. Yet while this current battle of the books has raged, none of Professor Bloom's supporters or detractors have generated anything like the mass appeal of Professor Bloom's initial assault.

Professor Levine's champions, however, remain optimistic. An unremitting attack by conservatives could be the key to maintaining public interest. Dr. Katz called the book "the first to make the case in a serious way for multiculturalism in higher education," and he thinks freshness will inspire debate.

Professor Gates, chairman of the department of Afro-American Studies at Harvard, called the book "highly readable," and Elliott Gorn, a professor of history at Miami University in Ohio, said he thought the positive "something's right with the academy" tone of the book would attract a following. Beacon Press plans a first printing of 40,000 copies, an unusually large press run for an academic treatise. Roger Kimball, managing editor of the neoconservative New Criterion, another who is criticized in Professor Levine's book, lashed out after reading it. "How can Levine say that nothing's wrong?" he said in an interview. "It is incontrovertible that the academy has been taken over by left-wing radicals. The riches of the humanistic tradition are being perverted by a conjury of ideological assaults. You can't deny that."

Professor Levine said he decided to write *The Opening of the American Mind*" when it struck him that Professor Bloom's desire "to rescue education from the virus of democracy" paralleled the way in which a turn-of-the-century elite captured for itself exclusively cultural icons like Shakespeare, art museums and symphony orchestras -- a development that inspired Professor Levine's earlier book, "Highbrow/Lowbrow."

"I became increasingly upset at myself and my colleagues for not explaining to students and their parents why we are teaching multiculturalism," he said. "We left ourselves vulnerable. There is a need to explain."

"We weren't turning our backs on Western Civilization. That hadn't even existed as a subject until just after the First World War. Thomas Jefferson never heard of something called Western Civilization."

Professor Levine said he was appalled by the fact that he graduated from the City College of New York in the 1950s "knowing very little about the vast majority of the people in the world." "We studied Northern and Western Europe," he said. "Nothing on Africa, Asia and Latin America. Even Canada was a great blank. My own father was an immigrant from Lithuania and my grandparents were from Odessa, but we talked only about Northern and Western Europe. There's something wrong with that."

[August 21, 1996, Wednesday]

Critical Thinking

1.   According to Professor Levine, what is "multiculturalism"?

2.   How is the information presented? What details, dialogue and support does Honan use? Write a brief outline of the argument on both sides of the issue as presented by Honan.

3.   Honan's article appeared in *The New York Times*. What are the advantages and disadvantages of reading an article? Did the article raise any questions? Did it spark your interest? Would you like to read any of the books mentioned in the piece?

Writing Assignments

1.   Write an essay from a first person point of view describing the ideal college curriculum.

2.   Write an argumentation essay about the debate over multiculturalism. Use your own college curriculum and your observations. You may want to add research. If so, go to the library and take out both *The Opening of the American Mind* by Lawrence W. Levine and *The Closing of the American Mind* by Allan Bloom.

3.   Professor Levine said that he graduated college with very little knowledge "about the vast majority of the people in the world." Consider what you learned in high school and are learning in college. Can you relate to his experience? Explain.

RELATING THE AUTHORS' IDEAS

1. Compare and contrast the two parenting techniques demonstrated in "Girl" and "The Swimming Lesson." Which do you think is more effective? Why?

2. Compare and contrast the self-education Malcolm X received with the social education the young girl receives in "Girl."

3. Many of us have experienced, at one point, the frustration of not being able to understand something. Ribner describes "a language with no meaning." Malcolm X also speaks of his frustration of not being able to understand the words on a page. Write an essay about a time when you were frustrated because you did not understand. How did you finally learn? Compare your own experience to Ribner's and Malcolm X's.

4. Honan's article includes information about both sides of the multiculturalism debate. How do you think Malcolm X would respond to the issues in Honan's article? In your opinion, which side of the debate would he defend? Explain.

Chapter IV

Contemplating

Career and Work

IV

Contemplating
Career and Work

Introduction

One of the most important decisions we make involves career choice. People often ask, "What do you do?" The response is usually "I am a . . ." Frequently, people define themselves by their career. Socially, career success is often recognized by wealth and status. As we contemplate career and work, it is necessary to ask ourselves: What is success? How do I define success?

The selections by Scott Tarkov, Virginia Woolf, Bonnie Smith-Yackel, Ruth Sidel, and Richard Selzer are about career and work. In "Making the Cut" John Tarkov defines what it means to make the cut, and to miss it. Drawing upon his own experience in "missing the cut," he states, "the message a man so easily hears [when he misses the cut] remains the same: *You aren't good enough.*" However, his definition of making the cut evolves. At the end of his piece he expands his definition, "There is absolute worth and pride due to a man who will simply continue. To do that, perhaps, is the finest measure of making the cut."

In order to make or miss the cut, we need an opportunity. What happens when none exists? In "Shakespeare's Sister" Virginia Woolf writes: "It is a perennial puzzle why no woman wrote a word of that extraordinary literature when every other man, it seemed, was capable of song or sonnet." Then, she imaginatively creates a situation. What if Shakespeare "had a wonderfully gifted sister, called Judith." After recreating the path Judith would take in life, Woolf surmises that Judith's would have been so "thwarted and hindered" that there would be no way for her to have succeeded.

As we will read in "My Mother Never Worked," women's work is seldom recognized as "real work." Bonnie Smith-Yackel cleverly frames her story with a phone call to the Death Benefits Office. While she is waiting on the phone, she recounts all of the contributions her mother made to the family and society by working all her life. Ironically, when the phone call resumes, she is informed that there is no death benefit check: "You see, your mother never worked."

Due to the women's movement young women working today have many more opportunities. In "The New American Dreamers," Ruth Sidel interviews young women.   She finds that these young women are turning away from traditional roles and moving towards work traditionally performed by men.   She states: "It is not sufficient, however, to become a doer in a traditionally female occupation, for, as we know, these occupations are notoriously underpaid and underesteemed."   "Among young women I interviewed," says Sidel, "the New American Dreamers stand apart in their intention to make their own way in the world and determine their own destiny."

Richard Selzer, a surgeon and writer, was fortunate enough to create his own "destiny" and pursue his dream to become a surgeon.   In "The Knife," Richard Selzer describes the intimate relationship between surgeon and knife: "So close is the joining of knife and surgeon that they are like the Centaur—the knife, below, all equine energy, the surgeon, above, with his delicate art."   As you read the essay, list the various references and images used by Selzer to describe the knife.   What sense do you get of his attitude towards his profession?   Also, think beyond the scope of the essay.   What tools do you use (or do you plan on using) in your trade?

Take time to contemplate career and work, as well as underlying attitudes about success and worth.   By examining our beliefs and attitudes towards the work we do, we will gain a greater understanding about the choices that we make.

"It is not the critic who counts, not the man who points out how the strong man stumbled, or where the doer of deeds could have done better. The credit belongs to the man who is actually in the arena; whose face is marred by dust and sweat and blood; who strives valiantly; who errs and comes short again and again; who knows the great enthusiasms, the great devotions and spends himself in a worthy cause; who at best knows in the end the triumph of high achievement; and who at the worst, if he fails, at least fails while daring greatly; so that his place shall never be with those cold and timid souls who know neither victory nor defeat."

— Theodore Roosevelt

"Making the Cut"[*]
John Tarkov

John Tarkov is a writer and journalist. He is a contributor to magazines and newspapers. In 1983, he was editor of Geo magazine. This article appeared in The New York Times, September 25, 1983.

THE LESSON is a hard one, and it gets no easier through repetition. I got an early dose of it in high school, when I was trying out for varsity basketball and—for reasons that must have made sense to me then—feeling confident about my chances. In the end, there was a piece of paper taped to the locker room door. On it were the names of the guys who had worn uniforms. I had to read the list more than once before I would believe it, as if my name was really up there, somewhere between the lines. After a while, I walked away.

Making the cut. The phrase comes from the vocabulary of sport, but the experience extends beyond the realm of gyms and practice fields. Getting a job,

[*] From *The New York Times*, September 25, 1983. Reprinted by permission.

starting out alone in a new city, stretching a paycheck, holding a marriage together, scavenging for status and power—whether the goal is commendable or open to question, if things work out poorly, the message a man so easily hears remains the same: *You aren't good enough.* That is the message of the cut.

There is a gear in a man's inner workings that grinds against those words. It a man cannot—or will not—come to terms with them, they can hound him into rage or into a fixed posture of defeat.

When I was in college, I worked after school in a furniture warehouse. One of my duties was to slip outside when I was asked to and return with a pint of whiskey for one of the regulars. He was in his 50s, and he was a decent man who had heard the message of the cut unrelentingly. I spent a winter assigned to his section, running his errand for him and helping him wrestle recliners and sofas onto racks and skids.

He liked to talk, and over the months the skeleton of his life emerged: He had taken to heart the idea that he was dull and without promise as a boy, dropped out of school, married very young, raised his four kids and never saw a paycheck that didn't belong to someone else as soon as it was handed to him. I wonder now if he heard the message of the cut each payday. I wonder how he felt on those Thursday afternoons.

One evening, working overtime and in a mood to show off, he took in too much liquor too fast. I tried to walk him around, but his legs had lost any sensible linkage to his brain. A friend of his helped me get him out through a side door, and he eased into stupor in the back seat of his friend's car. Later on, we sneaked his card into the time clock and punched him out, and his friend drove him home. The next day, he sent me out for a pint.

A man's response to missing the cut rests, naturally, on his temperament and on how deeply the message of the cut has taken root. I know men who have heard the message and been hurt by it many times, and yet they seem to shrug it off and proceed much as before. I have known others who retreated into a life of little risk. What you can never know is a man's tolerance for the message of the cut, or how much of it he holds hidden inside.

I once knew a man whose life in its externals was perfectly in place, all the details in enviable order. His high-school years were a time of celebrity, as an athlete in a town where high-school sports were a fulcrum to life. He did well in college and had moved on to a good job. His marriage was a new and happy one.

And yet the explanation he committed to paper before he put a bullet through his eye at the age of 24 could be distilled to this: *I'm not good enough.* It had echoed within him since a boyhood of deprivation, until he could listen to it no more. His sister called from the Middle West to tell me what had happened, weeping over the words and trying to make sense of them. Just then, you didn't want to make sense of them.

And so your Spirit livens every time the obverse message is heard: *You are good enough.* Not long ago, a friend wrote to say that he had moved from a dead-end job into management. I understood what the promotion and the extra money meant to him and his wife, with a third child on the way. Another friend has met a woman who is changing his life for the good. Another calls to tell me that his documentary on old Negro baseball leagues has been scheduled for early fall on PBS. I know about the years of effort he put into it. I know also how it must have felt when his own baseball career ended in the minor leagues after he ruined his pitching arm. To hear the news is to feel it as well. You know what it is to make the cut and you know what it is to miss it. And so there is a special moment of elation and shared understanding when the cut is made.

You come full circle to sports, finally, trying to explain and understand. The movie "Rocky" established a mythic character in the American consciousness: A man whose life consisted of nothing but missing the cut, but who was good enough in the end. Before the sequels to the film came out, the story ended on a note of purely personal triumph. A journeyman club fighter had lost a split decision to the heavyweight champion of the world. He was still standing after 15 brutal rounds. The man had earned a moment of uncomplicated worth and pride.

It is difficult to feel anything like pride just at the time you miss the cut. But then you find yourself proceeding with your life, for all the times you have perceived yourself in failure—as not being good enough. And you may want to rethink your definition of what failure means. I think of men who buckled under the message of the cut, and I see no failure there, no more than in a fighter who was overmatched and whose body and spirit finally gave way. I think of men who would not stay down and who went on, perhaps in more certainty of punishment than relief from it. Call it the grace to continue. There is absolute worth and pride due a man who will simply continue. To do that, perhaps, is the finest measure of making the cut.

And l look back to the man I worked with in the warehouse that winter long ago, fetching his booze for him and trusting him to balance his own breaking point against the breaking point of his paycheck and his debts. Think what you want about his drinking; you'll never know all the reasons, and neither will I. Perhaps they ran deeper than the lines of the self-portrait he sketched. Perhaps he compounded his own punishment. But judge him gently, if you have a need to judge. The man had the grace to continue. I wish that he were here right now so I could tell him that he didn't miss the cut at all.

Critical Thinking

1.   How does Tarkov define "making the cut"? Does this definition evolve?

2.   What word or group of words does Tarkov repeat throughout the essay? Why do you think he does this? What effect does it have?

3.   When referring to the man he worked with in the warehouse, Tarkov writes "think what you want about drinking…The man had the grace to continue. I wish that he were here right now so I could tell him that he didn't miss the cut at all." Do you agree or disagree with Tarkov's claim that his co-worker made the cut? If yes, why? If not, why not?

Writing Assignments

1.   Write an essay in which you recall an early memory where you first experienced not making the cut. Include the experience, how you felt, and how you reacted. For example, one of the characters in Tarkov'e essay reacts to not making the cut by drinking and another by committing suicide. In your essay include your reaction, whether negative or positive. Alternatively, write an essay recalling a time when you did make the cut and provide what the experience was, how you felt, and how you and others reacted.

2.   It's been said that suicide is a permanent solution to a temporary problem. What other alternative or alternatives could the 24-year-old who "put a bullet through his eye" have chosen? Write an essay in which you

compare his life to a person you know who seems to have success on an external level.

3.   Consider how the definition of making the cut might differ in another culture?

"We hold these truths to be self evident, that all men and women are created equal."
-- Elizabeth Cady Stanton, First Women's Rights Convention, Seneca, New York Declaration of Sentiment (July 19-20, 1848)

"Shakepeare's Sister"[*]
Virginia Woolf

Born in 1882, British writer, novelist, and essayist Viginia Woolf is best known for her innovative and experimental books, including To The Lighthouse (1927), Mrs. Dalloway (1925) and The Waves (1931). In 1917 she founded Hogarth Press with her husband Leonard Woolf. This excerpt is from her A Room of One's Own.[†]

IT WAS disappointing not to have brought back in the evening some important statement, some authentic fact. Women are poorer than men because—this or that. Perhaps now it would be better to give up seeking for the truth, and receiving on one's head an avalanche of opinion hot as lava, discoloured as dish-water. It would be better to draw the curtains; to shut out distractions; to light the lamp; to narrow the enquiry and to ask the historian, who records not opinions but facts, to describe under what conditions women lived, not throughout the ages, but in England, say in the time of Elizabeth.

For it is a perennial puzzle why no woman wrote a word of that extraordinary literature when every other man, it seemed, was capable of song or sonnet. What were the conditions in which women lived, I asked myself; for fiction, imaginative work that is, is not dropped like a pebble upon the ground, as science may be; fiction is like a spider's web, attached ever so lightly perhaps, but still attached to life at all four corners. Often the attachment is scarcely perceptible; Shakespeare's plays, for instance, seem to hang there complete by themselves. But when the web is pulled askew, hooked up at the edge, torn in the middle, one remembers that these webs are not spun in mid-air by incorporeal creatures, but are the work of suffering human beings, and are attached to grossly material things, like health and money and the houses we live in.

I went, therefore, to the shelf where the histories stand and took down one of the latest, Professor Trevelyan's *History of England*. Once more I looked up Women, found "position of," and turned to the pages indicated. "Wife-beating," I read, "was a recognised right of man, and was practised without shame by high as well as low. . . . Similarly," the historian goes on, "the daughter who refused to marry the gentleman of her parents' choice was liable to be locked up, beaten and flung about the room, without any shock being inflicted on public opinion. Marriage was not an affair of personal affection, but of family avarice, particularly in the 'chivalrous' upper classes. . . . Betrothal often took place while one or both of the parties was in the cradle, and marriage when they were scarcely out of the nurses' charge." That was about 1470, soon after Chaucer's time. The next reference to the position of women is some two hundred years later, in the time of the Stuarts. "It was still the exception for women of the upper and middle class to choose their own husbands, and when the husband had been assigned, he was lord and master, so far at least as law and custom could make him. Yet even so," Professor Trevelyan concludes, "neither Shakespeare's women nor those of authentic seventeenth-century memoirs, like the Verneys and the Hutchinsons, seem wanting in personality and character." Certainly, if we consider it, Cleopatra must have had a way with her; Lady Macbeth, one would suppose, had a will of her own; Rosalind, one might conclude, was an attractive girl. Professor Trevelyan is speaking no more than the truth when he remarks that Shakespeare's women do not seem wanting in personality and character. Not being a historian, one might go even further and say that women have burnt like beacons in all the works of all the poets from the beginning of time— Clytemnestra, Antigone, Cleopatra, Lady Macbeth, Phèdre, Cressida, Rosalind, Desdemona, the Duchess of Malfi, among the dramatists; then among the prose writers: Millamant, Clarissa, Becky Sharp, Anna Karenina, Emma Bovary, Madame de Guermantes—the names flock to mind, nor do they recall women "lacking in personality and character." Indeed, if woman had no existence save in the fiction written by men, one would imagine her a person of the utmost importance; very various; heroic and mean; splendid and sordid; infinitely beautiful and hideous in the extreme; as great as a man, some think even greater.[1] But this is woman in fiction. In fact, as Professor Trevelyan points out, she was locked up, beaten and flung about the room.

A very queer, composite being thus emerges. Imaginatively she is of the highest importance; practically she is completely insignificant. She pervades poetry from cover to cover; she is all but absent from history. She dominates the lives of kings and conquerors in fiction; in fact she was the slave of any boy whose parents forced a ring upon her finger. Some of the most inspired words, some of the most profound thoughts in literature fall from her lips; in real life she could hardly read, could scarcely spell, and was the property of her husband.

Illusion vs Reality

It was certainly an odd monster that one made up by reading the historians first and the poets afterwards—a worm winged like an eagle; the spirit of life and beauty in a kitchen chopping up suet. But these monsters, however amusing to the imagination, have no existence in fact. What one must do to bring her to life was to think poetically and prosaically at one and the same moment, thus keeping in touch with fact—that she is Mrs. Martin, aged thirty-six, dressed in blue, wearing a black hat and brown shoes; but not losing sight of fiction either—that she is a vessel in which all sorts of spirits and forces are coursing and flashing perpetually.   The moment, however, that one tries this method with the Elizabethan woman, one branch of illumination fails; one is held up by the scarcity of facts.   One knows nothing detailed, nothing perfectly true and substantial about her.   History scarcely mentions her.   And I turned to Professor

---

[1] "It remains a strange and almost inexplicable fact that in Athena's city, where women were kept in almost Oriental suppression as odalisques or drudges, the stage should yet have produced figures like Clytemnestra and Cassandra, Atossa and Antigone, Phèdre and Medea, and all the other heroines who dominate play after play of the 'misogynist' Euripides. But the paradox of this world where in real life a respectable woman could hardly show her face alone in the street, and yet on the stage woman equals or surpasses man, has never been satisfactorily explained. In modern tragedy the same predominance exists. At all events, a very cursory survey of Shakespeare's work (similarly with Webster, though not with Marlowe or Jonson) suffices to reveal how this dominance, this initiative of women, persists from Rosalind to Lady Macbeth. So too in Racine; six of his tragedies bear their heroines' names; and what male characters of his shall we set against Hermione and Andromaque, Bérnéice and Roxane, Phèdre and Athalie? So again with Ibsen; what men shall we match with Solveig and Nora, Hedda and Hilda Wangel and Rebecca West?—F. L. Lucas, Tragedy, pp. 114-15.

Trevelyan again to see what history meant to him. I found by looking at his chapter headings that it meant—

"The Manor Court and the Methods of Open-field Agriculture . . . The Cistercians and Sheep-farming . . . The Crusades . . . The University . . . The House of Commons . . . The Hundred Years' War . . . The Wars of the Roses . . . The Renaissance Scholars . . . The Dissolution of the Monasteries . . . Agrarian and Religious Strife . . . The Origin of English Sea-power . . . The Armada . . ." and so on. Occasionally an individual woman is mentioned, an Elizabeth, or a Mary; a queen or a great lady. But by no possible means could middle-class women with nothing but brains and character at their command have taken part in any one of the great movements which, brought together, constitute the historian's view of the past. Nor shall we find her in any collection of anecdotes. Aubrey hardly mentions her. She never writes her own life and scarcely keeps a diary; there are only a handful of her letters in existence. She left no plays or poems by which we can judge her. What one wants, I thought—and why does not some brilliant student at Newnham or Girton supply it?—is a mass of information; at what age did she marry; how many children had she as a rule; what was her house like; had she a room to herself; did she do the cooking; would she be likely to have a servant? All these facts lie somewhere, presumably, in parish registers and account books; the life of the average Elizabethan woman must be scattered about somewhere, could one collect it and make a book of it. It would be ambitious beyond my daring, I thought, looking about the shelves for books that were not there, to suggest to the students of those famous colleges that they should re-write history, though I own that it often seems a little queer as it is, unreal, lop-sided; but why should they not add a supplement to history? calling it, of course, by some inconspicuous name so that women might figure there without impropriety? For one often catches a glimpse of them in the lives of the great, whisking away into the background, concealing, I sometimes think, a wink, a laugh, perhaps a tear. And, after all, we have lives enough of Jane Austen; it scarcely seems necessary to consider again the influence of the tragedies of Joanna Baillie upon the poetry of Edgar Allan Poe; as for myself, I should not mind if the homes and haunts of Mary Russell Mitford were closed to the public for a century at least. But what I find deplorable, I continued, looking about the bookshelves again, is that nothing is known about women before the eighteenth century. I have no model in my mind to turn about this way and that. Here am I asking why women did not write poetry in the Elizabethan age, and I am not sure how they were educated; whether they were taught to write; whether they had sitting-rooms to

There is more of women before this time and only in the on the Professions

themselves; how many women had children before they were twenty-one; what, in short, they did from eight in the morning till eight at night. They had no money evidently; according to Professor Trevelyan they were married whether they liked it or not before they were out of the nursery, at fifteen or sixteen very likely. It would have been extremely odd, even upon this showing, had one of them suddenly written the plays of Shakespeare, I concluded, and I thought of that old gentleman, who is dead now, but was a bishop, I think, who declared that it was impossible for any woman, past, present, or to come, to have the genius of Shakespeare. He wrote to the papers about it. He also told a lady who applied to him for information that cats do not as a matter of fact go to heaven, though they have, he added, souls of a sort. How much thinking those old gentlemen used to save one! How the borders of ignorance shrank back at their approach! Cats do not go to heaven. Women cannot write the plays of Shakespeare.

Sadly but true

Be that as it may, I could not help thinking, as I looked at the works of Shakespeare on the shelf, that the bishop was right at least in this; it would have been impossible, completely and entirely, for any woman to have written the plays of Shakespeare in the age of Shakespeare. Let me imagine, since facts are so hard to come by, what would have happened had Shakespeare had a wonderfully gifted sister, called Judith, let us say. Shakespeare himself went, very probably—his mother was an heiress—to the grammar school, where he may have learnt Latin—Ovid, Virgil and Horace—and the elements of grammar and logic. He was, it is well known, a wild boy who poached rabbits, perhaps shot a deer, and had, rather sooner than he should have done, to marry a woman in the neighbourhood, who bore him a child rather quicker than was right. That escapade sent him to seek his fortune in London. He had, it seemed, a taste for the theatre; he began by holding horses at the stage door. Very soon he got work in the theatre, became a successful actor, and lived at the hub of the universe, meeting everybody, knowing everybody, practising his art on the boards, exercising his wits in the streets, and even getting access to the palace of the queen. Meanwhile his extraordinarily gifted sister, let us suppose, remained at home. She was as adventurous, as imaginative, as agog to see the world as he was. But she was not sent to school. She had no chance of learning grammar and logic, let alone of reading Horace and Virgil. She picked up a book now and then, one of her brother's perhaps, and read a few pages. But then her parents came in and told her to mend the stockings or mind the stew and not moon about with books and papers. They would have spoken sharply but kindly, for they were substantial people who knew the conditions of life for a woman and loved their daughter—indeed, more likely than not she was the apple of her father's eye. Perhaps she scribbled some pages up in an apple loft on the sly, but was careful to hide them or set fire to them. Soon, however, before she was out of her teens, she was to be betrothed to the son of a neighbouring wool-stapler. She cried out that marriage was hateful to her, and for that she was severely beaten by her father. Then he ceased to scold her. He begged her instead not to hurt him, not to shame him in this matter of her marriage. He would give her a chain of beads or a fine petticoat, he said; and there were tears in his eyes. How could she disobey him? How could she break his heart? The force of her own gift alone drove her to it. She made up a small parcel of her belongings, let herself down by a rope one summer's night and took the road to London. She was not seventeen. The birds that sang in the hedge were not more musical than she was. She had the quickest fancy, a gift like her brother's, for the tune of words. Like him, she had a taste for the theatre. She stood at the stage door; she wanted to act, she said. Men laughed in her face. The manager—a fat, loose-lipped man—guffawed. He bellowed something about poodles dancing and women acting—no woman, he said, could possibly be an actress. He hinted—you can imagine what. She could get no training in her craft. Could she even seek her dinner in a tavern or roam the streets at midnight? Yet her genius was for fiction and lusted to feed abundantly upon the lives of men and women and the study of their ways. At last—for she was very young, oddly like Shakespeare the poet in her face, with the same grey eyes and rounded brows—at last Nick Greene the actor-manager took pity on her; she found herself with child by that gentleman and so—who shall measure the heat and violence of the poet's heart when caught and tangled in a woman's body?—killed herself one winter's night and lies buried at some cross-roads where the omnibuses now stop outside the Elephant and Castle.

That, more or less, is how the story would run, I think, if a woman in Shakespeare's day had had Shakespeare's genius. But for my part, I agree with the deceased bishop, if such he was—it is unthinkable that any woman in Shakespeare's day should have had Shakespeare's genius. For genius like Shakespeare's is not born among labouring, uneducated, servile people. It was not born in England among the Saxons and the Britons. It is not born today among the working classes. How, then, could it have been born among women whose work began, according to Professor Trevelyan, almost before they were out of the nursery, who were forced to it by their parents and held to it by all the power of law and custom? Yet genius of a sort must have existed among women as it must have existed among the working classes. Now and again an Emily

Brontë or a Robert Burns blazes out and proves its presence. But certainly it never got itself on to paper. When, however, one reads of a witch being dunked, of a woman possessed by devils, of a wise woman selling herbs, or even of a very remarkable man who had a mother, then I think we are on the track of a lost novelist, a suppressed poet, of some mute and inglorious Jane Austen, some Emily Brontë who dashed her brains out on the moor or mopped and mowed about the highways crazed with the torture that her gift had put her to. Indeed, I would venture to guess that Anon, who wrote so many poems without signing them, was often a woman. It was a woman Edward Fitzgerald, I think, suggested who made the ballads and the folk-songs, crooning them to her children, beguiling her spinning with them, or the length of the winter's night.

This may be true or it may be false—who can say?—but what is true in it, so it seemed to me, reviewing the story of Shakespeare's sister as I had made it, is that any woman born with a great gift in the sixteenth century would certainly have gone crazed, shot herself, or ended her days in some lonely cottage outside the village, half witch, half wizard, feared and mocked at. For it needs little skill in psychology to be sure that a highly gifted girl who had tried to use her gift for poetry would have been so thwarted and hindered by other people, so tortured and pulled asunder by her own contrary instincts, that she must have lost her health and sanity to a certainty.

Critical Thinking

1.   In the first couple of lines Woolf makes a bold assertion. What is it? Does she support this assertion with sufficient evidence?

2.   How, according to Woolf, are women portrayed in fiction? In history?

3.   In the final lines of her essay, Woolf's female character commits suicide, after finding herself pregnant by the theatre stage manager. Why do you think Woolf created such a tragic ending? Do you find this ending realistic? Why or why not?

Writing Assignments

1. Would you describe Woolf's essay as feminist?   Why or why not? Include a definition from a dictionary or encyclopedia in your answer.

2. Write a persuasive essay explaining why people should pursue a career, marriage, or education of their choice.

3. Studies show that men and women see situations from different perspectives.   Pretend Virginia Woolf is a man and rewrite the essay "Shakespeare's Sister" from the perspective of a man.

> *"Woman has always been man's dependent, if not his slave; the two sexes have never shaped the world in equality. And even today woman is heavily handicapped, though her situation is beginning to change."*
>
> *- Simone De Beauvoir,*
> <u>*The Second Sex*</u> *(1953)*

"My Mother Never Worked"[*]
Bonnie Smith-Yackel

Born in 1937, the sixth of Ben and Martha Smith's eight children, Bonnie Smith-Yackel was shaped by her parents' example of hard work, honest ethics, and keen social conscience. As a former suburban housewife and mother of three children, she wrote and published extensively. Upon retirement from the corporate world, Bonnie Smith-Yackel once again resumed her first passion-writing.[†]

"Social Security Office." (The voice answering the telephone sounds very self-assured.)

"I'm calling about . . . I . . . my mother just died . . . I was told to call you and see about a . . . death-benefit check, I think they call it. . . ."

"I see. Was your mother on Social Security? How old was she?"

"Yes . . . she was seventy-eight . . ."

"Do you know her number?"

"No . . . I, ah . . . don't you have a record?"

"Certainly. I'll look it up. Her name?"

"Smith. Martha Smith. Or maybe she used Martha Ruth Smith . . . . Sometimes she used her maiden name . . . Martha Jerabek Smith."

"If you'd care to hold on, I'll check our records—it'll be a few minutes."

"Yes . . . . "

Her love letters—to and from Daddy—were in an old box, tied with ribbons and stiff, rigid-with-age leather thongs: 1918 through 1920; hers written on stationery from the general store she had worked in full-time and managed, single-handed, after her graduation from high school in 1913; and his, at first, on YMCA or Soldiers and Sailors Club stationery dispensed to the fighting men of World War 1. He wooed her thoroughly and persistently by mail, and though she reciprocated all his feelings for her, she dreaded marriage . . . .

"It's so hard for me to decide when to have my wedding day—that's all I've thought about these last two days. I have told you dozens of times that I won't be afraid of married life, but when it comes down to setting the date and then picturing myself a married woman with half a dozen or more kids to look after, it just makes me sick . . . . I am weeping right now—I hope that some day I can look back and say how foolish I was to dread it all."

They married in February, 1921, and began farming. Their first baby, a daughter, was born in January, 1922, when my mother was 26 years old. The second baby, a son, was born in March, 1923. They were renting farms; my father, besides working his own fields, also was a hired man for two other farmers. They had no capital initially, and had to gain it slowly, working from dawn until midnight every day. My town-bred mother learned to set hens and raise chickens, feed pigs, milk cows, plant and harvest a garden, and can every fruit and vegetable she could scrounge. She carried water nearly a quarter of a mile from the well to fill her wash boilers in order to do her laundry on a scrub board. She learned to shuck grain, feed threshers, shock and husk corn, feed corn pickers. In September, 1925, the third baby came, and in June, 1927, the fourth child—both daughters. In 1930, my parents had enough money to buy their own farm, and that March they moved all their livestock and belongings themselves, 55 miles over rutted, muddy roads.

In the summer of 1930 my mother and her two eldest children reclaimed a 40-acre field from Canadian thistles, by chopping them all out with a hoe. In the other fields, when the oats and flax began to head out, the green and blue of the crops were hidden by the bright yellow of wild mustard. My mother walked the fields day after day, pulling each mustard plant. She raised a new flock of baby chicks—500—and she spaded up, planted, hoed, and harvested a half-acre garden.

During the next spring their hogs caught cholera and died. No cash that fall.

And in the next year the drought hit. My mother and father trudged from the well to the chickens, the well to the calf pasture, the well to the barn, and from the well to the garden. The sun came out hot and bright, endlessly, day after day. The crops shriveled and died. They harvested half the corn, and ground the other half, stalks and all, and fed it to the cattle as fodder. With the price at four cents a bushel for the harvested crop, they couldn't afford to haul it into town. They burned it in the furnace for fuel that winter.

In 1934, in February, when the dust was still so thick in the Minnesota air that my parents couldn't always see from the house to the barn, their fifth child— a fourth daughter—was born. My father hunted rabbits daily, and my mother stewed them, fried them, canned them, and wished out loud that she could taste hamburger once more. In the fall the shotgun brought prairie chickens, ducks, pheasant, and grouse. My mother plucked each bird, carefully reserving the breast feathers for pillows.

In the winter she sewed night after night, endlessly, begging cast-off clothing from relatives, ripping apart coats, dresses, blouses, and trousers to remake them to fit her four daughters and son. Every morning and every evening she milked cows, fed pigs and calves, cared for chickens, picked eggs, cooked meals, washed dishes, scrubbed floors, and tended and loved her children. In the spring she planted a garden once more, dragging pails of water to nourish and sustain the vegetables for the family. In 1936 she lost a baby in her sixth month.

In 1937 her fifth daughter was born. She was 42 years old. In 1939 a second son, and in 1941 her eighth child—and third son.

But the war had come, and prosperity of a sort. The herd of cattle had grown to 30 head; she still milked morning and evening. Her garden was more than a half acre—the rains had come, and by now the Rural Electricity Administration and indoor plumbing. Still she sewed—dresses and jackets for the children, house dresses and aprons for herself, weekly patching of jeans, overalls, and denim shirts. Still she made pillows, using the feathers she had plucked, and quilts every year—intricate patterns as well as patchwork, stitched as well as tied—all necessary bedding for her family. Every scrap of cloth too small to be used in quilts was carefully saved and painstakingly sewed together in strips to make rugs. She still went out in the fields to help with the haying whenever there was a threat of rain.

In 1959 my mother's last child graduated from high school. A year later the cows were sold. She still raised chickens and ducks, plucked feathers, made pillows, baked her own bread, and every year made a new quilt—now for a married child or for a grandchild. And her garden, that huge, undying symbol of sustenance, was as large and cared for as in all the years before. The canning, and now freezing, continued.

In 1969, on a June afternoon, mother and father started out for town so that she could buy sugar to make rhubarb jam for a daughter who lived in Texas. The car crashed into a ditch. She was paralyzed from the waist down.

In 1970 her husband, my father, died. My mother struggled to regain some competence and dignity and order in her life. At the rehabilitation institute, where they gave her physical therapy and trained her to live usefully in a wheelchair, the therapist told me: "She did fifteen pushups today—fifteen! She's almost seventy-five years old! I've never known a woman so strong!"

From her wheelchair she canned pickles, baked bread, ironed clothes, wrote dozens of letters weekly to her friends and her "half dozen or more kids," and made three patchwork housecoats and one quilt. She made balls and balls of carpet rags-enough for five rugs. And kept all her love letters.

"I think I've found your mother's records-Martha Ruth Smith; married to Ben F. Smith?"

"Yes, that's right."

"Well, I see that she was getting a widow's pension . . . . "

"Yes, that's right."

"Well, your mother isn't entitled to our $255 death benefit."

"Not entitled! But why?"

The voice on the telephone explains patiently:

"Well, you see—your mother never worked."

Critical Thinking

1.   What do you think is the purpose of the essay? Be specific.

2.   Why does the author frame her story? Is it an effective technique? Explain.

3.   Describe Smith-Yackel's mother. What details does Smith-Yackel use to sketch the portrait of her mother?

Writing Assignments

1.   Experiment with the framing technique used by Smith-Yackel. Write a personal essay about an important social issue using the framing technique.

2.   Compare and contrast your own observations of a mother, grandmother or aunt who works in the home to Smith-Yackel's observations of her mother's work.

3.   Write an essay enumerating the many trades that can evolve from domestic work.

"Some of us are becoming the men we wanted to marry."
—Gloria Steinem, Speech at Yale University [September 1981]

"The New American Dreamers"[*]
Ruth Sidel

Ruth Sidel is professor of sociology at Hunter College, New York City. She is a writer of several books, including On Her Own, Battling Bias: the Struggle for Identity and Community on College Campuses, *and* Women and Children Last*. This excerpt is from her book* On Her Own.[†]

She is the prototype of today's young woman—confident, outgoing, knowledgeable, involved. She is active in her school, church, or community. She may have a wide circle of friends or simply a few close ones, but she is committed to them and to their friendship. She is sophisticated about the central issues facing young people today—planning for the future, intimacy, sex, drugs, and alcohol—and discusses them seriously, thoughtfully, and forthrightly. She wants to take control of her life and is trying to figure out how to get from where she is to where she wants to go. Above all, she is convinced that if she plans carefully, works hard, and makes the right decisions, she will be a success in her chosen field; have the material goods she desires; in time, marry if she wishes; and, in all probability, have children. She plans, as the expression goes, to "have it all."

She lives in and around the major cities of the United States, in the towns of New England, in the smaller cities of the South and Midwest, and along the West Coast. She comes from an upper-middle-class family, from the middle class, from the working class, and even sometimes from the poor. What is clear is that she has heard the message that women today should be the heroines of their own lives. She looks toward the future, seeing herself as the central character, planning her career, her apartment, her own success story. These young women do not see themselves as playing supporting roles in someone else's life script; it is their own journeys they are planning. They see their lives in terms of *their* aspirations, *their* hopes, *their* dreams.

Beth Conant is a sixteen-year-old high-school junior who lives with her mother and stepfather in an affluent New England college town. She has five brothers, four older and one several years younger. Her mother is a librarian, and her stepfather is a stock broker. A junior at a top-notch public high school, she hopes to study drama in college, possibly at Yale, "like Meryl Streep." She would like to live and act in England for a time, possibly doing Shakespeare. She hopes to be living in New York by the age of twenty-five, in her own apartment or condo, starting on her acting career while working at another job by which she supports herself. She wants to have "a great life," be "really independent," and have "everything that's mine—crazy furniture, everything my own style."

By the time she's thirty ("that's so boring"), she feels, she will need to be sensible, because soon she will be "tied down." She hopes that by then her career will be "starting to go forth" and that she will be getting good roles. By thirty-five she'll have a child ("probably be married beforehand"), be working in New York and have a house in the country. How will she manage all this? Her husband will share responsibilities. She's not going to be a "supermom." They'll both do child care. He won't do it as a favor; it will be their joint responsibility. Moreover, if she doesn't have the time to give to a child, she won't have one. If necessary, she'll work for a while, then have children, and after that "make one movie a year."

Amy Morrison is a petite, black, fifteen-year-old high-school sophomore who lives in Ohio. Her mother works part-time, and her father works for a local art museum. She plans to go to medical school and hopes to become a surgeon. She doesn't want to marry until she has a good, secure job but indicates that she might be living with someone. She's not sure about having children but says emphatically that she wants to be successful, to make money, to have cars. In fact, originally she wanted to become a doctor "primarily for the money," but now she claims other factors are drawing her to medicine.

Jacqueline Gonzalez is a quiet, self-possessed, nineteen-year-old Mexican-American woman who is a sophomore at a community college in southern California. She describes her father as a "self-employed contractor" and her mother as a "housewife." Jacqueline, the second-youngest of six children, is the first in her family to go to college. Among her four brothers and one sister, only her sister has finished high school. Jacqueline's goal is to go to law school and then to go into private practice. While she sees herself as eventually married with "one or two children," work, professional achievement, and an upper-middle-class life-style are central to her plans for her future.

If in the past, and to a considerable extent still today, women have hoped to find their identity through marriage, have sought to find "validation of . . . [their] uniqueness and importance by being singled out among all other women by a man,"[1] the New American Dreamers are setting out on a very different quest for self-realization. They are, in their plans for the future, separating identity from intimacy, saying that they must first figure out who they are and that then and only then will they form a partnership with a man. Among the young women I interviewed, the New American Dreamers stand apart in their intention to make their own way in the world and determine their own destiny prior to forming a significant and lasting intimate relationship.

Young women today do not need to come from upper-middle-class homes such as Beth's or middle-class homes such as Amy's or working-class homes such as Jacqueline's to dream of "the good life." Even young women with several strikes against them see material success as a key prize at the end of the rainbow. Some seem to feel that success is out there for the taking. Generally, the most prestigious, best-paying careers are mentioned; few women of any class mention traditional women's professions such as teaching or nursing. A sixteen-year-old unmarried Arizona mother of a four-and-a-half-month-old baby looks forward to a "professional career either in a bank or with a computer company," a "house that belongs to me," a "nice car," and the ability to buy her son "good clothes." She sees herself in the future as dating but not married. "There is not so much stress on marriage these days," she says.

Yet another young woman, a seventeen-year-old black unmarried mother of an infant, hopes to be a "professional model," have "lots of cash," be "rich," maybe have another child. When asked if a man will be part of the picture, she responds, "I don't know."

An eighteen-year-old Hispanic unmarried mother hopes to "be my own boss" in a large company, have a "beautiful home," send her daughter to "the best schools." She wants, in her words, to "do it, make it, have money."

These young women are bright, thoughtful, personable. And they are quintessentially American: they believe that with enough hard work they will "make it" in American society. No matter what class they come from, their fantasies are of upward mobility, a comfortable life filled with personal choice and material possessions. The upper-middle-class women fantasize a life even more upper-middle-class; middle-class and working-class women look toward a life of high status in which they have virtually everything they want; and some young women who come from families with significant financial deprivation and numerous other problems dream of a life straight out of "Dallas," "Dynasty," or "L.A. Law." According to one young woman, some of her friends are so determined to be successful that they are "fearful that there will be a nuclear war and that they will die before they have a chance to live their lives. If there is a nuclear war," she explained, "they won't live long enough to be successful."

Young women are our latest true believers. They have bought into the image of a bright future. Many of them see themselves as professional women, dressed in handsome clothes, carrying a briefcase to work, and coming home to a comfortable house or condo, possibly to a loving, caring husband and a couple of well-behaved children. How widespread is the dream? How realistic is it? What is the function of this latest American dream? What about those young women who cling to a more traditional dream? What about those who feel their dreams must be deferred? What about those with no dream at all? And what about those who "share the fantasy," as the Chanel No. 5 perfume advertisement used to say, but have little or no chance of achieving it?

Perhaps the most poignant example of the impossible dream is Simone Baker, a dynamic, bright, eighteen-year-old black woman from Louisiana. Simone's mother is a seamstress who has been off and on welfare over the years, and her father is a drug addict. Simone herself has been addicted to drugs of one kind or another since she was five. She has been in and out of drug-abuse facilities, and although she attended school for many years and was passed from grade to grade, she can barely read and write. When I met her in a drug rehabilitation center, she was struggling to become drug free so that she could join the Job Corps, finish high school, and obtain some vocational training. Her dream of the future is so extraordinary, given her background, that she seems to epitomize the Horatio Alger myth of another era. When asked what she would like her life to be like in the future, Simone replies instantly, her eyes shining: "I want to be a model. I want to have a Jacuzzi. I want to have a *big*, BIG house and a BIG family—three girls and two boys."

"And what about the man?" I ask her.

"He'll be a lawyer. He'll be responsible, hardworking, and sensitive to my feelings. Everything will be fifty-fifty. And he'll take the little boys out to play football and I'll have the girls inside cooking. That would be a dream come true!"

Simone's dream is an incredible mixture of the old and the new Dick-and-Jane reader updated. And she's even mouthing the supreme hope of so many women in this age of the therapeutic solution to personal problems—that she'll find a man who is "sensitive to her feelings." She has lived a life far from the traditional middle class and yet has the quintessential image of the good life as it has been formulated in the last quarter of the twentieth century. But for Simone, it is virtually an impossible dream. One wishes that that were not so; listening to her, watching her excitement and hope at the mere thought of such a life, one gets caught up and wants desperately for it all to happen. The image is clear: the white house in the suburbs with the brass knocker on the front door, the leaves on the lawn in the fall, the boys playing football with this incredibly wonderful husband/father, and Simone sometimes the successful model, other times at home, cooking with her daughters. But we know how very unlikely it is that this particular dream will come true. And yet, maybe . . .

How have young women come to take on the American Dream as their own? That this is a relatively new dream for women is clear. Until recent years women, for the most part, did not perceive themselves as separate, independent entities with their own needs and agendas. Women fit themselves into other people's lives, molded their needs to fit the needs of others. For the full-time homemaker the day began early enough to enable husband and children to get to work and school on time. Chores had to be done between breakfast and lunch or between lunch and the end of school. Dinnertime was when the man of the house returned from work. When a woman worked outside of the home, her work hours were often those that fit into the schedules of other family members. Her needs were determined by the needs of others, as often her identity rested on her affiliation with them.

What some women seem to be saying now is that they will form their own identities, develop their own styles, and meet their own needs. They will be the central characters in their stories. They will work at jobs men work at, earn the money men earn; but many of them also plan at the same time to play all the roles women have traditionally played.

What has become clear in talking with young women throughout the country is that many of them are planning for their future in terms of their "public" roles as well as their "domestic" roles, that they are "laying claim to significant and satisfying work . . . as a normal part of their lives and laying claim also to the authority, prestige, power, and salary that   . . . [that] work commands."[2]   Historically, women have been confined primarily to the "domestic" sphere of life, particularly to child rearing and homemaking, and men, for the most part, have participated in the "public" sphere—that is, in social, economic, and political institutions and forms of association in the broader social structure.   This dichotomy between "public" and "domestic" has led to "an asymmetry in the cultural evaluation of male and female that appears to be universal."[3]   Margaret Mead noted this asymmetry when she observed that "whatever the arrangements in regard to descent or ownership of property, and even if these formal outward arrangements are reflected in the temperamental relations between the sexes, the prestige values always attach to the activities of men."[4]

In New Guinea, women grow sweet potatoes and men grow yams; yams are the prestige food.   In societies where women grow rice, the staple food, and men hunt for meat, meat is the most valued food.[5]   Traditionally, the more exclusively male the activity, the more cultural value is attached to it.   Because male activities have been valued over female activities and women have become "absorbed primarily in domestic activities because of their role as mothers,"[6] women's work of caring has traditionally been devalued.   However, as political scientist Joan Tronto has pointed out, it is not simply the dichotomy between the public and the private that results in the devaluation of the female but the immense difference in power between the two spheres.[7]   So long as men have a monopoly on the public sphere and it in turn wields great power within society, women, identified with the private sphere which is seen as relatively powerless, will be devalued.

Since the emergence of the women's movement in the 1960s, women in the U.S. as well as in many other parts of the world have been questioning the traditional asymmetry between men and women, seeking to understand its roots, its causes, and its consequences, and attempting to modify the male monopoly of power. Many strategies have developed toward this end: laws have been passed in an attempt to eliminate discrimination; groups have formed to elect more women to positions of power; those already in power have been urged to appoint more women to administrative roles; dominant, high-status, high-income professions have been pressured to admit more women to their hallowed ranks; and strategies to bring greater equity to male and female salaries have been developed.

Great stress has been placed on raising the consciousness of both women and men concerning this imbalance of power, but particular attention has been devoted to raising the consciousness of women. Discussion about the relative powerlessness of the non-wage-earning "housewife" has been widespread. Books and articles about the impoverishment of the divorced woman, the problems of the displaced homemaker, and the often desperate plight of the single, female head of household have been directed at women. During the 1970s and 1980s, the message suddenly became clear to many women: perhaps they are entitled to play roles formerly reserved for men; perhaps they would enjoy these challenges; perhaps they have something special to offer and can make a difference in the practice of medicine or law or in running the country. Moreover, it became clear that if women want power, prestige, and paychecks similar to those men receive, if they want to lessen the asymmetry between male and female, then perhaps they must enter those spheres traditionally reserved for men. If men grow yams, must women grow yams? If men hunt and women gather, must women purchase a bow and arrow? If men are in the public sphere while women are at home caring for children and doing the laundry, the consensus seems to say that women must enter the public sphere. If men are doctors and lawyers and earn great rewards while women are nurses and teachers and earn meager rewards, then women see what they obviously must do. If men have focused on doing while women have focused on caring, then clearly women must become doers.

It is not sufficient, however, to become a doer in a traditionally female occupation, for, as we know, these occupations are notoriously underpaid and underesteemed. Women must become real doers in the arena that counts: they must learn to play hardball, or, as Mary Lou Retton says in her breakfast-cereal advertisements, "eat what the big boys eat." For real power, status, money, and "success," it's law, medicine, and finance—also, possibly, acting, modeling, or working in the media, if one is very lucky.

An illustration of the current emphasis on male-dominated careers as the road to success for young women are the career goals of *Glamour* magazine's "Top Ten College Women '88." One woman hopes to become an astronaut; a second plans to work in the area of public policy, another to be a biologist, another to obtain a degree in business administration, yet another to obtain a degree in acting; and one young woman is currently working in journalism. One college senior is undecided between journalism and law, and the last three are planning to go to law school. These young women, according to *Glamour*, "possess the talents and ambition necessary to shape tomorrow's society." It is noteworthy that none of the women Glamour chose to honor are entering any traditionally female occupation or any "helping" profession—not even medicine. Don't nurses, teachers, and social workers "possess the talents and ambition necessary to shape tomorrow's society?" The word has gone out and continues to go out that the way to "make it" in American society and the way to "shape tomorrow's society" is the traditional male route.[8]

Once singled out, these young women play their part in spreading the ideology of the American Dream. Three of the ten honorees appeared on NBC's "Today" show. When asked about the significance of their being chosen, one woman replied without hesitation that if you work hard, you can do whatever you want to do. This statement was greeted by smiles and nods; she had clearly given the right message.

In addition to wanting to break out of the mold of a secondary worker receiving inferior wages and benefits and having little authority or opportunity for advancement, women have been motivated to make real money and to acquire valued skills and some semblance of security because of their relatively recent realization that women, even women with children, may well be forced to care for themselves or, at the very least, to participate in providing for the family unit. Women have come to realize that whether because of divorce (which leaves women on the average 73 percent poorer and men on the average 42 percent richer),[9] childbearing outside of marriage, the inability of many men to earn an adequate "family wage," or their remaining single—either through design or through circumstance—they must be prepared to support themselves and anyone else for whom they feel responsible.

But what of all that caring women used to do—for children, for elderly parents, for sick family members, for the home? What about Sunday dinner, baking chocolate-chip cookies with the kids eating up half the batter, serving Kool-Aid in the backyard on a hot summer day? What about sitting with a child with a painful ear infection until the antibiotic takes effect, going with a four-year-old to nursery school the first week until the child feels comfortable letting you leave, being available when there's an accident at school and your second-grader must be rushed to the emergency room? Who's going to do the caring? Who is going to do the caring in a society in which few institutions have been developed to take up the slack, a society in which men have been far more reluctant to become carers than women have been to become doers. Members of the subordinate group may gain significantly in status, in self-image, and in material rewards when they take on the activities and characteristics of the dominant group, but there is little incentive for members of the dominant group to do the reverse.

Above all, how do young women today deal with these questions? How do they feel about doing and caring, about power, prestige, and parenting? What messages is society giving them about the roles they should play, and how are they sorting out these messages?

A key message the New American Dreamers are both receiving and sending is one of optimism—the sense that they can do whatever they want with their lives. Many Americans, of course—not just young people or young women—have a fundamentally optimistic attitude toward the future. Historically, Americans have believed that progress is likely, even inevitable, and that they have the ability to control their own destinies. A poll taken early in 1988 indicates that while the American public was concerned about the nation's future and indeed more pessimistic about "the way things [were] going in the United States" than they had been at any other time since the Carter presidency in the late 1970s, they nonetheless believed that they could "plan and regulate their own lives, even while the national economy and popular culture appear[ed] to be spinning out of control."[10] As one would expect, those with higher incomes and more education are more optimistic than those with less; Republicans are more optimistic than Democrats or Independents; and, significantly, men are more hopeful than women.[11] In looking toward the future, young men clearly dream of "the good life," of upward mobility and their share of material possessions. While young women historically have had far less control over their lives than men, for the past twenty-five years they have been urged to take greater control, both in the workplace and in their private lives, and they have clearly taken the message very much to heart.

Angela Dawson, a sixteen-year-old high-school junior from southern California, sums up the views of the New American Dreamers: "It's your life. You have to live it yourself. You must decide what you want in high school, plan your college education, and from there you can basically get what you want. If you work hard enough, you will get there. You must be in control of your life, and then somehow it will all work out."

Notes

1.   Rachel M. Brownstein, *Becoming a Heroine: Reading About Women in Novels* (New York: Penguin, 1984), p. xv.

2.   Nadya Aisenberg and Mona Harrington, *Women of Academe: Outsiders in the Sacred Grove* (Amherst, Mass.: University of Massachusetts Press, 1988), p. 3.

3.   Michelle Zimbalist Rosaldo, "Women, Culture, and Society: An Overview," in *Women, Culture, and Society*, Michelle Zimbalist Rosaldo and Louise Lamphere, eds. (Stanford, Calif.: Stanford University Press, 1974), p. 19.

4.   Ibid.

5.   Ibid.

6.   Ibid., p. 24.

7.   Joan C. Tronto, "Women and Caring: What Can Feminists Learn About Morality from Caring?" in *Body, Gender and Knowledge*, Alison Jagger and Susan Brodo, eds. (New Brunswick, NJ.: Rutgers University Press, in press). See also Linda Imray and Audrey Middleton, "Public and Private: Marking the Boundaries," in *The Public and the Private*, Eva Gamarnikow et al., eds. (London: Heinemann, 1983), pp. 12-27.

8.   *Glamour* (August 1988), pp. 208-9.

9.   Terry Arendell, *Mothers and Divorce: Legal, Economic, and Social Dilemmas* (Los Angeles: University of California Press, 1986), p. 2.

10.   Steven V. Roberts, "Poll Finds Less Optimism in U.S. on Future, a First Under Reagan," *The New York Times*, February 21, 1988.

11.   Ibid.

Critical Thinking

1.   Describe "The New American Dreamers."

2.   What evidence does Sidel use? Be specific.

3.   About Simon Baker, why does Sidel qualify the statement, "We all know how unlikely it is that this particular dream will come true" with "And yet maybe . . ."?

Writing Assignments

1.   Take an informal poll of your friends and family. Write down your results. How do they compare with Sidel's findings?

2.   Sidel asks a very important question, "Who's going to do all the caring?" Write a one page response with your own list of solutions.

3.   Do you agree with the statement, "If you work hard, you can achieve anything"? Write an essay in which you support or refute this statement. Use evidence from your own experience, observations and reading.

*"Man is a tool-using animal . . . .
Without tools he is nothing, with
tools he is all."*
*- Thomas Carlyle, <u>Sartor Resartus</u>
(1833-34), Book 1, Ch. 4*

"The Knife"[*]
Richard Selzer

*Surgeon, physican, essayist, and writer Richard Selzer is best
known for his compelling essays about his profession. This essay
is from his book <u>Mortal Lessons: Notes on the Art of Surgery</u>.*[†]

One holds the knife as one holds the bow of a cello or a tulip—by the
stem. Not palmed nor gripped nor grasped, but lightly, with the tips of the
fingers. The knife is not for pressing. It is for drawing across the field of skin.
Like a slender fish, it waits, at the ready, then, go! It darts, followed by a fine
wake of red. The flesh parts, falling away to yellow globules of fat. Even now,
after so many times, I still marvel at its power—cold, gleaming, silent. More, I
am still struck with a kind of dread that it is I in whose hand, the blade travels,
that my hand is its vehicle, that yet again this terrible steel-bellied thing and I
have conspired for a most unnatural purpose, the laying open of the body of a
human being.

A stillness settles in my heart and is carried to my hand. It is the quietude
of resolve layered over fear. And it is this resolve that lowers us, my knife and
me, deeper and deeper into the person beneath. It is an entry into the body that is
nothing like a caress; still, it is among the gentlest of acts. Then stroke and stroke
again, and we are joined by other instruments, hemostats and forceps, until the

[†] "Richard Selzer." *Contemporary Authors Online.* The Gale Group, 2001. 15 June 2001.
January 26, 2002 <http://www.galenet.com/servlet/LitRC?c=1&ai=80197&ste=6&docNum=H
1000089429&bConts=2191&tab=1&vrsn=3&ca=1&tbst=arp&ST=Selzer%2C+Richard&srchtp=a
thr&n=10&locID=nypl&OP=contains>.

wound blooms with strange flowers whose looped handles fall to the sides in steely array.

There is sound, the tight click of clamps fixing teeth into severed blood vessels, the snuffle and gargle of the suction machine clearing the field of blood for the next stroke, the litany of monosyllables with which one prays his way down and in: *clamp, sponge, suture, tie, cut.* And there is color. The green of the cloth, the white of the sponges, the red and yellow of the body. Beneath the fat lies the fascia, the tough fibrous sheet encasing the muscles. It must be sliced and the red beef of the muscles separated. Now there are retractors to hold apart the wound. Hands move together, part, weave. We are fully engaged, like children absorbed in a game or the craftsmen of some place like Damascus.

Deeper still. The peritoneum, pink and gleaming and membranous, bulges into the wound. It is grasped with forceps, and opened. For the first time we can see into the cavity of the abdomen. Such a primitive place. One expects to find drawings of buffalo on the walls. The sense of trespassing is keener now, heightened by the world's light illuminating the organs, their secret colors revealed—maroon and salmon and yellow. The vista is sweetly vulnerable at this moment, a kind of welcoming. An arc of the liver shines high and on the right, like a dark sun. It laps over the pink sweep of the stomach, from whose lower border the gauzy omentum is draped, and through which veil one sees, sinuous, slow as just-fed snakes, the indolent coils of the intestine.

You turn aside to wash your gloves. It is a ritual cleansing. One enters this temple doubly washed. Here is man as microcosm, representing in all his parts the earth, perhaps the universe.

I must confess that the priestliness of my profession has ever been impressed on me. In the beginning there are vows, taken with all solemnity. Then there is the endless harsh novitiate of training, much fatigue, much sacrifice. At last one emerges as celebrant, standing close to the truth lying curtained in the Ark of the body. Not surplice and cassock but mask and gown are your regalia. You hold no chalice, but a knife. There is no wine, no wafer. There are only the facts of blood and flesh.

And if the surgeon is like a poet, then the scars you have made on countless bodies are like verses into the fashioning of which you have poured your soul. I think that if years later I were to see the trace from an old incision of mine, I should know it at once, as one recognizes his pet expressions.

But mostly you are a traveler in a dangerous country, advancing into the moist and jungly cleft your hands have made. Eyes and ears are shuttered from the land you left behind; mind empties itself of all other thought. You are the root of groping fingers. It is a fine hour for the fingers, their sense of touch so enhanced. The blind must know this feeling. Oh, there is risk everywhere. One goes lightly. The spleen. No! No! Do not touch the spleen that lurks below the left leaf of the diaphragm, a manta ray in a coral cave, its bloody tongue protruding. One poke and it might rupture, exploding with sudden hemorrhage. The filmy omentum must not be torn, the intestine scraped or denuded. The hand finds the liver, palms it, fingers running along its sharp lower edge, admiring. Here are the twin mounds of the kidneys, the apron of the omentum hanging in front of the intestinal coils. One lifts it aside and the fingers dip among the loops, searching, mapping territory, establishing boundaries. Deeper still, and the womb is touched, then held like a small muscular bottle—the womb and its earlike appendages, the ovaries. How they do nestle in the cup of a man's hand, their power all dormant. They are frailty itself.

There is a hush in the room. Speech stops. The hands of the others, assistants and nurses, are still. Only the voice of the patient's respiration remains. It is the rhythm of a quiet sea, the sound of waiting. Then you speak, slowly, the terse entries of a Himalayan climber reporting back.

"The stomach is okay. Greater curvature clean. No sign of ulcer. Pylorus, duodenum fine. Now comes the gallbladder. No stones. Right kidney, left, all right. Liver . . . uh-oh."

Your speech lowers to a whisper, falters, stops for a long, long moment, then picks up again at the end of a sigh that comes through your mask like a last exhalation.

"Three big hard ones in the left lobe, one on the right. Metastatic deposits. Bad, bad. Where's the primary? Got to be coming from somewhere."

The arm shifts direction and the fingers drop lower and lower into the pelvis—the body impaled now upon the arm of the surgeon to the hilt of the elbow.

"Here it is."

The voice goes flat, all business now.

"Tumor in the sigmoid colon, wrapped all around it, pretty tight. We'll take out a sleeve of the bowel. No colostomy. Not that, anyway. But, God, there's a lot of it down there. Here, you take a feel."

You step back from the table, and lean into a sterile basin of water, resting on stiff arms, while the others locate the cancer.

When I was a small boy, I was taken by my father, a general practitioner in Troy, New York, to St. Mary's Hospital, to wait while he made his rounds. The solarium where I sat was all sunlight and large plants. It smelled of soap and starch and clean linen. In the spring, clouds of lilac billowed from the vases; and in the fall, chrysanthemums crowded the magazine tables. At one end of the great high-ceilinged, glass-walled room was a huge cage where colored finches streaked and sang. Even from the first, I sensed the nearness of that other place, the Operating Room, knew that somewhere on these premises was that secret dreadful enclosure where *surgery* was at that moment happening. I sat among the cut flowers, half drunk on the scent, listening to the robes of the nuns brush the walls of the corridor, and felt the awful presence of *surgery*.

Oh, the pageantry! I longed to go there. I feared to go there. I imagined surgeons bent like storks over the body of the patient, a circle of red painted across the abdomen. Silence and dignity and awe enveloped them, these surgeons; it was the bubble in which they bent and straightened. Ah, it was a place I would never see, a place from whose walls the hung and suffering Christ turned his affliction to highest purpose. It is thirty years since I yearned for that old Surgery. And now I merely break the beam of an electric eye, and double doors swing open to let me enter, and as I enter, always, I feel the surging of a force that I feel in no other place. It is as though I am suddenly stronger and larger, heroic. Yes, that's it!

The operating room is called a theatre. One walks onto a set where the cupboards hold tanks of oxygen and other gases. The cabinets store steel cutlery of unimagined versatility, and the refrigerators are filled with bags of blood. Bodies are stroked and penetrated here, but no love is made. Nor is it ever allowed to grow dark, but must always gleam with a grotesque brightness. For the special congress into which patient and surgeon enter, the one must have his senses deadened, the other his sensibilities restrained. One lies naked, blind, offering; the other stands masked and gloved. One yields; the other does his will.

I said no love is made here, but love happens. I have stood aside with lowered gaze while a priest, wearing the purple scarf of office, administers Last Rites to the man I shall operate upon. I try not to listen to those terrible last questions, the answers, but hear, with scorching clarity, the words that formalize the expectation of death. For a moment my resolve falters before the resignation, the *attentiveness*, of the other two. I am like an executioner who hears the cleric comforting the prisoner. For the moment I am excluded from the centrality of the event, a mere technician standing by. But it is only for the moment.

The priest leaves, and we are ready. Let it begin.

Later, I am repairing the strangulated hernia of an old man. Because of his age and frailty, I am using local anesthesia. He is awake. His name is Abe Kaufman, and he is a Russian Jew. A nurse sits by his head, murmuring to him. She wipes his forehead. I know her very well. Her name is Alexandria, and she is the daughter of Ukrainian peasants. She has a flat steppe of a face and slanting eyes. Nurse and patient are speaking of blintzes, borscht, piroshki—Russian food that they both love. I listen, and think that it may have been her grandfather who raided the shtetl where the old man lived long ago, and in his high boots and his blouse and his fury this grandfather pulled Abe by his side curls to the ground and stomped his face and kicked his groin. Perhaps it was that ancient kick that caused the hernia I am fixing. I listen to them whispering behind the screen at the head of the table. I listen with breath held before the prism of history.

"Tovarich," she says, her head bent close to his.

He smiles up at her, and forgets that his body is being laid open.

"You are an angel," the old man says.

One can count on absurdity. There, in the midst of our solemnities, appears, small and black and crawling, an insect: The Ant of the Absurd. The belly is open; one has seen and felt the catastrophe within. It seems the patient is already vaporizing into angelhood in the heat escaping therefrom. One could warm one's hands in that fever. All at once that ant is there, emerging from beneath one of the sterile towels that border the operating field. For a moment one does not really see it, or else denies the sight, so impossible it is, marching precisely, heading briskly toward the open wound.

Drawn from its linen lair, where it snuggled in the steam of the great sterilizer, and survived, it comes. Closer and closer, it hurries toward the incision. Ant, art thou in the grip of some fatal *ivresse*? Wouldst hurtle over these scarlet cliffs into the very boil of the guts? Art mad for the reek we handle? Or in some secret act of formication engaged?

The alarm is sounded. An ant! An ant! And we are unnerved. Our fear of defilement is near to frenzy. It is not the mere physical contamination that we loathe. It is the evil of the interloper, that he scurries across our holy place, and filthies our altar. He *is* disease—that for whose destruction we have gathered. Powerless to destroy the sickness before us, we turn to its incarnation with a vengeance, and pluck it from the lip of the incision in the nick of time. Who would have thought an ant could move so fast?

Between thumb and forefinger, the intruder is crushed. It dies as quietly as it lived. Ah, but now there is death in the room. It is a perversion of our purpose. Albert Schweitzer would have spared it, scooped it tenderly into his hand, and lowered it to the ground.

The corpselet is flicked into the specimen basin. The gloves are changed. New towels and sheets are placed where it walked. We are pleased to have done something, if only a small killing. The operation resumes, and we draw upon ourselves once more the sleeves of office and rank. Is our reverence for life in question?

In the room the instruments lie on trays and tables. They are arranged precisely by the scrub nurse, in an order that never changes, so that you can reach blindly for a forceps or hemostat without looking away from the operating field. The instruments lie *thus*! Even at the beginning, when all is clean and tidy and no blood has been spilled, it is the scalpel that dominates. It has a figure the others do not have, the retractors and the scissors. The scalpel is all grace and line, a fierceness. It grins. It is like a cat—to be respected, deferred to, but which returns no amiability. To hold it above a belly is to know the knife's force—as though were you to give it slightest rein, it would pursue an intent of its own, driving into the flesh, a wild energy.

In a story by Borges, a deadly knife fight between two rivals is depicted. It is not, however, the men who are fighting. It is the knives themselves that are settling their own old score. The men who hold the knives are mere adjuncts to the weapons. The unguarded knife is like the unbridled war-horse that not only carries its helpless rider to his death, but tramples all beneath its hooves. The hand of the surgeon must tame this savage thing. He is a rider reining to capture a pace.

So close is the joining of knife and surgeon that they are like the Centaur—the knife, below, all equine energy, the surgeon, above, with his delicate art. One holds the knife back as much as advances it to purpose. One is master of the scissors. One is partner, sometimes rival, to the knife. In a moment it is like the long red fingernail of the Dragon Lady. Thus does the surgeon curb in order to create, restraining the scalpel, governing it shrewdly, setting the action of the operation into a pattern, giving it form and purpose.

It is the nature of creatures to live within a tight cuirass that is both their constriction and their protection. The carapace of the turtle is his fortress and retreat, yet keeps him writhing on his back in the sand. So is the surgeon rendered impotent by his own empathy and compassion. The surgeon cannot weep. When he cuts the flesh, his own must not bleed. Here it is all work. Like an asthmatic hungering for air, longing to take just one deep breath, the surgeon struggles not to feel. It is suffocating to press the feeling out. It would be easier to weep or mourn—for you know that the lovely precise world of proportion contains, just beneath, *there*, all disaster, all disorder. In a surgical operation, a risk may flash into reality: the patient dies . . . of *complication.* The patient knows this too, in a more direct and personal way, and he is afraid.

And what of that *other*, the patient, you, who are brought to the operating room on a stretcher, having been washed and purged and dressed in a white gown? Fluid drips from a bottle into your arm, diluting you, leaching your body of its personal brine. As you wait in the corridor, you hear from behind the closed door the angry clang of steel upon steel, as though a battle were being waged. There is the odor of antiseptic and ether, and masked women hurry up and down the halls, in and out of rooms. There is the watery sound of strange machinery, the tinny beeping that is the transmitted heartbeat of yet another *human being.* And all the while the dreadful knowledge that soon you will be taken, laid beneath great lamps that will reveal the secret linings of your body. In the very act of lying down, you have made a declaration of surrender. One lies down gladly for sleep or for love. But to give over one's body and will for surgery, to *lie down* for it, is a yielding of more than we can bear.

Soon a man will stand over you, gowned and hooded. In time the man will take up a knife and crack open your flesh like a ripe melon. Fingers will rummage among your viscera. Parts of you will be cut out. Blood will run free. Your blood. All the night before you have turned with the presentiment of death upon you. You have attended your funeral, wept with your mourners. You think, "I should never have had surgery in the springtime." It is too cruel. Or on a Thursday. It is an unlucky day.

Now it is time. You are wheeled in and moved to the table. An injection is given. "Let yourself go," I say. "It's a pleasant sensation," I say. "Give in," I say.

Let go? Give in? When you know that you are being tricked into the hereafter, that you will end when consciousness ends? As the monstrous silence of anesthesia falls discourteously across your brain, you watch your soul drift off.

Later, in the recovery room, you awaken and gaze through the thickness of drugs at the world returning, and you guess, at first dimly, then surely, that you have not died. In pain and nausea you will know the exultation of death averted, of life restored.

What is it, then, this thing, the knife, whose shape is virtually the same as it was three thousand years ago, but now with its head grown detachable? Before steel, it was bronze. Before bronze, stone—then back into unencumbered time. Did man invent it or did the knife precede him here, hidden under ages of vegetation and hoofprints, lying in wait to be discovered, picked up, used?

The scalpel is in two parts, the handle and the blade. Joined, it is six inches from tip to tip. At one end of the handle is a narrow notched prong upon which the blade is slid, then snapped into place. Without the blade, the handle has a blind, decapitated look. It is helpless as a trussed maniac. But slide on the blade, click it home, and the knife springs instantly to life. It is headed now, edgy, leaping to mount the fingers for the gallop to its feast.

Now is the moment from which you have turned aside, from which you have averted your gaze, yet toward which you have been hastened. Now the scalpel sings along the flesh again, its brute run unimpeded by germs or other frictions. It is a slick slide home, a barracuda spurt, a rip of embedded talon. One listens, and almost hears the whine—nasal, high, delivered through that gleaming metallic snout. The flesh splits with its own kind of moan. It is like the penetration of rape.

The breasts of women are cut off, arms and legs sliced to the bone to make ready for the saw, eyes freed from sockets, intestines lopped. The hand of the surgeon rebels. Tension boils through his pores, like sweat. The flesh of the patient retaliates with hemorrhage, and the blood chases the knife wherever it is withdrawn.

Within the belly a tumor squats, toadish, fungoid. A gray mother and her brood. The only thing it does not do is croak. It too is hacked from its bed as the carnivore knife lips the blood, turning in it in a kind of ecstasy of plenty, a gluttony after the long fast. It is just for this that the knife was created, tempered, heated, its violence beaten into paper-thin force.

At last a little thread is passed into the wound and tied. The monstrous booming fury is stilled by a tiny thread. The tempest is silenced. The operation is over. On the table, the knife lies spent, on its side, the bloody meal smear-dried upon its flanks. The knife rests.

And waits.

Critical Thinking

1.   What were your initial reactions to the essay?

2.   Identify the various references to the knife and to the "priestliness" of his profession. What metaphors and similes does he use? Are any of them too graphic? Why or why not?

3.   What do you make of the conclusion?

Writing Assignments

1.   Write a stylistic analysis. Identify the literary, religious, travelling, sexual, and equestrian analogies. How does his use of stylistic detail tie into the theme(s) of the essay?

2.   Selzer uses medical vocabulary. Is it appropriate?

3.   Write a descriptive essay using metaphor and simile to describe a tool used in any trade.

RELATING THE AUTHORS' IDEAS

1. What is your definition of success? Compare and contrast your definition of success to the views presented by any two authors in this chapter?

2. Look at the lives of women as presented by Woolf and Smith-Yackel. What attitudes toward women emerge?

3. Explore the issue of male power and the powerlessness of women, as it is presented in Woolf and Sidel.

4. Which characters in the selections possess a passion for the work they do? Which do not? Do you think it is important to have a passion for the work you choose? Why? If not, then, what is more important than passion? Is it financial security or other? Explain.

Chapter V

Entertaining the Self

V

Entertaining the Self

Introduction

Entertainment is natural, necessary and vital to the enjoyment of life. Numerous forms of entertainment satisfy our cravings for connection, distraction, laughter, and diversion.

In this chapter, E. B. White, Pat Mora, Elizabeth Kolbert, Stephen King, and Joan Didion observe the values, motivations and effects of several favorite pastimes—specifically, the circus, museums, television, and film. In "The Ring of Time," E.B. White writes about the beauty of the circus "before it has been put together." As he observes the circus performers, he discovers a parallel to the world: "The circus comes as close to being the world in microcosm as anything I know." In "The Dance within My Heart" Pat Mora describes a visit to the museum. Museums have the power to affect her intellectually, emotionally, and physically: "For me, museums are pleasure havens. When I enter, my breathing changes." Art has a positive effect on her, it expands her interior self. She says, "Art is not a luxury: it nourishes our parched spirits. It is essential."

For Mora, museums have a positive, uplifting effect. But are there forms of entertainment that have negative influences on our lives? In "Americans Despair of Popular Culture," Elizabeth Kolbert asks Americans about their attitudes toward television and its effect on teenage violence. The findings of a *New York Times* opinion poll reveal that "although the average adult in the United States watches television for more than four hours a day, a little more than half of the adults polled could not think of a single good thing to say about television, or about movies or popular music." In fact, "9 out of 10 of those polled could think of something bad to say about popular culture."

Stephen King, on the other hand, discovers redeeming factors in popular culture, specifically horror. In "Why we Crave Horror Movies," bestselling horror writer Stephen King explores the motivations behind the public's cravings for horror and outlines the benefits of watching horror films. They are not just fun, he writes, but necessary outlets for anti-civilized emotions. He insists that our "anti-civilization emotions don't go away, and they demand periodic exercise." King's bestselling books have been turned into blockbuster movies and he knows the genre well. He states, "The mythic horror movie . . . appeals to all that is the worst in us." He observes that "the best horror films, like the best fairy tales, manage to be reactionary, anarchistic, and revolutionary all at the same time."

The final essay in this chapter is "Goodbye to All That" by Joan Didion. In this essay, she explores her experiences as a young woman living in New York. She describes how she fell *in love* with New York—the excitement of the city, the parties, and the people—and then, *out of love* with the city. Didion says, "I want to explain to you, and in the process perhaps to myself, why I no longer live in New York."

As writers, let's examine our sources of entertainment, and record our observations. Perhaps, by doing so, we will gain a greater understanding of ourselves and world we live in.

*"For me the circus is at its best
before it has been put together."*

-- E. B. White

"The Ring of Time"[*]
E. B. White

*Born in 1899, E.B. White is an award winning writer, novelist, and
essayist. He is the recipient of numerous nominations and awards.
His bestselling children's book, particularly Charlotte's Web and
Stuart Little are highly acclaimed. In 1978, he received the
Pulitzer Prize (special citation). He is also recognized for his
highly popular book The Elements of Style, 2nd Edition, with
William Strunk, Jr.[†]*

FIDDLER BAYOU, MARCH 22, 1956

After the lions had returned to their cages, creeping angrily through the
chutes, a little bunch of us drifted away and into an open doorway nearby, where
we stood for a while in semidarkness, watching a big brown circus horse go
harumphing around the practice ring. His trainer was a woman of about forty, and
the two of them, horse and woman, seemed caught up in one of those desultory
treadmills of afternoon from which there is no apparent escape. The day was hot,
and we kibitzers were grateful to be briefly out of the sun's glare. The long rein,
or tape, by which the woman guided her charge counterclockwise in his dull
career formed the radius of their private circle, of which she was the revolving
center; and she, too, stepped a tiny circumference of her own, in order to
accommodate the horse and allow him his maximum scope. She had on a
short-skirted costume and a conical straw hat. Her legs were bare and she wore
high heels, which probed deep into the loose tanbark and kept her ankles in a state
of constant turmoil. The great size and meekness of the horse, the repetitious

[*] "The Ring of Time" from *The Points of the Compass* by E.B. White. Copyright © 1956 by E.B.
White. Originally appeared in *The New Yorker*. Reprinted by permission of HarperCollins
Publishers Inc.

[†] "E.B. White," *Contemporary Authors Online*. The Gale Group, 2001. 10 October 1996.
January 26, 2002. <http://www.galenet.com/servlet/LitRC?c=1&ai=94220&ste=6&docNum=H10
00105504&bConts=15279&tab=1&vrsn=3&ca=1&tbst=arp&ST=White%2C+E.B.&srchtp=athr&
n=10&locID=nypl&OP=contains>.

It was there job & had no choice but to do it.

So that girls presence which brought a glow to the place

exercise, the heat of the afternoon, all exerted a hypnotic charm that invited boredom; we spectators were experiencing a languor—we neither expected relief nor felt entitled to any. We had paid a dollar to get into the grounds, to be sure, but we had got our dollar's worth a few minutes before, when the lion trainer's whiplash had got caught around a toe of one of the lions. What more did we want for a dollar?

Behind me I heard someone say, "Excuse me, please," in a low voice. She was halfway into the building when I saw her—a girl of sixteen or seventeen, politely threading her away through us onlookers who blocked the entrance. As she emerged in front of us, I saw that she was barefoot, her dirty little feet fighting the uneven ground. In most respects she was like any of two or three dozen showgirls you encounter if you wander about the winter quarters of Mr. John Ringling North's circus, in Sarasota—cleverly proportioned, deeply browned by the sun, dusty, eager, and almost naked. But her grave face and the naturalness of her manner gave her a sort of quick distinction and brought a new note into the gloomy octagonal building where we had to all cast our lot for a few moments. As soon as she had squeezed through the crowd, she spoke a word or two to the older woman, whom I took to be her mother, *I assumed it was the ladies daughter* stepped to the ring, and waited while the horse coasted to a stop in front of her. She gave the animal a couple of affectionate swipes on his enormous neck and then swung herself aboard. The horse immediately resumed his rocking canter, the woman goading him on, chanting something that sounded like "Hop! Hop!"

In attempting to recapture this mild spectacle, I am merely acting as recording secretary for one of the oldest of societies—the society of those who, at one time or another, have surrendered, without even a show of resistance, to the bedazzlement of a circus rider. As a writing man, or secretary, I have always felt charged with the safekeeping of all unexpected items of worldly and unworldly enchantment, as though I might be held personally responsible if even a small one were to be lost. But it is not easy to communicate anything of this nature. The circus comes as close to being the world in microcosm as anything I know; in a way, it puts all the rest of show business in the shade. Its magic is universal and complex. Out of its wild disorder comes order; from its rank smell rises the good aroma of courage and daring; out of its preliminary shabbiness comes the final splendor. And buried in the familiar boasts of its advance agents lies the modesty of most of its people. For me the circus is at its best before it has been put together. It is at its best at certain moments when it comes to a point, as through a

Little girls perform mance

burning glass, in the activity and destiny of a single performer out of so many. One ring is always bigger than three. One rider, one aerialist, is always greater than six. In short, a man has to catch the circus unawares to experience its full impact and share its gaudy dream.

The ten-minute ride the girl took achieved—as far as I was concerned, who wasn't looking for it, and quite unbeknownst to her, who wasn't even striving for it—the thing that is sought by performers everywhere, on whatever stage, whether struggling in the tidal currents of Shakespeare or bucking the difficult motion of a horse. I somehow got the idea she was just cadging a ride, improving a shining ten minutes in the diligent way all serious artists seize free moments to hone the blade of their talent and keep themselves in trim. Her brief tour included only elementary postures and tricks, perhaps because they were all she was capable of, perhaps because her warm-up at this hour was unscheduled and the ring was not rigged for a real practice session. She swung herself off and on the horse several times, gripping his mane. She did a few knee-stands—or whatever they are called—dropping to her knees and quickly bouncing back up on her feet again. Most of the time she simply rode in a standing position, well aft on the beast, her hands hanging easily at her sides, her head erect, her straw-colored ponytail lightly brushing her shoulders, the blood of exertion showing faintly through the tan of her skin. Twice she managed a one-foot stance—a sort of ballet pose, with arms outstretched. At one point the neck strap of her bathing suit broke and she went twice around the ring in the classic attitude of a woman making minor repairs to a garment. The fact that she was standing on the back of a moving horse while doing this invested the matter with a clownish significance that perfectly fitted the spirit of the circus—jocund, yet charming. She just rolled the strap into a neat ball and stowed it inside her bodice while the horse rocked and rolled beneath her in dutiful innocence. The bathing suit proved as self-reliant as its owner and stood up well enough without benefit of strap.

The richness of the scene was in its plainness, its natural condition—of horse, of ring, of girl, even to the girl's bare feet that gripped the bare back of her proud and ridiculous mount. The enchantment grew not out of anything that happened or was performed but out of something that seemed to go round and around and around with the girl, attending her, a steady gleam in the shape of a circle—a ring of ambition, of happiness, of youth. (And the positive pleasures of equilibrium under difficulties.) In a week or two, all would be changed, all (or almost all) lost: the girl would wear makeup, the horse would wear gold, the ring

would become different

would be painted, the bark would be clean for the feet of the horse, the girl's feet would be clean for the slippers that she'd wear. All, all would be lost.

As I watched with the others, our jaws adroop, our eyes alight, I became painfully conscious of the element of time. Everything in the hideous old building seemed to take the shape of a circle, conforming to the course of the horse. The rider's gaze, as she peered straight ahead, seemed to be circular, as though bent by force of circumstance; then time itself began running in circles, and so the beginning was where the end was, and the two were the same, and one thing ran into the next and time went round and around and got nowhere. The girl wasn't so young that she did not know the delicious satisfaction of having a perfectly behaved body and the fun of using it to do a trick most people can't do, but she was too young to know that time does not really move in a circle at all. I thought: "She will never be as beautiful as this again"—a thought that made me acutely unhappy—and in a flash my mind (which is too much of a busy body to suit me) had projected her twenty-five years ahead, and she was now in the center of the ring, on foot, wearing a conical hat and high-heeled shoes, the image of the older woman, holding the long rein, caught in the treadmill of an afternoon long in the future. "She is at that enviable moment in life [I thought] when she believes she can go once around the ring, make one complete circuit, and at the end be exactly the same age as at the start." Everything in her movements, her expression, told you that for her the ring of time was perfectly formed, changeless, predictable, without beginning or end, like the ring in which she was traveling at this moment with the horse that wallowed under her. And then I slipped back into my trance, and time was circular again—time, pausing quietly with the rest of us, so as not to disturb the balance of a performer.

nosense

Her ride ended as casually as it had begun. The older woman stopped the horse, and the girl slid to the ground. As she walked toward us to leave, there was a quick, small burst of applause. She smiled broadly, in surprise and pleasure; then her face suddenly regained its gravity and she disappeared through the door.

It has been ambitious and plucky of me to attempt to describe what is indescribable, and I have failed, as I knew I would. But I have discharged my duty to my society; and besides, a writer, like an acrobat, must occasionally try a stunt that is too much for him. At any rate, it is worth reporting that long before the circus comes to town, its most notable performances have already been given. Under the bright lights of the finished show, a performer need only reflect the electric candle power that is directed upon him; but in the dark and dirty old training rings and in the makeshift cages, whatever light is generated, whatever excitement, whatever beauty, must come from original sources—from internal fires of professional hunger and delight, from the exuberance and gravity of youth. It is the difference between planetary light and the combustion of stars.

[FIDDLER BAYOU, MARCH 22, 1956]

Critical Thinking

1.   Why does E.B. White prefer the circus "before it has been put together"? What will be lost when the circus opens?

2.   Find all images that relate to geometric shapes. How do they relate to the theme(s) of the essay?

3.   What, according to White, is the duty of a writer?

Writing Assignments

1.   Attend any event before "it has been put together." For example, you could attend a fleamarket before it opens. Write a descriptive essay. Include sensory images. What do you see, hear, feel, touch, and taste?

2.   Write an essay in which you compare and/or contrast White's ideas about the duty of a writer to your own.

3.   Write a stylistic analysis essay showing how White's use of word choice and imagery ties into the theme(s) of the essay.

"The Dance Within My Heart"[*]
Pat Mora

Pat Mora is a contemporary writer and poet. She is a contributor to various magazines and newspapers. Her publications include <u>My Own True name: New and Selected Poems for Young Adults, 1984-1999</u> *and* <u>Agua Santa: Holy Water</u> *(1995). She is the recipient of numerous awards and fellowships. This selection is from* <u>Nepantla: Essays from the Land in the Middle</u>.[†]

For a Southwesterner, early spring in the Midwest is a time for jubilation. Another winter survived. Why, then, on a soft spring Saturday would I choose to leave the dogwoods and daffodils and spend my day inside museums?

Certainly, I didn't spend my youth enduring trips through solemn rooms, being introduced to "culture." There was only one small art museum in my hometown, and I'm not sure how comfortable my parents would have felt there. My father worked evenings and weekends to support the four of us and to give us what he and my mother hadn't had, a youth without financial worries. And my mother not only helped him in his optical business but as our willing chauffeur in addition to assisting the grandmother and aunt who lived with us, our extended Mexican American family.

But as an adult I began to visit those echoing buildings. A fellowship allowed trips to modest and grand museums in New York, Paris, Washington, Mexico, Hawaii, and the Dominican Republic. And much to my surprise, I even found myself directing a small university museum for a time, having the opportunity to convince people of all ages and backgrounds that indeed the museum was theirs. I was hooked for life.

For me, museums are pleasure havens. When I enter, my breathing changes just as it does when I visit aquariums, zoos, botanical gardens. These latter sites offer a startling array of living species. Unless we have become totally desensitized to nature's grandeur, to its infinite variations, arboretums and nature centers inspire us to treat our planet with more care, to be more attentive to the life around us, no matter how minute. I stand entranced by the sprightliness of glass shrimp, the plushness of the jaguar, the haughtiness of birds in paradise in bloom. Parrots make me laugh, fins spin my blood, ferns hush my doubts. I leave refreshed.

When they were younger, my children could far more easily understand my desire to visit displays of living creatures that they could my penchant for natural history and art museums, for gazing at baskets and pottery, at sculpture and flashing neon. It sounded like work walking through room after room, up and down stairs, being relatively quiet, not eating, reading small carts of text, staring at "weird" objects. This is fun?

But museums remind me of the strength and inventiveness of the human imagination through time. They remind me that offering beauty to a community is a human habit, a needed reminder in a society with little time for observing, listening, appreciating. I gaze at African masks crusted with cowrie shells, at drums and carvings of old, wrinkled wood, at the serenity of Buddha. I watch my fellow visitors, drawn to cases both by the beauty and craft but also as a kind of testimony to humans who once sat under our sun and moon and with rough hands graced our world.

I walk on to see the sturdy pre-Columbian female figures from Nayarit, Mexico, women of broad dimensions who occupy space rather than shrink as we sometimes do. I see pan pipes and bone flutes from Peru, 180 B.C., back then, high in the Andes, hear a man transforming his breath into music.

Room after room I watch light and shadow play on sandstone, silver, wood, bronze, earthenware, copper, ivory, hemp, oil, acrylic, watercolor, straw, gold. I study toenails on a headless marble statue, watch light stroke the soft curves, wish I could touch her outstretched Roman hand. The next room, or turning a corner, can yield surprise, the halls and rooms a pleasure maze. I stand in Chagall's blue light, see his glass bird poised to fly from room to room.

I ignore the careful museum maps, enjoying the unexpected, the independence of viewing at will, the private pleasure of letting myself abandon order and logic room to room. Purposeless wandering? Not really, for I now know I come not only for the intellectual and sensory stimulation but for comfort. I come to be with humans I admire, with those who produced these drums and breathing dances, who through the ages added beauty to this world. Their work gives me hope, reminds me that art is not a luxury: it nourishes our parched spirits. It is essential.

I think again of how privileged I am to be in these quiet rooms, not having to wait for a free day, having time to spend wandering these galleries rather than having to care for someone else's children while mine are alone, or having to iron clothes that I will never wear.

And certainly free days and increased public programming—the democratization of museums—are an improvement from past eras, an acknowledgment, although sometimes grudgingly, that not only the "washed and worthy" deserve entrance. Museums are slowly changing, realizing that artifacts and art belong to all people, not some people. Museums are even becoming a bit embarrassed about how they acquired what they own, about why they arrogantly ushered certain groups past their polished doors. The faces viewing with me have been more varied in recent years.

I walk on. I, who can barely sew a button, study an array of quilts, glad that such women's art is now displayed, think of the careful fingers—stitch, stitch, stitch— and probably careful voices that produced these works. The text of a bronze of Shiva says that her dance takes place within her heart. I study her and think of that dance, of the private nature of that spring of emotion. I watch a group of teenage girls walk by and wonder if they can hear or feel their private dance in a world that equates noise and brutality with entertainment.

The contemporary art halls most baffled my children when they were young. "Why, I could do that!" they would scoff staring at a Jackson Pollock. I smile secretly when my youngest, now taller than I am, asks, "Where are our favorite rooms?" meaning, yes, those rooms with massive canvases, with paint everywhere, the rooms that loosen me up inside, that provide escape from the confines of the predictable.

I walk outside glad to breathe in sky and wind but also brimming with all I saw and felt, hearing the dance within my heart.

Critical Thinking

1. Describe the effects museums have on Mora.

2. What examples does Mora use to support her ideas?

3. Why does she refer to the "democratization" of museums? What purpose do her statements serve?

Writing Assignments

1. Write a descriptive essay in which you recall a visit to a museum, zoo, or botanical garden. Be sure to describe not only what you see and hear, but also how you feel.

2. Compare and contrast your own ideas about the value of art to Mora's.

3. Mora says "Museums are even becoming a bit embarrassed about how they acquired what they own." Conduct research on this topic and write an essay supporting or refuting this statement.

"Disparagement of television is second only to watching television as an American pastime."
-- George F. Will, "Prisoners of TV," <u>The Pursuit of Happiness and Other Sobering Thoughts</u> (1978)

"Americans Despair of Popular Culture"[*]
Elizabeth Kolbert

Elizabeth Kolbert is a writer and journalist. She is a contributor to many magazines and newspapers, including <u>The New Yorker</u> and <u>The New York Times</u>. This essay was printed in <u>The New York Times</u>, Sunday, August 20, 1995.

AMERICANS HAVE A STARKLY NEGATIVE VIEW of popular culture, and blame television more than any other single factor for teen-age sex and violence. By a large margin, they favor measures like ratings that would give parents more information about what their children are watching and listening to. But by almost as large a margin, they say they believe that such measures would not actually succeed in preventing children from viewing or hearing material that is inappropriate.

These are among the findings of a *New York Times* poll examining Americans' attitudes about the influence of popular culture. The results of the poll suggest that Americans are deeply ambivalent about their own diversions. Although the average adult in the United States watches television for more than four hours a day, a little more than half of the adults polled could not think of a single good thing to say about television, or about movies or popular music. In contrast, 9 out of 10 of those polled could think of something bad to say about popular culture, with a large proportion mentioning too much sex, violence and vulgar language and a smaller percentage pointing to bias and just plain stupidity.

Many Americans say they believe there is a direct connection between the fictional world young people are exposed to and the way they behave in real life. Half of those surveyed said they believed portrayals of sex and violence on television, in movies and in music lyrics contribute "a lot" to whether teen-agers

[*] From 8/20/1995 *The New York Times*. Reprinted by permission.

become sexually active or violent. A quarter said they believed such portrayals contribute "some." Only a fifth said they believed that the portrayals of sex and violence in popular culture had "little" or "no" influence on teen-agers' behavior. "I think it has a bad influence." said Robert Bowden, a 50-year-old father of five from Cottage Grove, Tenn., in a follow-up telephone interview after the poll was completed. "That's your future generation. It's what we've made them. Two parents are working all the time. They can't be with the family like they used to. They don't know what's going on while they're not home."

Asked to name for themselves what is most to blame for teen-age violence, 21 percent of those polled volunteered "television." Six percent blamed "the media" more generally, while 4 percent cited movies. Altogether, 33 percent of those polled named some aspect of popular culture, making it the most often cited cause; and 33 percent cited some aspect of family life, including lack of parental discipline and family breakdown. Smaller percentages cited causes like "drugs," "boredom" and "economics."

The poll suggests that politicians who denounce the sex and violence in popular culture—as Senator Bob Dole did in May in his much-publicized presidential campaign speech attacking Hollywood—have hit on a theme that resonates deeply with the American public. At the same time, the poll suggests that these politicians should not expect to get too much credit for their attacks. Only one out of five respondents said that politicians who criticize popular culture were "sincere," while three out of five said such politicians were simply speaking out "for political gain."

THE POLL, CONDUCTED JULY 23 through July 26, surveyed 1,209 adults. Of those, 411 (34 percent) were parents who have children ages 2 through 17 living with them. The poll—which has a margin of sampling error of plus or minus 3 percentage points over all, and plus or minus 5 percentage points for those with children living at home—found little difference between the opinions of parents and those of adults in general. Questions about the influence of popular culture on society and about what, if anything, should be done to combat it have occupied psychological researchers and social scientists for years. Increasingly, as polls have shown growing public concern about such questions, they have become a matter of political debate as well.

The *New York Times* poll, the first by the newspaper measuring attitudes about pop culture, suggests that while Americans are deeply concerned about the impact of popular culture, they are also concerned about government intrusion into the entertainment industry and skeptical that measures that are currently being debated in Washington will really make much difference.   Asked, for example, whether television shows should have ratings as movies now do, 84 percent of those polled said yes.   But when they were asked whether those ratings should be required by the Federal Government, the proportion answering yes was only 39 percent.   And when they were asked whether ratings would "succeed in keeping children from seeing inappropriate material," the proportion saying yes dropped to just 30 percent.   Roughly the same pattern emerged from questions about rating music recordings and video games.

The one form of ratings that exists—movie ratings—received mixed reviews in the poll.   Fifty-two percent of those polled said that the movie rating system, established voluntarily by the movie industry in 1968, did "a good job in informing people about how much sex and violence to expect," while 43 percent said it did not.   Only 20 percent said that the rating system actually succeeds in keeping children away from inappropriate movies, while 76 percent said, it did not.   Raymond Dieter, a 46-year-old father of four from Essexville, Mich., said in a follow-up interview that he tried to monitor what his children watch and listen to, and that ratings for television shows and music recordings "would help some." But, he added, "Kids are always going to want to watch what we don't want them to."

A majority of the parents polled said they had forbidden their children from watching specific movies or television shows because of content. Eighty-four percent of the parents said they had forbidden their children from watching a specific television show at some point; 64 percent said they had done so in the last six months.   Sixty-four percent said they had forbidden their children from seeing a specific movie, 42 percent in the last six months.   The television show that was most frequently mentioned as forbidden was MTV's "Beavis and Butt-head," followed by Fox's "Mighty Morphine Power Rangers."   No one movie was singled out by parents as off limits; movies ranging from the science fiction thriller "Species" to the goofy comedy "Dumb and Dumber" each received a few mentions.

Less than half of the parents polled, 42 percent, said they had forbidden their children from listening to a specific musical recording, 29 percent in the last six months.   The category of music most frequently mentioned as forbidden was rap.

ALTHOUGH AMERICANS SEEM eager to exert more control over what their children are exposed to, on the issue of the so-called V-chip, by which televisions could be programmed to block out shows with certain ratings, they also seem concerned about the possibility of too much government intrusion into the entertainment industry. Both houses of Congress have recently voted to require all new television sets to carry V-chips (the "V" stands for violence). Proponents of V-chips, including President Clinton, say they would provide parents with a powerful new tool to help restrict what their children watch. Opponents of the chips, including Senator Dole and most of the television industry, argue that they would lead to an indirect form of censorship. Asked whether the government should require the installation of V-chips, or whether that would "involve too much government regulation," 31 percent of those polled said the chips should be required while 60 percent said such a requirement would involve too much regulation.

Kelly Stenquist, 32, a mother of three from Sandy, Utah, said in a follow-up interview that she had originally been in favor of the V-chip but reconsidered after her husband argued that the television industry could use the existence of the chip to justify putting even more violent or salacious shows on in prime time. "It's kind of scary, she said. "I'm kind of torn."

Members of the entertainment industry, as well as many more-disinterested observers of popular culture, argue that the concerns about mass entertainment's impact are overstated and that no clear-cut connection has ever been demonstrated between, say, the violence children see on television and in movies and the crimes they commit on the streets. And, indeed, many of the studies on the topic have failed to come up with a strong statistical correlation between what children watch and what they do.

Among social scientists, however, there is a broad consensus that there is at least an indirect relationship between popular culture and behavior. And as many have pointed out, the television industry at least implicitly believes this to be the case. Otherwise, how can television executives make the case to advertisers that buying air time will boost their sales?

Most of the parents interviewed as a follow-up to the poll said that they saw direct evidence of the connection between popular culture and behavior, noting that their children imitated behavior and language they picked up from television, movies and the radio. "It's the way they talk and the way they view life in general," said 41-year-old Denise O'Hara of Roswell, Ga., the mother of two teen-age boys. "They say 'I'm going to kill you' like it's O.K., like it's nothing. They don't understand that you kill someone, that's it, they're gone. It's like 'Oh, cool, oh neat, watching this is great.'" Even though they sometimes prevent their children from watching specific television programs or movies, most of the parents interviewed also said they felt powerless to prevent their children from seeing and hearing all inappropriate entertainment. Dave Hull, a 40-year-old father of two from Lake Worth, Fla., was another person who pointed out that because both parents in many families are working these days, it is becoming more and more difficult to keep children from being exposed to whatever is on the air or in the cinemas. "Parents are not around," said Mr. Hull, who works days as a cook and whose wife works nights as a security guard. "So kids are going to get a hold of what they want no matter what. I don't see how you can keep them away."

As for ratings for television shows, videos and musical recordings, Mr. Hull said he wasn't sure they would be "worth the money or the bureaucracy." "Something should be done," he said. "But there's no easy answer." Mark Mellman, a political pollster who has studied Americans' attitudes toward popular culture, said that concern about the influence of the entertainment industry has been rising precisely because many people feel that parents no longer spend enough time with their kids. "Behind every major issue, like crime or welfare, people look at it and see declining values as key," he said. "The family is the place where good values should be taught. But because of economic circumstances, both parents are working just to provide necessities, and people have less time to inculcate values. So people see TV, movies and other kids inculcating values, and they're the wrong values."

One reason Americans seem so skeptical about regulatory solutions to the problem. he said, is that there is no way for the government to make parents less busy. "There's not some chip that can give people more time," he said. "That's a much more difficult problem to get your hands around."

Critical Thinking

1. What is the thesis?

2. What evidence does she use to support her main idea? Is it credible? Why or why not?

3. Why are citizens concerned about "government intrusion in the entertainment industry"?

Writing Assignments

1. Take an informal poll of your friends and family about their attitudes toward television. What are your findings?

2. What is the usefulness of polls? Write an essay exploring the advantages and the disadvantages of polls.

3. Write an argumentation essay about the issue of censorship.

> *"When we pay our four or five bucks and seat ourselves at tenth-row center in a theater showing a horror movie, we are daring the nightmare."*
> —*Stephen King*

"Why We Crave Horror Movies"[*]
Stephen King

Bestselling author Stephen King is known for his horror novels, short stories and films. He has written numerous books, including Carrie, The Shining, Misery, *and* The Green Mile. *In this essay, the master of the genre explores the psychology behind our insatiable craving for horror.[†]*

I think that we're all mentally ill; those of us outside the asylums only hide it a little better—and maybe not all that much better, after all. We've all known people who talk to themselves, people who sometimes squint their faces into horrible grimaces when they believe no one is watching, people who have some hysterical fear—of snakes, the dark, the tight place, the long drop . . . and, of course, those final worms and grubs that are waiting so patiently underground.

When we pay our four or five bucks and seat ourselves at tenth-row center in a theater showing a horror movie, we are daring the nightmare.

Why? Some of the reasons are simple and obvious. To show that we can, that we are not afraid, that we can ride this roller coaster. Which is not to say that a really good horror movie may not surprise a scream out of us at some point, the way we may scream when the roller coaster twists through a complete 360 or plows through a lake at the bottom of the drop. And horror movies, like roller coasters, have always been the special province of the young; by the time one turns 40 or 50, one's appetite for double twists or 360-degree loops may be considerably depleted.

[†] "Stephen King: The Man." *Stephen King Website* <http://sids.com/king/man.htm>.

We also go to re-establish our feelings of essential normality; the horror movie is innately conservative, even reactionary. Freda Jackson as the horrible melting woman in *Die, Monster Die!* confirms for us that no matter how far we may be removed from the beauty of a Robert Redford or a Diana Ross, we are still light-years from true ugliness.

And we go to have fun.

Ah, but this is where the ground starts to slope away, isn't it? Because this is a very peculiar sort of fun indeed. The fun comes from seeing others menaced—sometimes killed. One critic has suggested that if pro football has become the voyeur's version of combat, then the horror film has become the modern version of the public lynching.

It is true that the mythic, "fairytale" horror film intends to take away the shades of gray. . . . It urges us to put away our more civilized and adult penchant for analysis and to become children again, seeing things in pure blacks and whites. It may be that horror movies provide psychic relief on this level because this invitation to lapse into simplicity, irrationality and even outright madness is extended so rarely. We are told we may allow our emotions a free rein . . . or no rein at all.

If we are all insane, then sanity becomes a matter of degree. If your insanity leads you to carve up women like Jack the Ripper or the Cleveland Torso Murderer, we clap you away in the funny farm (but neither of those two amateur-night surgeons was ever caught, heh-heh-heh); if, on the other hand, your insanity leads you only to talk to yourself when you're under stress or to pick your nose on the morning bus, then you are left alone to go about your business . . . though it is doubtful that you will ever be invited to the best parties.

The potential lyncher is in almost all of us (excluding saints, past and present; but then, most saints have been crazy in their own ways), and every now and then, he has to be let loose to scream and roll around in the grass. Our emotions and our fears form their own body, and we recognize that it demands its own exercise to maintain proper muscle tone. Certain of these emotional muscles are accepted—even exalted—in civilized society; they are, of course, the emotions that tend to maintain the status quo of civilization itself. Love, friendship, loyalty, kindness—these are all the emotions that we applaud, emotions that have been immortalized in the couplets of Hallmark cards and in the verses (I don't dare call it poetry) of Leonard Nimoy.

When we exhibit these emotions, society showers us with positive reinforcement; we learn this even before we get out of diapers. When, as children, we hug our rotten little puke of a sister and give her a kiss, all the aunts and uncles smile and twit and cry, "Isn't he the sweetest little thing?" Such coveted treats as chocolate-covered graham crackers often follow. But if we deliberately slam the rotten little puke of a sister's fingers in the door, sanctions follow—angry remonstrance from parents, aunts and uncles; instead of a chocolate-covered graham cracker, a spanking.

But anticivilization emotions don't go away, and they demand periodic exercise. We have such "sick" jokes as, "What's the difference between a truckload of bowling balls and a truckload of dead babies?" (You can't unload a truckload of bowling balls with a pitchfork . . . a joke, by the way, that I heard originally from a ten-year-old.) Such a joke may surprise a laugh or a grin out of us even as we recoil, a possibility that confirms the thesis: If we share a brotherhood of man, then we also share an insanity of man. None of which is intended as a defense of either the sick joke or insanity but merely as an explanation of why the best horror films, like the best fairy tales, manage to be reactionary, anarchistic, and revolutionary all at the same time.

The mythic horror movie, like the sick joke, has a dirty job to do. It deliberately appeals to all that is worst in us. It is morbidity unchained, our most base instincts let free, our nastiest fantasies realized . . . and it all happens, fittingly enough, in the dark. For those reasons, good liberals often shy away from horror films. For myself, I like to see the most aggressive of them, *Dawn of the Dead*, for instance—as lifting a trap door in the civilized forebrain and throwing a basket of raw meat to the hungry alligators swimming around in that subterranean river beneath.

Why bother? Because it keeps them from getting out, man. It keeps them down there and me up here. It was Lennon and McCartney who said that all you need is love, and I would agree with that.

As long as you keep the gators fed.

Critical Thinking

1.   Respond to the first line of the essay: "I think that we're all mentally ill; those of us outside the asylums only hide it a little better—and maybe not all that much better."

2.   What support does King use to persuade the reader?

3.   What are the differences between anti-civilized emotions and civilized emotions?

Writing Assignments

1.   Write an essay similar to King's essay on a subject other than horror. Begin the title with "Why We Crave _____."

2.   Write an essay in which you compare King's ideas about horror movies to your own.

3.   Write a letter to King agreeing or disagreeing with his views on "anti-civilized emotions."

"Nature did not say to me, 'Do not be poor'; still less, 'Be rich'; but she cried out to me, 'Be independent.'"

--Chamfort

"Goodbye to All That"[*]
Joan Didion

Joan Didion is a prolific essayist, novelist and screenplay writer. She has won numerous awards and nominations. She was nominated for the National Book Award in Fiction (1971) for Play It as It Lays. *Her most recent book is* Political Fictions (Knopf, 2001). *This essay is from her bestselling book* Slouching Towards Bethlehem. [†]

How many miles to Babylon?
Three score miles and ten—
Can I get there by candlelight?
Yes, and back again—
If your feet are nimble and light
You can get there by candlelight.

IT IS EASY to see the beginnings of things, and harder to see the ends. I can remember now, with a clarity that makes the nerves in the back of my neck constrict, when New York began for me, but I cannot lay my finger upon the moment it ended, can never cut through the ambiguities and second starts and broken resolves to the exact place on the page where the heroine is no longer as optimistic as she once was. When I first saw New York I was twenty and it was

---

[*] Reprinted by permission of Farrar, Straus and Giroux, LLC: "Goodbye to All That" from *Slouching Towards Bethlehem* by Joan Didion. Copyright © 1966, 1968, renewed 1996 by Joan Didion.

[†] "Joan Didion," *Contemporary Authors Online.* The Gale Group, 2001. 4 April 2001. January 26, 2002 < http://www.galenet.com/servlet/LitRC?c=1&ai=24249&ste=6&docNum= H1000 0254 98 &bConts=16303&tab=1&vrsn=3&ca=1&tbst=arp&ST=Didion%2C+Joan&srchtp=athr&n=10 &locID=nypl&OP=contains>.

summertime, and I got off a DC-7 at the old Idlewild temporary terminal in a new dress which had seemed very smart in Sacramento but seemed less smart already, even in the old Idlewild temporary terminal, and the warm air smelled of mildew and some instinct, programmed by all the movies I had ever seen and all the songs I had ever heard sung and all the stories I had ever read about New York, informed me that it would never be quite the same again. In fact it never was. Some time later there was a song on all the jukeboxes on the Upper East Side that went "but where is the schoolgirl who used to be me," and if it was late enough at night I used to wonder that. I know now that almost everyone wonders something like that, sooner or later and no matter what he or she is doing, but one of the mixed blessings of being twenty and twenty-one and even twenty-three is the conviction that nothing like this, all evidence to the contrary notwithstanding, has ever happened to anyone before.

Of course it might have been some other city, had circumstances been different and the time been different and had I been different, might have been Paris or Chicago or even San Francisco, but because I am talking about myself I am talking here about New York. That first night I opened my window on the bus into town and watched for the skyline, but all I could see were the wastes of Queens and the big signs that said MIDTOWN TUNNEL THIS LANE and then a flood of summer rain (even that seemed remarkable and exotic, for I had come out of the West where there was no summer rain), and for the next three days I sat wrapped in blankets in a hotel room air-conditioned to 35° and tried to get over a bad cold and a high fever. It did not occur to me to call a doctor, because I knew none, and although it did occur to me to call the desk and ask that the air conditioner be turned off, I never called, because I did not know how much to tip whoever might come—was anyone ever so young? I am here to tell you that someone was. All I could do during those three days was talk long-distance to the boy I already knew I would never marry in the spring. I would stay in New York, I told him, just six months, and I could see the Brooklyn Bridge from my window. As it turned out the bridge was the Triborough, and I stayed eight years.

foot of innocence

In retrospect it seems to me that those days before I knew the names of all the bridges were happier than the ones that came later, but perhaps you will see that as we go along. Part of what I want to tell you is what it is like to be young in New York, how six months can become eight years with the deceptive ease of a film dissolve, for that is how those years appear to me now, in a long sequence of

sentimental dissolves and old-fashioned trick shots—the Seagram Building
fountains dissolve into snowflakes, I enter a revolving door at twenty and come
out a good deal older, and on a different street. But most particularly I want to
explain to you, and in the process perhaps to myself, why I no longer live in New
York. It is often said that New York is a city for only the very rich and the very
poor. It is less often said that New York is also, at least for those of us who came
there from somewhere else, a city for only the very young.

I remember once, one cold bright December evening in New York,
suggesting to a friend who complained of having been around too long that he
come with me to a party where there would be, I assured him with the bright
resourcefulness of twenty-three, "new faces." He laughed literally until he
choked, and I had to roll down the taxi window and hit him on the back. "New
faces," he said finally, "don't tell me about *new faces*." It seemed that the last
time he had gone to a party where he had been promised "new faces," there had
been fifteen people in the room, and he had already slept with five of the women
and owed money to all but two of the men. I laughed with him, but the first snow
had just begun to fall and the big Christmas trees glittered yellow and white as far
as I could see up Park Avenue and I had a new dress and it would be a long while
before I would come to understand the particular moral of the story.

It would be a long while because, quite simply, I was in love with New
York. I do not mean "love" in any colloquial way, I mean that I was in love with
the city, the way you love the first person who ever touches you and never love
anyone quite that way again. I remember walking across Sixty-second Street one
twilight that first spring, or the second spring, they were all alike for a while. I
was late to meet someone but I stopped at Lexington Avenue and bought a peach
and stood on the corner eating it and knew that I had come out of the West and
reached the mirage. I could taste the peach and feel the soft air blowing from a
subway grating on my legs and I could smell lilac and garbage and expensive
perfume and I knew that it would cost something sooner or later—because I did
not belong there, did not come from there—but when you are twenty-two or
twenty-three, you figure that later you will have a high emotional balance, and be
able to pay whatever it costs. I still believed in possibilities then, still had the
sense, so peculiar to New York, that something extraordinary would happen any
minute, any day, any month. I was making only $65 or $70 a week then ("Put
yourself in Hattie Carnegie's hands," I was advised without the slightest trace of
irony by an editor of the magazine for which I worked), so little money that some

she didn't succeed

weeks I had to charge food at Bloomingdale's gourmet shop in order to eat, a fact which went unmentioned in the letters I wrote to California. I never told my father that I needed money because then he would have sent it, and I would never know if I could do it by myself. At that time making a living seemed a game to me, with arbitrary but quite inflexible rules. And except on a certain kind of winter evening—six-thirty in the Seventies, say, already dark and bitter with a wind off the river, when I would be walking very fast toward a bus and would look in the bright windows of brownstones and see cooks working in clean kitchens and imagine women lighting candles on the floor above and beautiful children being bathed on the floor above that—except on nights like those, I never felt poor; I had the feeling that if I needed money I could always get it. I could write a syndicated column for teenagers under the name "Debbi Lynn" or I could smuggle gold into India or I could become a $100 call girl, and none of it would matter.

Nothing was irrevocable; everything was within reach. Just around every corner lay something curious and interesting, something I had never before seen or done or known about. I could go to a party and meet someone who called himself Mr. Emotional Appeal and ran The Emotional Appeal Institute or Tina Onassis Blandford or a Florida cracker who was then a regular on what he called "the Big C," the Southampton—El Morocco circuit ("I'm well-connected on the Big C, honey," he would tell me over collard greens on his vast borrowed terrace), or the widow of the celery king of the Harlem market or a piano salesman from Bonne Terre, Missouri, or someone who had already made and lost two fortunes in Midland, Texas. I could make promises to myself and to other people and there would be all the time in the world to keep them. I could stay up all night and make mistakes, and none of it would count.

You see I was in a curious position in New York: it never occurred to me that I was living a real life there. In my imagination I was always there for just another few months, just until Christmas or Easter or the first warm day in May. For that reason I was most comfortable in the company of Southerners. They seemed to be in New York as I was, on some indefinitely extended leave from wherever they belonged, disinclined to consider the future, temporary exiles who always knew when the flights left for New Orleans or Memphis or Richmond or, in my case, California. Someone who lives always with a plane schedule in the drawer lives on a slightly different calendar. Christmas, for example, was a difficult season. Other people could take it in stride, going to Stowe or going abroad or going for the day to their mothers' places in Connecticut; those of us who believed that we lived somewhere else would spend it making and canceling airline reservations, waiting for weather-bound flights as if for the last plane out of Lisbon in 1940, and finally comforting one another, those of us who were left, with the oranges and mementos and smoked-oyster stuffings of childhood, gathering close, colonials in a far country.

Which is precisely what we were. I am not sure that it is possible for anyone brought up in the East to appreciate entirely what New York, the idea of New York, means to those of us who came out of the West and the South. To an Eastern child, particularly a child who has always had an uncle on Wall Street and who has spent several hundred Saturdays first at F. A. O. Schwarz and being fitted for shoes at Best's and then waiting under the Biltmore clock and dancing to Lester Lanin, New York is just a city, albeit *the* city, a plausible place for people to live. But to those of us who came from places where no one had heard of Lester Lanin and Grand Central Station was a Saturday radio program, where Wall Street and Fifth Avenue and Madison Avenue were not places at all but abstractions ("Money," and "High Fashion," and "The Hucksters"), New York was no mere city. It was instead an infinitely romantic notion, the mysterious nexus of all love and money and power, the shining and perishable dream itself. To think of "living" there was to reduce the miraculous to the mundane; one does not "live" at Xanadu.

In fact it was difficult in the extreme for me to understand those young women for whom New York was not simply an ephemeral Estoril but a real place, girls who bought toasters and installed new cabinets in their apartments and committed themselves to some reasonable future. I never bought any furniture in New York. For a year or so I lived in other people's apartments; after that I lived in the Nineties in an apartment furnished entirely with things taken from storage by a friend whose wife had moved away. And when I left the apartment in the Nineties (that was when I was leaving everything, when it was all breaking up) I left everything in it, even my winter clothes and the map of Sacramento County I had hung on the bedroom wall to remind me who I was, and I moved into a monastic four-room floor-through on Seventy-fifth Street. "Monastic" is perhaps misleading here, implying some chic severity; until after I was married and my husband moved some furniture in, there was nothing at all in those four rooms except a cheap double mattress and box springs, ordered by telephone the day I decided to move, and two French garden chairs lent me by a friend who imported them. (It strikes me now that the people I knew in New York all had curious and self-defeating sidelines. They imported garden chairs which did not sell very well at Hammacher Schlemmer or they tried to market hair straighteners in Harlem or they ghosted exposés of Murder Incorporated for Sunday supplements. I think that perhaps none of us was very serious, *engagé* only about our most private lives.)

All I ever did to that apartment was hang fifty yards of yellow theatrical silk across the bedroom windows, because I had some idea that the gold light would make me feel better, but I did not bother to weigh the curtains correctly and all that summer the long panels of transparent golden silk would blow out the windows and get tangled and drenched in the afternoon thunderstorms. That was the year, my twenty-eighth, when I was discovering that not all of the promises would be kept, that some things are in fact irrevocable and that it had counted after all, every evasion and every procrastination, every mistake, every word, all of it.

That is what it was all about, wasn't it? Promises? Now when New York comes back to me it comes in hallucinatory flashes, so clinically detailed that I sometimes wish that memory would effect the distortion with which it is commonly credited. For a lot of the time I was in New York I used a perfume called *Fleurs de Rocaille,* and then *L'Air du Temps,* and now the slightest trace of either can short-circuit my connections for the rest of the day. Nor can I smell Henri Bendel jasmine soap without falling back into the past, or the particular mixture of spices used for boiling crabs. There were barrels of crab boil in a Czech place in the Eighties where I once shopped. Smells, of course, are notorious memory stimuli, but there are other things which affect me the same way. Blue-and-white striped sheets. Vermouth cassis. Some faded nightgowns which were new in 1959 or 1960, and some chiffon scarves I bought about the same time.

I suppose that a lot of us who have been young in New York have the same scenes on our home screens. I remember sitting in a lot of apartments with a slight headache about five o'clock in the morning. I had a friend who could not sleep, and he knew a few other people who had the same trouble, and we would watch the sky lighten and have a last drink with no ice and then go home in the early morning light, when the streets were clean and wet (had it rained in the night? we never knew) and the few cruising taxis still had their headlights on and the only color was the red and green of traffic signals. The White Rose bars opened very early in the morning; I recall waiting in one of them to watch an astronaut go into space, waiting so long that at the moment it actually happened I had my eyes not on the television screen but on a cockroach on the tile floor. I liked the bleak branches above Washington Square at dawn, and the monochromatic flatness of Second Avenue, the fire escapes and the grilled storefronts peculiar and empty in their perspective.

It is relatively hard to fight at six-thirty or seven in the morning without any sleep, which was perhaps one reason we stayed up all night, and it seemed to me a pleasant time of day. The windows were shuttered in that apartment in the Nineties and I could sleep a few hours and then go to work, I could work then on two or three hours' sleep and a container of coffee from Chock Full O' Nuts. I liked going to work, liked the soothing and satisfactory rhythm of getting out a magazine, liked the orderly progression of four-color closings and two-color closings and black-and-white closings and then The Product, no abstraction but something which looked effortlessly glossy and could be picked up on a newsstand and weighed in the hand I liked all the minutiae of proofs and layouts, liked working late on the nights the magazine went to press, sitting and reading *Variety* and waiting for the copy desk to call. From my office I could look across town to the weather signal on the Mutual of New York Building and the lights that alternately spelled out TIME and LIFE above Rockefeller Plaza; that pleased me obscurely, and so did walking uptown in the mauve eight o'clocks of early summer evenings and looking at things, Lowestoft tureens in Fifty-seventh Street windows, people in evening clothes trying to get taxis, the trees just coming into full leaf, the lambent air, all the sweet promises of money and summer.

Some years passed, but I still did not lose that sense of wonder about New York. I began to cherish the loneliness of it, the sense that at any given time no one need know where I was or what I was doing. I liked walking, from the East River over to the Hudson and back on brisk days, down around the Village on warm days. A friend would leave me the key to her apartment in the West Village when she was out of town, and sometimes I would just move down there, because by that time the telephone was beginning to bother me (the canker, you see, was already in the rose) and not many people had that number. I remember one day when someone who did have the West Village number came to pick me up for lunch there, and we both had hangovers, and I cut my finger opening him a beer and burst into tears, and we walked to a Spanish restaurant and drank Bloody

Marys and *gazpacho* until we felt better. I was not then guilt-ridden about spending afternoons that way, because I still had all the afternoons in the world.

And even that late in the game I still liked going to parties, all parties, bad parties, Saturday-afternoon parties given by recently married couples who lived in Stuyvesant Town, West Side parties given by unpublished or failed writers who served cheap red wine and talked about going to Guadalajara, Village parties where all the guests worked for advertising agencies and voted for Reform Democrats, press parties at Sardi's, the worst kinds of parties. You will have perceived by now that I was not one to profit by the experience of others, that it was a very long time indeed before I stopped believing in new faces and began to understand the lesson in that story, which was that it is distinctly possible to stay too long at the Fair.

I could not tell you when I began to understand that. All I know is that it was very bad when I was twenty-eight. Everything that was said to me I seemed to have heard before, and I could no longer listen. I could no longer sit in little bars near Grand Central and listen to someone complaining of his wife's inability to cope with the help while he missed another train to Connecticut. I no longer had any interest in hearing about the advances other people had received from their publishers, about plays which were having second-act trouble in Philadelphia, or about people I would like very much if only I would come out and meet them. I had already met them, always. There were certain parts of the city which I had to avoid. I could not bear upper Madison Avenue on weekday mornings (this was a particularly inconvenient aversion, since I then lived just fifty or sixty feet east of Madison), because I would see women walking Yorkshire terriers and shopping at Gristede's, and some Veblenesque gorge would rise in my throat. I could not go to Times Square in the afternoon, or to the New York Public Library for any reason whatsoever. One day I could not go into a Schrafft's; the next day it would be Bonwit Teller.

I hurt the people I cared about, and insulted those I did not. I cut myself off from the one person who was closer to me than any other. I cried until I was not even aware when I was crying and when I was not, cried in elevators and in taxis and in Chinese laundries, and when I went to the doctor he said only that I seemed to be depressed, and should see a "specialist." He wrote down a psychiatrist's name and address for me, but I did not go.

Instead I got married, which as it turned out was a very good thing to do but badly timed, since I still could not walk on upper Madison Avenue in the mornings and still could not talk to people and still cried in Chinese laundries. I had never before understood what "despair" meant, and I am not sure that I understand now, but I understood that year. Of course I could not work. I could not even get dinner with any degree of certainty, and I would sit in the apartment on Seventy-fifth Street paralyzed until my husband would call from his office and say gently that I did not have to get dinner, that I could meet him at Michael's Pub or at Toots Shor's or at Sardi's East. And then one morning in April (we had been married in January) he called and told me that he wanted to get out of New York for a while, that he would take a six-month leave of absence, that we would go somewhere.

It was three years ago that he told me that, and we have lived in Los Angeles since. Many of the people we knew in New York think this a curious aberration, and in fact tell us so. There is no possible, no adequate answer to that, and so we give certain stock answers, the answers everyone gives. I talk about how difficult it would be for us to "afford" to live in New York right now, about how much "space" we need. All I mean is that I was very young in New York, and that at some point the golden rhythm was broken, and I am not that young any more. The last time I was in New York was in a cold January, and everyone was ill and tired. Many of the people I used to know there had moved to Dallas or had gone on Antabuse or had bought a farm in New Hampshire. We stayed ten days, and then we took an afternoon flight back to Los Angeles, and on the way home from the airport that night I could see the moon on the Pacific and smell jasmine all around and we both knew that there was no longer any point in keeping the apartment we still kept in New York. There were years when I called Los Angeles "the Coast," but they seem a long time ago.

[1967]

Critical Thinking

1.   Why the title "Goodbye to all that"?

2.   Describe Didion's attitude toward New York City.

3.   In the second to last paragraph, Didion says, "Instead I got married."
       What was your reaction to that switch? Why do you think she got
       married?

Writing Assignments

1.   Didion writes, "It is easy to see the beginning of things, and harder to see
       the endings." Write an essay about a time in your life when you clearly
       remember the beginning, but find it harder to see the ending.

2.   Didion states "smells are notorious stimuli." Do you agree? Write about a
       time when you recalled a memory because of the sense of smell.

3.   Write an essay about a very exciting time in your life that is now over.
       Try to re-create the initial excitement.

RELATING THE AUTHORS' IDEAS

1. Compare and/or contrast why White, Mora and Didion record their experiences.

2. How do you think Stephen King would react to the findings of the *New York Times* poll in Elizabeth Kolbert's article?

3. Compare the effects museums have on Mora to the effects horror films have on King.

4. Write an essay about youth and the passing of time. Consider White's description of the young circus performer and Didion's description of being young and in New York.

Chapter VI

Connecting With
Our Natural World

VI

Connecting With Our

Natural World

Introduction

Throughout the ages, writers have gazed upon the beauty of our natural world and have contemplated the connections between ourselves and other inhabitants of the planet.

In this chapter, Loren Eiseley, Virginia Woolf, Louise Erdrich, E.B. White, and Annie Dillard, observe the natural world. In "The Brown Wasps," Loren Eiseley draws powerful analogies between the plight of human beings and it's fellow creatures. He observes, "It is as though all living creatures, and particularly the more intelligent, can survive only by fixing or transforming a bit of time and pace or by securing a bit of space with its objects immortalized and made permanent in time." He senses a powerful affinity: "I spoke for myself, one field mouse, and several pigeons. We were all out of touch but somehow permanent. It was the world that had changed."

Virginia Woolf's keen observation skills are revealed by her reflections on a moth: "Watching him, it seemed as if a fibre, very thin but pure, of the enormous energy of the world had been thrust into his frail and diminutive body." The moth's mortality parallels our own mortality: "Oh yes, he seemed to say, death is stronger than I." By extension, "stronger" than us all. Death and time are themes that emerge in E.B. White's "Once More to the Lake." It is the lake and its surroundings that conjure up a sense of timelessness and mortality. During his stay at the lake with his son, White experiences a blurred sense of time: "I began to sustain the illusion that he was I, and therefore, by simple transposition, that I was my father." The appearance of a dragonfly had the power to thrust him back in time: "There had been no years between the ducking of this dragonfly and other one-the one that was part of memory. I looked at the boy, who was silently watching his fly and it was my hands the held his rod, my eyes watching. I felt dizzy and didn't know which rod I was at the end of."

Likewise, in "The Blue Jay's Dance," Louise Erdrich's observations of a blue jay leads her to a reflection about her daughter and her responsibilities: "Since the two of us are still in the process of differentiating, since my acts are hers and I do not even think, yet, where I stop for her or where her needs, exactly, begin, I must dance for her. I must be the one to dip and twirl in the cold glare and I must teach her, as she grows, the unlikely steps." In "The Deer at Providencia" Annie Dillard parallels the torture of a deer to that of a man and asks: "Will someone please explain to Alan McDonald in his dignity, to the deer at Providencia in his dignity, what is going on? And mail me the carbon."

As writers, let's observe nature with all of our senses—sight, smell, hearing, taste, and touch—make connections, draw analogies, and ask questions. Perhaps, you too will be inspired to draw new insights about our place in this mysterious and beautiful world.

"Are animals consciously aware of anything, or are they all 'zombies' incapable of conscious thoughts or emotional feeling."

--Donald R. Griffin, <u>Animal Minds: Beyond Cognition to Consciousness</u> (2001)

"The Brown Wasps"[*]
Loren Eiseley

Naturalist, scientist, essayist, and poet, Loren Eiseley is the recipient of numerous awards, fellowships and nominations. Eiseley is a contributor to many magazines and newspapers, including <u>Saturday Evening Post</u>, <u>Harper's</u> magazine, and <u>The New York Times</u>. His books include <u>The Unexpected Universe</u>, <u>Notes of an Alchemist</u>, and <u>The Night Country</u>. This essay is from his book <u>The Night Country</u>.[†]

THERE is a corner in the waiting room of one of the great Eastern stations where women never sit. It is always in the shadow and overhung by rows of lockers. It is, however, always frequented—not so much by genuine travelers as by the dying. It is here that a certain element of the abandoned poor seeks a refuge out of the weather, clinging for a few hours longer to the city that has fathered them. In a precisely similar manner I have seen, on a sunny day in midwinter, a few old brown wasps creep slowly over an abandoned wasp nest in a thicket. Numbed and forgetful and frost-blackened, the hum of the spring hive still resounded faintly in their sodden tissues. Then the temperature would fall and they would drop away into the white oblivion of the snow. Here in the station it is in no way different save that the city is busy in its snows. But the old ones

[*] Reprinted with the permission of Scribner, a Division of Simon & Schuster, Inc., from *The Night Country* by Loren Eiseley. Copyright © 1971 by Loren Eiseley.
[†] "Loren Eiseley," *Contemporary Authors Online*. The Gale Group, 2001. 30 October, 1997. January 26, 2002. <http://www.galenet.com/servlet/LitRC?c=1&ai=26939&ste=6&docNum=H1000028663&bConts=2191&tab=1&vrsn=3&ca=1&tbst=arp&ST=Eiseley%2C+Loren+Corey&srchtp=athr&n=10&locID=nypl&OP=contains>.

cling to their seats as though these were symbolic and could not be given up. Now and then they sleep, their gray old heads resting with painful awkwardness on the backs of the benches.

Also they are not at rest. For an hour they may sleep in the gasping exhaustion of the ill-nourished and aged who have to walk in the night. Then a policeman comes by on his round and nudges them upright.

"You can't sleep here," he growls.

A strange ritual then begins. An old man is difficult to waken. After a muttered conversation the policeman presses a coin into his hand and passes fiercely along the benches prodding and gesturing toward the door. In his wake, like birds rising and settling behind the passage of a farmer through a cornfield, the men totter up, move a few paces, and subside once more upon the benches.

One man, after a slight, apologetic lurch, does not move at all. Tubercularly thin, he sleeps on steadily. The policeman does not look back. To him, too, this has become a ritual. He will not have to notice it again officially for another hour.

Once in a while one of the sleepers will not awake. Like the brown wasps, he will have had his wish to die in the great droning center of the hive rather than in some lonely room. It is not so bad here with the shuffle of footsteps and the knowledge that there are others who share the bad luck of the world. There are also the whistles and the sounds of everyone, everyone in the world, starting on journeys. Amidst so many journeys somebody is bound to come out all right. Somebody.

Maybe it was on a like thought that the brown wasps fell away from the old paper nest in the thicket. You hold till the last, even if it is only to a public seat in a railroad station. You want your place in the hive more than you want a room or a place where the aged can be eased gently out of the way. It is the place that matters, the place at the heart of things. It is life that you want, that bruises your gray old head with the hard chairs; a man has a right to his place.

But sometimes the place is lost in the years behind us. Or sometimes it is a thing of air, a kind of vaporous distortion above a heap of rubble. We cling to a time and a place because without them man is lost, not only man but life. This is why the voices, real or unreal, which speak from the floating trumpets at spiritualist seances are so unnerving. They are voices out of nowhere whose only reality lies in their ability to stir the memory of a living person with some fragment of the past. Before the medium's cabinet both the dead and the living revolve endlessly about an episode, a place, an event that has already been engulfed by time.

This feeling runs deep in life; it brings stray cats running over endless miles, and birds homing from the ends of the earth. It is as though all living creatures, and particularly the more intelligent, can survive only by fixing or transforming a bit of time into space or by securing a bit of space with its objects immortalized and made permanent in time. For example, I once saw, on a flower pot in my own living room, the efforts of a field mouse to build a remembered field. I have lived to see this episode repeated in a thousand guises, and since I have spent a large portion of my life in the shade of a nonexistent tree I think I am entitled to speak for the field mouse.

One day as I cut across the field which at that time extended on one side of our suburban shopping center, I found a giant slug feeding from a runnel of pink ice cream in an abandoned Dixie cup. I could see his eyes telescope and protrude in a kind of dim uncertain ecstasy as his dark body bunched and elongated in the curve of the cup. Then, as I stood there at the edge of the concrete, contemplating the slug, I began to realize it was like standing on a shore where a different type of life creeps up and fumbles tentatively among the rocks and sea wrack. It knows its place and will only creep so far until something changes. Little by little as I stood there I began to see more of this shore that surrounds the place of man. I looked with sudden care and attention at things I had been running over thoughtlessly for years. I even waded out a short way into the grass and the wild-rose thickets to see more. A huge black-belted bee went droning by and there were some indistinct scurryings in the underbrush.

Then I came to a sign which informed me that this field was to be the site of a new Wanamaker suburban store. Thousands of obscure lives were about to perish, the spores of puffballs would go smoking off to new fields, and the bodies of little white-footed mice would be crunched under the inexorable wheels of the bulldozers. Life disappears or modifies its appearances so fast that everything takes on an aspect of illusion—a momentary fizzing and boiling with smoke rings, like pouring dissident chemicals into a retort. Here man was advancing, but in a few years his plaster and bricks would be disappearing once more into the insatiable maw of the clover. Being of an archaeological cast of mind, I thought of this fact with an obscure sense of satisfaction and waded back through the rose thickets to the concrete parking lot. As I did so, a mouse scurried ahead of me, frightened of my steps if not of that ominous Wanamaker sign. I saw him vanish in the general direction of my apartment house, his little body quivering with fear in the great open sun on the blazing concrete. Blinded and confused, he was running straight away from his field. In another week scores would follow him.

I forgot the episode then and went home to the quiet of my living room. It was not until a week later, letting myself into the apartment, that I realized I had a visitor. I am fond of plants and had several ferns standing on the floor in pots to avoid the noon glare by the south window.

As I snapped on the light and glanced carelessly around the room, I saw a little heap of earth on the carpet and a scrabble of pebbles that had been kicked merrily over the edge of one of the flower pots. To my astonishment I discovered a fullfledged burrow delving downward among the fern roots. I waited silently. The creature who had made the burrow did not appear. I remembered the wild field then, and the flight of the mice. No house mouse, no Mus domesticus, had kicked up this little heap of earth or sought refuge under a fern root in a flower pot. I thought of the desperate little creature I had seen fleeing from the wild-rose thicket. Through intricacies of pipes and attics, he, or one of his fellows, had climbed to this high green solitary room. I could visualize what had occurred. He had an image in his head, a world of seed pods and quiet, of green sheltering leaves in the dim light among the weed stems. It was the only world he knew and it was gone.] —*We cannot destroy what it, someones home*

Somehow in his flight he had found his way to this room with drawn shades where no one would come till nightfall. And here he had smelled green leaves and run quickly up the flower pot to dabble his paws in common earth. He had even struggled half the afternoon to carry his burrow deeper and had failed. I examined the hole, but no whiskered twitching face appeared. He was gone. I gathered up the earth and refilled the burrow. I did not expect to find traces of him again.

Yet for three nights thereafter I came home to the darkened room and my ferns to find the dirt kicked gaily about the rug and the burrow reopened, though I was never able to catch the field mouse within it. I dropped a little food about the mouth of the burrow, but it was never touched. I looked under beds or sat reading with one ear cocked for rustlings in the ferns. It was all in vain; I never saw him. Probably he ended in a trap in some other tenant's room.

But before he disappeared I had come to look hopefully for his evening burrow. About my ferns there had begun to linger the insubstantial vapor of an autumn field, the distilled essence, as it were, of a mouse brain in exile from its home. It was a small dream, like our dreams, carried a long and weary journey along pipes and through spider webs, past holes over which loomed the shadows of waiting cats, and finally, desperately, into this room where he had played in the shuttered daylight for an hour among the green ferns on the floor. Every day these invisible dreams pass us on the street, or rise from beneath our feet, or look out upon us from beneath a bush.

Some years ago the old elevated railway in Philadelphia was torn down and replaced by a subway system. This ancient El with its barnlike stations containing nut-vending machines and scattered food scraps has, for generations, been the favorite feeding ground of flocks of pigeons, generally one flock to a station along the route of the El. Hundreds of pigeons were dependent upon the system. They flapped in and out of its stanchions and steel work or gathered in watchful little audiences about the feet of anyone who rattled the peanut-vending machines. They even watched people who jingled change in their hands, and prospected for food under the feet of the crowds who gathered between trains. Probably very few among the waiting people who tossed a crumb to an eager pigeon realized that this El was like a food-bearing river, and that the life which haunted its banks was dependent upon the running of the trains with their human freight.

I saw the river stop.

The time came when the underground tubes were ready; the traffic was transferred to a realm unreachable by pigeons. It was like a great river subsiding suddenly into desert sands. For a day, for two days, pigeons continued to circle over the El or stand close to the red vending machines. They were patient birds, and surely this great river which had flowed through the lives of unnumbered generations was merely suffering from some momentary drought.

They listened for the familiar vibrations that had always heralded an approaching train; they flapped hopefully about the head of an occasional workman walking along the steel runways. They passed from one empty station to another, all the while growing hungrier. Finally they flew away.

I thought I had seen the last of them about the El, but there was a revival and it provided a curious instance of the memory of living things for a way of life or a locality that has long been cherished. Some weeks after the El was abandoned workmen began to tear it down. I went to work every morning by one particular station, and the time came when the demolition crews reached this spot. Acetylene torches showered passers-by with sparks, Pneumatic drills hammered at the base of the structure, and a blind man who, like the pigeons, had clung with his cup to a stairway leading to the change booth, was forced to give up his place.

It was then, strangely, momentarily, one morning that I witnessed the return of a little band of the familiar pigeons. I even recognized one or two members of the flock that had lived around this particular station before they were dispersed into the streets. They flew bravely in and out among the sparks and the hammers and the shouting workmen. They had returned—and they had returned because the hubbub of the wreckers had convinced them that the river was about to flow once more. For several hours they flapped in and out through the empty windows, nodding their heads and watching the fall of girders with attentive little eyes. By the following morning the station was reduced to some burned-off stanchions in the street. My bird friends had gone. It was plain, however, that they retained a memory for an insubstantial structure now compounded of air and time. Even the blind man clung to it. Someone had provided him with a chair, and he sat at the same corner staring sightlessly at an invisible stairway where, so far as he was concerned, the crowds were still ascending to the trains.

I have said my life has been passed in the shade of a nonexistent tree, so that such sights do not offend me. Prematurely I am one of the brown wasps and I often sit with them in the great droning hive of the station, dreaming sometimes of a certain tree. It was planted sixty years ago by a boy with a bucket and a toy spade in a little Nebraska town. That boy was myself. It was a cottonwood sapling and the boy remembered it because of some words spoken by his father and because everyone died or moved away who was supposed to wait and grow old under its shade. The boy was passed from hand to hand, but the tree for some intangible reason had taken root in his mind. It was under its branches that he sheltered; it was from this tree that his memories, which are my memories, led away into the world.

After sixty years the mood of the brown wasps grows heavier upon one. During a long inward struggle I thought it would do me good to go and look upon that actual tree. I found a rational excuse in which to clothe this madness. I purchased a ticket and at the end of two thousand miles I walked another mile to an address that was still the same. The house had not been altered.

I came close to the white picket fence and reluctantly, with great effort, looked down the long vista of the yard. There was nothing there to see. For sixty years that cottonwood had been growing in my mind. Season by season its seeds had been floating farther on the hot prairie winds. We had planted it lovingly there, my father and I, because he had a great hunger for soil and live things growing, and because none of these things had long been ours to protect. We had planted the little sapling and watered it faithfully, and I remembered that I had run out with my small bucket to drench its roots the day we moved away. And all the years since it had been growing in my mind, a huge tree that somehow stood for my father and the love I bore him. I took a grasp on the picket fence and forced myself to look again.

A boy with the hard bird eye of youth pedaled a tricycle slowly up beside me.

"What'cha lookin' at?" he asked curiously.

"A tree," I said.

"What for?" he said.

"It isn't there," I said, to myself mostly, and began to walk away at a pace just slow enough not to seem to be running.

"What isn't there?" the boy asked. I didn't answer. It was obvious I was attached by a thread to a thing that had never been there, or certainly not for long. Something that had to be held in the air, or sustained in the mind, because it was part of my orientation in the universe and I could not survive without it. There was more than an animal's attachment to a place. There was something else, the attachment of the spirit to a grouping of events in time; it was part of our mortality.

So I had come home at last, driven by a memory in the brain as surely as the field mouse who had delved long ago into my flower pot or the pigeons flying forever amidst the rattle of nut-vending machines. These, the burrow under the greenery in my living room and the red-bellied bowls of peanuts now hovering in midair in the minds of pigeons, were all part of an elusive world that existed nowhere and yet everywhere. I looked once at the real world about me while the persistent boy pedaled at my heels.

It was without meaning, though my feet took a remembered path. In sixty years the house and street had rotted out of my mind. But the tree, the tree that no longer was, that had perished in its first season, bloomed on in my individual mind, unblemished as my father's words. "We'll plant a tree here, son, and we're not going to move any more. And when you're an old, old man you can sit under it and think how we planted it here, you and me, together."

I began to outpace the boy on the tricycle.

"Do you live here, Mister?" he shouted after me suspiciously. I took a firm grasp on airy nothing—to be precise, on the bole of a great tree. "I do," I said. I spoke for myself, one field mouse, and several pigeons. We were all out of touch but somehow permanent. It was the world that had changed.

Critical Thinking

1. What do you consider to be the theme of the essay?

2. What words and/or phrases are used in the first paragraph to set up a comparison between the wasps and the men?

3. In the conclusion, Eiseley states, "I spoke for myself, one field mouse, and several pigeons. We were all out of touch but somehow permanent. It was the world that had changed." Explain.

Writing Assignments

1. Write an essay about a time in your life when you experienced a connection to nature. Explore the effect the experience had on your life.

2. Identify the various analogies in the text. In your opinion, are they effective? Why or why not?

3. Explain the significance of the cottonwood tree. What is it symbolic of?

"Until death, it is all life."
-Cervantes, Don Quixote
(1605-15)

"The Death of the Moth"[*]
Virginia Woolf

Born in 1882, British writer, novelist and essayist Virginia Woolf is best known for her innovative and experimental books, including To The Lighthouse *(1927),* Mrs. Dalloway *(1925) and* The Waves *(1931). In 1917 she founded Hogarth Press with her husband Leonard Woolf. This excerpt is from her* A Room of One's Own.[†]

MOTHS that fly by day are not properly to be called moths; they do not excite that pleasant sense of dark autumn nights and ivy-blossom which the commonest yellow-underwing asleep in the shadow of the curtain never fails to rouse in us. They are hybrid creatures, neither gay like butterflies nor sombre like their own species. Nevertheless the present specimen, with his narrow hay-coloured wings, fringed with a tassel of the same colour, seemed to be content with life. It was a pleasant morning, mid-September, mild, benignant, yet with a keener breath than that of the summer months. The plough was already scoring the field opposite the window, and where the share had been, the earth was pressed flat and gleamed with moisture. Such vigour came rolling in from the fields and the down beyond that it was difficult to keep the eyes strictly turned upon the book. The rooks too were keeping one of their annual festivities; soaring round the tree tops until it looked as if a vast net with thousands of black knots in it had been cast up into the air; which, after a few moments sank slowly down upon the trees until every twig seemed to have a knot at the end of it. Then, suddenly, the net would be thrown into the air again in a wider circle this time, with the utmost clamour and vociferation, as though to be thrown into the air and settle slowly down upon the tree tops were a tremendously exciting experience.

[*] "The Death of the Moth" from *The Death of the Moth and Other Essays* by Virginia Woolf, copyright © 1942 by Harcourt, Inc. and renewed 1970 by Marjorie T. Parsons, Executrix, reprinted by permission of the publisher.
[†] "Virgina Woolf," *Contemporary Authors Online.* The Gale Group, 2001. 15 June 2001. January 26, 2002. <http://www.galenet.com/servlet/LitRC?ST=Woolf%2C+Virginia&ste= 4&sk povr=1&vrsn=3&tbst=arp&srchtp=athr&n=10&locID=nypl&OP=contains>.

The same energy which inspired the rooks, the ploughmen, the horses, and even, it seemed, the lean bare-backed downs, sent the moth fluttering from side to side of his square of the window-pane. One could not help watching him. One was, indeed, conscious of a queer feeling of pity for him. The possibilities of pleasure seemed that morning so enormous and so various that to have only a moth's part in life, and a day moth's at that, appeared a hard fate, and his zest in enjoying his meagre opportunities to the full, pathetic. He flew vigorously to one corner of his compartment, and, after waiting there a second, flew across to the other. What remained for him but to fly to a third corner and then to a fourth? That was all he could do, in spite of the size of the downs, the width of the sky, the far-off smoke of houses, and the romantic voice, now and then, of a steamer out at sea. What he could do he did. Watching him, it seemed as if a fibre, very thin but pure, of the enormous energy of the world had been thrust into his frail and diminutive body. As often as he crossed the pane, I could fancy that a thread of vital light became visible. He was little or nothing but life.

Yet, because he was so small, and so simple a form of the energy that was rolling in at the open window and driving its way through so many narrow and intricate corridors in my own brain and in those of other human beings, there was something marvellous as well as pathetic about him. It was as if someone had taken a tiny bead of pure life and decking it as lightly as possible with down and feathers, had set it dancing and zigzagging to show us the true nature of life. Thus displayed one could not get over the strangeness of it. One is apt to forget all about life, seeing it humped and bossed and garnished and cumbered so that it has to move with the greatest circumspection and dignity. Again, the thought of all that life might have been had he been born in any other shape caused one to view his simple activities with a kind of pity.

After a time, tired by his dancing apparently, he settled on the window ledge in the sun, and, the queer spectacle being at an end, I forgot about him. Then, looking up, my eye was caught by him. He was trying to resume his dancing, but seemed either so stiff or so awkward that he could only flutter to the bottom of the window-pane; and when he tried to fly across it he failed. Being intent on other matters I watched these futile attempts for a time without thinking, unconsciously waiting for him to resume his flight, as one waits for a machine, that has stopped momentarily, to start again without considering the reason of its failure. After perhaps a seventh attempt he slipped from the wooden ledge and fell, fluttering his wings, on to his back on the window sill. The helplessness of his attitude roused me. It flashed upon me that he was in difficulties; he could no longer raise himself; his legs struggled vainly. But, as I stretched out a pencil, meaning to help him to right himself, it came over me that the failure and awkwardness were the approach of death. I laid the pencil down again.

The legs agitated themselves once more. I looked as if for the enemy against which he struggled. I looked out of doors. What had happened there? Presumably it was midday, and work in the fields had stopped. Stillness and quiet had replaced the previous animation. The birds had taken themselves off to feed in the brooks. The horses stood still. Yet the power was there all the same, massed outside indifferent, impersonal, not attending to anything in particular. Somehow it was opposed to the little hay-coloured moth. It was useless to try to do anything. One could only watch the extraordinary efforts made by those tiny legs against an oncoming doom which could, had it chosen, have submerged an entire city, not merely a city, but masses of human beings; nothing, I knew had any chance against death. Nevertheless after a pause of exhaustion the legs fluttered again. It was superb this last protest, and so frantic that he succeeded at last in righting himself. One's sympathies, of course, were all on the side of life. Also, when there was nobody to care or to know, this gigantic effort on the part of an insignificant little moth, against a power of such magnitude, to retain what no one else valued or desired to keep, moved one strangely. Again, somehow, one saw life, a pure bead. I lifted the pencil again, useless though I knew it to be. But even as I did so, the unmistakable tokens of death showed themselves. The body relaxed, and instantly grew stiff. The struggle was over. The insignificant little creature now knew death. As I looked at the dead moth, this minute wayside triumph of so great a force over so mean an antagonist filled me with wonder. Just as life had been strange a few minutes before, so death was now as strange. The moth having righted himself now lay most decently and uncomplainingly composed. O yes, he seemed to say, death is stronger than I am.

Critical Thinking

1.   What is the theme of this essay?

2.   Examine Woolf's use of word choice. How does she demonstrate the ebb and flow of life and death through watching a "day moth" have its life's journey?

3.   How does Woolf make the moth interesting? Why does she choose the definite article "the" in her title, instead of "a" moth? How does that complement her theme(s)?

Writing Assignments

1.   Sit down in front of a window in your home (or on a break from work or school) and write a description of what you see and feel about what you see.

2.   Observe an animal or insect. Write an essay of similar length to Woolf's.

3.   What can you decipher about Woolf from this essay? How does she convey more global themes by writing about such a small subject?

"The bluebird carries the sky on his back."

—Henry David Thoreau

"The Blue Jay's Dance"[*]
Louise Erdrich[†]

Poet, novelist and essayist Louise Erdrich is an award winning Native American writer. She has received numerous awards and nominations, including the 2001 National Book Award nomination for The Last Report on the Miracles at Little No Horse. This essay is from her book The Blue Jay's Dance: A Birth Year (1995).

THE HAWK SWEEPS OVER, LIGHT SHINING through her rust red tail. She makes an immaculate cross in flight, her shadow running along the ground behind her as I'm walking below. Our shadows join, momentarily, and then separate, both to our appointed rounds. Always, she hunts flying into the cast of the sun, making a pass east to west. Once inside, I settle baby, resettle baby, settle and resettle myself, and have just lowered my head into my hands to proofread a page when a blur outside my vision causes me to look up.

The hawk drops headfirst out of a cloud. She folds her wings hard against her and plunges into the low branches of the apple tree, moving at such dazzling speed I can barely follow. She strikes at one of the seven blue jays who make up the raucous gang, and it tumbles before her, head over feet, end over end. She plunges after it from the branches, flops in the sun. They both light on the ground and square off, about a foot apart in the snow.

The struck jay thrusts out its head, screams, raises its wings, and dances toward the gray hawk. The plain of snow must seem endless, an arena without

[†] "Louise Erdrich," *Contemporary Authors Online.* The Gale Group, 2001. 11 October, 2001. January 26, 2002. <http://www.galenet.com/servlet/LitRC?ai=27779&ste= 6&docNum = H1000029621&b Conts=16047&tab=1&vrsn=3&ca=1&tbst=arp&ST=Erdrich%2C+Louise&sr ch tp= athr&n= 10&locID=nypl&OP =contains>.

shelter, and the bird gets no help from the other six jays except loud encouragement at a safe distance. I hardly breathe. The hawk, on the ground, its wings clattering against the packed crust, is so much larger than its shadow, which has long brushed in and out of mine. It screams back, eyes filled with yellow light. Its hooked beak opens and it feints with its neck. Yet the jay, ridiculous, continues to dance, hopping forward, hornpiping up and down with tiny leaps, all of its feathers on end to increase its size. Its crest is sharp, its beak open in a continual shriek, its eye-mask fierce. It pedals its feet in the air. The hawk steps backward. She seems confused, cocks her head, and does not snap the blue jay's neck. She watches. Although I know nothing of the hawk and cannot imagine what moves her, it does seem to me that she is fascinated, that she puzzles at the absurd display before she raises her wings and lifts off.

PAST the gray moralizing and the fierce Roman Catholic embrace of suffering and fate that so often clouds the subject of suicide, there is the blue jay's dance. Beyond the impossible corners, stark cliffs, dark wells of trapped longing, there is that manic, successful jig—cocky, exuberant, entirely a bluff, a joke. That dance makes me clench down hard on life. But it is also a dance that in other circumstances might lead me, you, anyone, to choose a voluntary death. I see in that small bird's crazy courage some of what it took for my grandparents to live out the tough times. I peer around me, stroke my own skin, look into this baby's eyes that register me as a blurred self-extension, as a function of her will. I have made a pact with life: if I were to die now it would be a form of suicide for her. Since the two of us are still in the process of differentiating, since my acts are hers and I do not even think, yet, where I stop for her or where her needs, exactly, begin, I must dance for her. I must be the one to dip and twirl in the cold glare and I must teach her, as she grows, the unlikely steps.

Critical Thinking

1.   Why the title "The Blue Jay's Dance"?

2.   Make a list of the verbs. What do they convey?

3.   Locate references to Catholicism. In what context does Erdrich refer to Catholicism?

Writing Assignments

1. Write a one paragraph description of a bird in flight (or any other animal in motion). Use verbs and adjectives.

2. According to Erdrich, what are a parent's responsibilities to a child? Do you agree with her?

3. Erdrich discusses the courage it took for her grandparents "to live out the tough times." Write a one-page response about courage. How do you define courage? What are, in your opinion, courageous acts?

*"In looking at objects of Nature . . .
I seem rather to be seeking . . . for
something within me that already
and forever exists, than observing
anything new."*

—Samuel Taylor Coleridge
Anima Poetae [1805], Ch. 4

"Once More to the Lake"[*]
E.B. White

Born in 1899, E.B. White is an award winning writer, novelist, and essayist. He is the recipient of numerous nominations and awards. His bestselling children's book, particularly Charlotte's Web and Stuart Little are highly acclaimed. In 1978, he received the Pulitzer Prize (special citation). He is also recognized for his highly popular book The Elements of Style, 2nd Edition, with William Strunk, Jr.[†]

One summer, along about 1904, my father rented a camp on a lake in Maine and took us all there for the month of August. We all got ringworm from some kittens and had to rub Pond's Extract on our arms and legs night and morning, and my father rolled over in a canoe with all his clothes on; but outside of that the vacation was a success and from then on none of us ever thought there was any place in the world like that lake in Maine. We returned summer after summer—always on August 1 for one month. I have since become a salt-water man, but sometimes in summer there are days when the restlessness of the tides and the fearful cold of the sea water and the incessant wind that blows across the afternoon and into the evening make me wish for the placidity of a lake in the woods. A few weeks ago this feeling got so strong I bought myself a couple of

---

bass hooks and a spinner and returned to the lake where we used to go, for a week's fishing and to revisit old haunts.

I took along my son, who had never had any fresh water up his nose and who had seen lily pads only from train windows. On the journey over to the lake I began to wonder what it would be like. I wondered how time would have marred this unique, this holy spot—the coves and streams, the hills that the sun set behind, the camps and the paths behind the camps. I was sure that the tarred road would have found it out, and I wondered in what other ways it would be desolated. It is strange how much you can remember about places like that once you allow your mind to return into the grooves that lead back. You remember one thing, and that suddenly reminds you of another thing. I guess I remembered clearest of all the early mornings, when the lake was cool and motionless, remembered how the bedroom smelled of the lumber it was made of and of the wet woods whose scent entered through the screen. The partitions in the camp were thin and did not extend clear to the top of the rooms, and as I was always the first up I would dress softly so as not to wake the others, and sneak out into the sweet outdoors and start out in the canoe, keeping close along the shore in the long shadows of the pines. I remembered being very careful never to rub my paddle against the gunwale for fear of disturbing the stillness of the cathedral.

The lake had never been what you would call a wild lake. There were cottages sprinkled around the shores, and it was in farming country although the shores of the lake were quite heavyily wooded. Some of the cottages were owned by nearby farmers, and you would live at the shore and eat your meals at the farmhouse. That's what our family did. But although it wasn't wild, it was a fairly large and undisturbed lake and there were places in it that, to a child at least, seemed infinitely remote and primeval.

I was right about the tar: it led to within half a mile of the shore. But when I got back there, with my boy, and we settled into a camp near a farmhouse and into the kind of summertime I had known, I could tell that it was going to be pretty much the same as it had been before—I knew it, lying in bed the first morning, smelling the bedroom and hearing the boy sneak quietly out and go off along the shore in a boat. I began to sustain the illusion that he was I, and therefore, by simple transposition, that I was my father. This sensation persisted, kept cropping up all the time we were there. It was not an entirely new feeling, but in this setting it grew much stronger. I seemed to be living a dual existence. I would be in the middle of some simple act, I would be picking up a bait box or laying down a table fork, or I would be saying something, and suddenly it would be not I but my father who was saying the words or making the gesture. It gave me a creepy sensation.

We went fishing the first morning. I felt the same damp moss covering the worms in the bait can, and saw the dragonfly alight on the tip of my rod as it hovered a few inches from the surface of the water. It was the arrival of this fly that convinced me beyond any doubt that everything was as it always had been, that the years were a mirage and that there had been no years. The small waves were the same, chucking the rowboat under the chin as we fished at anchor, and the boat was the same boat, the same color green and the ribs broken in the same places, and under the floorboards the same fresh-water leavings and débris—the dead helgramite, the wisps of moss, the rusty discarded fishhook, and dried blood from yesterday's catch. We stared silently at the tips of our rods, at the dragonflies that came and went. I lowered the tip of mine into the water, tentatively, pensively dislodging the fly, which darted two feet away, poised, darted two feet back, and came to rest again a little farther up the rod. There had been no years between the ducking of this dragonfly and the other one—the one that was part of memory. I looked at the boy, who was silently watching his fly, and it was my hands that held his rod, my eyes watching. I felt dizzy and didn't know which rod I was at the end of.

We caught two bass, hauling them in briskly as though they were mackerel, pulling them over the side of the boat in a businesslike manner without any landing net, and stunning them with a blow on the back of the head. When we got back for a swim before lunch, the lake was exactly where we had left it, the same number of inches from the dock, and there was only the merest suggestion of a breeze. This seemed an utterly enchanted sea, this lake you could leave to its own devices for a few hours and come back to, and find that it had not stirred, this constant and trustworthy body of water. In the shallows, the dark, water-soaked sticks and twigs, smooth and old, were undulating in clusters on the bottom against the clean ribbed sand, and the track of the mussel was plain. A school of minnows swam by, each minnow with its small individual shadow, doubling the attendance, so clear and sharp in the sunlight. Some of the other campers were in swimming, along the shore, one of them with a cake of soap and the water felt thin and clear and unsubstantial. Over the years there had been this person with the cake of soap, this cultist, and here he was. There had been no years.

Up to the farmhouse to dinner through the teeming, dusty field, the road under our sneakers was only a two-track road. The middle track was missing, the one with the marks of the hooves and the splotches of dried, flaky manure. There had always been three tracks to choose from in choosing which track to walk in; now the choice was narrowed down to two. For a moment I missed terribly the middle alternative. But the way led past the tennis court, and something about the way it lay there in the sun reassured me; the tape had loosened along the backline, the alleys were green with plantains and other weeds, and the net (installed in June and removed in September) sagged the dry noon, and the whole place steamed with midday heat and hunger and emptiness. There was a choice of pie for dessert, and one was blueberry and one was apple, and the waitresses were the same country girls, there having been no passage of time, only the illusion of it as in a dropped curtain—the waitresses were still fifteen; their hair had been washed, that was the only difference—they had been to the movies and seen the pretty girls with the clean hair.

Summertime, oh, summertime, pattern of life indelible, the fade-proof lake, the woods unshatterable, the pasture with the sweetfern and the juniper forever and ever, summer without end; this was the background, and the life along the shore was the design, the cottagers with their innocent and tranquil design, their tiny docks with the flagpole and the American flag floating against the white clouds in the blue sky, the little paths over the roots of the trees leading from camp to camp and the paths leading back to the outhouses and the can of lime for sprinkling, and at the souvenir counters at the store the miniature birch-bark canoes and the postcards that showed things looking a little better than they looked. This was the American family at play, escaping the city heat, wondering whether the newcomers in the camp at the head of the cove were "common" or "nice," wondering whether it was true that the people who drove up for Sunday dinner at the farmhouse were turned away because there wasn't enough chicken.

It seemed to me, as I kept remembering all this, that those times and those summers had been infinitely precious and worth saving. There had been jollity and peace and goodness. The arriving (at the beginning of August) had been so big a business in itself, at the railway station the farm wagon drawn up, the first smell of the pine-laden air, the first glimpse of the smiling farmer, and the great importance of the trunks and your father's enormous authority in such matters, and the feel of the wagon under you for the long ten-mile haul, and at the top of the last long hill catching the first view of the lake after eleven months of not seeing this cherished body of water. The shouts and cries of the other campers when they saw you, and the trunks to be unpacked, to give up their rich burden. (Arriving was less exciting nowadays, when you sneaked up in your car and parked it under a tree near the camp and took out the bags and in five minutes it was all over, no fuss, no loud wonderful fuss about trunks.)

Peace and goodness and jollity. The only thing that was wrong now, really, was the sound of the place, an unfamiliar nervous sound of the outboard motors. This was the note that jarred, the one thing that would sometimes break the illusion and set the years moving. In those other summertimes all motors were inboard; and when they were at a little distance, the noise they made was a sedative, an ingredient of summer sleep. They were one-cylinder and two-cylinder engines, and some were make-and-break and some were jump-spark, but they all made a sleepy sound across the lake. The one-lungers throbbed and fluttered, and the twin-cylinder ones purred and purred, and that was a quiet sound, too. But now the campers all had outboards. In the daytime, in the hot mornings, these motors made a petulant, irritable sound; at night, in the still evening when the afterglow lit the water, they whined about one's ears like mosquitoes. My boy loved our rented outboard, and his great desire was to achieve single-handed mastery over it and authority, and he soon learned the trick of choking it a little (but not too much), and the adjustment of the needle valve. Watching him I would remember the things you could do with the old one-cylinder engine with the heavy flywheel, how you could have it eating out of your hand if you got really close to it spiritually. Motorboats in those days didn't have clutches, and you would make a landing by shutting off the motor at the proper time and coasting in with a dead rudder. But there was a way of reversing them, if you learned the trick, by cutting the switch and putting it on again exactly on the final dying revolution of the flywheel, so that it would kick back against compression and begin reversing. Approaching a dock in a strong following breeze, it was difficult to slow up sufficiently by the ordinary coasting method, and if a boy felt he had complete mastery over his motor, he was tempted to keep it running beyond its time and then reverse it a few feet from the dock. It took a cool nerve because if you threw the switch a twentieth of a second too soon you would catch the flywheel when it still had speed enough to go up past center, and the boat would leap ahead, charging bull-fashion at the dock.

We had a good week at the camp. The bass were biting well and the sun shone endlessly, day after day. We would be tired at night and lie down in the accumulated heat of the little bedrooms after the long hot day and the breeze would stir almost imperceptibly outside and the smell of the swamp drift in through the rusty screens. Sleep would come easily and in the morning the red squirrel would be on the roof, tapping out his gay routine. I kept remembering everything, lying in bed in the mornings—the small steamboat that had a long rounded stern like the lip of a Ubangi, and how quietly she ran on the moonlight sails, when the older boys played their mandolins and the girls sang and we ate doughnuts dipped in sugar, and how sweet the music was on the water in the shining night, and what it had felt like to think about girls then. After breakfast we would go up to the store and the things were in the same place—the minnows in a bottle, the plugs and spinners disarranged and pawed over by the youngsters from the boys camp, the Fig Newtons and the Beeman's gum. Outside, the road was tarred and cars stood in front of the store. Inside, all was just as it had always been, except there was more Coca-Cola and not so much Moxie and root beer and birch beer and sarsaparilla. We would walk out with the bottle of pop apiece and sometimes the pop would backfire up our noses and hurt. We explored the streams, quietly, where the turtles slid off the sunny logs and dug their way into the soft bottom; and we lay on the town wharf and fed worms to the tame bass. Everywhere we went I had trouble making out which was I, the one walking at my side, the one walking in my pants.

One afternoon while we were there at that lake a thunderstorm came up. It was like the revival of an old melodrama that I had seen long ago with childish awe. The second-act climax of the drama of the electrical disturbance over a lake in America had not changed in any important respect. This was the big scene, still the big scene. The whole thing was so familiar, the first feeling of oppression and heat and a general air around camp of not wanting to go very far away. In mid-afternoon (it was all the same) a curious darkening of the sky, and a lull in everything that had made life tick; and then the way the boats suddenly swung the other way at their moorings with the coming of a breeze out of the new quarter, and the premonitory rumble. Then the kettle drum, then the snare, then the bass drum and cymbals, then crackling light against the dark, and the gods grinning and licking their chops in the hills. Afterward the calm, the rain steadily rustling in the calm lake, the return of light and hope and spirits, and the campers running out in joy and relief to go swimming in the rain, their bright cries perpetuating the deathless joke about how they were getting simply drenched, and the children screaming with delight at the new sensation of bathing in the rain, and the joke about getting drenched linking the generations in a strong indestructible chain. And the comedian who waded in carrying an umbrella.

When the others went swimming, my son said he was going in, too. He pulled his dripping trunks from the line where they had hung all through the shower and wrung them out. Languidly, and with no thought of going in, I watched him, his hard little body, skinny and bare, saw him wince slightly as he pulled up around his vitals the small, soggy, icy garment. As he buckled the swollen belt, suddenly my groin felt the chill of death.

[AUGUST 1941]

Critical Thinking

1.   Why the title "Once More to the Lake"?

2.   Examine the word choice. How does White describe the lake as it is? As it was? What has changed?

3.   How does White blur the lines between the past and present?

Writing Assignments

1.   Write a descriptive essay about a family vacation.

2.   Write an essay about a family member you have a strong bond with. It could be with your father, mother, grandmother, or grandfather. Describe the person, your relationship, and how you feel when you are with them.

3.   In general, how reliable are our memories of events? Explain.

"There slowly grew up in me an unshakable conviction that we have no right to inflict suffering and death on another living creature unless there is some unavoidable necessity for it, and that we ought to feel what a horrible thing it is to cause suffering and death out of mere thoughtlessness."

—Albert Schweitzer, M.D.

"The Deer at Providencia"[*]
Annie Dillard[†]

Annie Dillard is an award-winning essayist, poet, and novelist. She has written numerous books and has received many nominations and awards, including the Pulitzer Prize (general non-fiction) in 1975 for Pilgrim a Tinker Creek. *This essay is from* Teaching A Stone To Talk: Expeditions and Encounters.

The first thing we saw when we climbed the riverbank to the village of Providencia was the deer. It was roped to a tree on the grass clearing near the thatch shelter where we would eat lunch.

The deer was small, about the size of a whitetail fawn, but apparently full-grown. It had a rope around its neck and three feet caught in the rope.

---

[*] "The Deer at Providencia" from *Teaching a Stone to Talk: Expeditions and Encounters* by Annie Dillard. Copyright © 1982 by Annie Dillard. Reprinted by permission of HarperCollins Publishers Inc.
[†] "Dillard, Annie," *Contemporary Authors Online.* The Gale Group, 2001. 30 October, 1997. January 26, 2002. <http://www.galenet.com/servlet/LitRC?c=1&ai=2 4347&ste =6& doc Num =H1000 025609&bCon ts=16303&tab=1&vrsn=3&ca=1&tbst=arp&ST=Dillard%2C+Annie&sr chtp=athr&n=10&locID=nypl&OP=contains>.

Someone said that the dogs had caught it that morning and the villagers were going to cook and eat it that night.

This clearing lay at the edge of the little thatched-hut village. We could see the villagers going about their business, scattering feed corn for hens about their houses, and wandering down paths to the river to bathe. The village headman was our host; he stood beside us as we watched the deer struggle. Several village boys were interested in the deer; they formed part of the circle we made around it in the clearing. So also did four businessmen from Quito who were attempting to guide us around the jungle. Few of the very different people standing in this circle had a common language. We watched the deer, and no one said much.

The deer lay on its side at the rope's very end, so the rope lacked slack to let it rest its head in the dust. It was "pretty," delicate of bone like all deer, and thin-skinned for the tropics. Its skin looked virtually hairless, in fact, and almost translucent, like a membrane. Its neck was no thicker than my wrist; it was rubbed open on the rope, and gashed. Trying to paw itself free of the rope, the deer had scratched its own neck with its hooves. The raw underside of its neck showed red stripes and some bruises bleeding inside the muscles. Now three of its feet were hooked in the rope under its jaw. It could not stand, of course, on one leg, so it could not move to slacken the rope and ease the pull on its throat and enable it to rest its head.

Repeatedly the deer paused, motionless, its eyes veiled, with only its rib cage in motion, and its breaths the only sound. Then, after I would think, "It has given up; now it will die," it would heave. The rope twanged; the tree leaves clattered; the deer's free foot beat the ground. We stepped back and held our breaths. It thrashed, kicking, but only one leg moved; the other three legs tightened inside the rope's loop. Its hip jerked; its spine shook. Its eyes rolled; its tongue, thick with spittle, pushed in and out. Then it would rest again. We watched this for fifteen minutes.

Once three young native boys charged in, released its trapped legs, and jumped back to the circle of people. But instantly the deer scratched up its neck with its hooves and snared its forelegs in the rope again. It was easy to imagine a third and then a fourth leg soon stuck, like Brer Rabbit and the Tar Baby.

We watched the deer from the circle, and then we drifted on to lunch. Our palm-roofed shelter stood on a grassy promontory from which we could see the deer tied to the tree, pigs and hens walking under village houses, and black-and-white cattle standing in the river. There was even a breeze.

Lunch, which was the second and better lunch we had that day, was hot and fried. There was a big fish called *doncella*, a kind of catfish, dipped whole in corn flour and beaten egg, then deep fried. With our fingers we pulled soft fragments of it from its sides to our plates, and ate; it was delicate fish-flesh, fresh and mild. Someone found the roe, and I ate of that too—it was fat and stronger, like egg yolk, naturally enough, and warm.

There was also a stew of meat in shreds with rice and pale brown gravy. I had asked what kind of deer it was tied to the tree; Pepe had answered in Spanish, "*Gama*." Now they told us this was *gama* too, stewed. I suspect the word means merely game or venison. At any rate, I heard that the village dogs had cornered another deer just yesterday, and it was this deer which we were now eating in full sight of the whole article. It was good. I was surprised at its tenderness. But it is a fact that high levels of lactic acid, which builds up in muscle tissues during exertion, tenderizes.

After the fish and meat we ate bananas fried in chunks and served on a tray; they were sweet and full of flavor. I felt terrific. My shirt was wet and cool from swimming; I had had a night's sleep, two decent walks, three meals, and a swim—everything tasted good. From time to time each one of us, separately, would look beyond our shaded roof to the sunny spot where the deer was still convulsing in the dust. Our meal completed, we walked around the deer and back to the boats.

That night I learned that while we were watching the deer, the others were watching me.

We four North Americans grew close in the jungle in a way that was not the usual artificial intimacy of travelers. We liked each other. We stayed up all that night talking, murmuring, as though we rocked on hammocks slung above time. The others were from big cities: New York, Washington, Boston. They all said that I had no expression on my face when I was watching the deer—or at any rate, not the expression they expected.

They had looked to see how I, the only woman, and the youngest, was taking the sight of the deer's struggles. I looked detached, apparently, or hard, or

calm, or focused, still. I don't know. I was thinking. I remember feeling very old
and energetic. I could say like Thoreau that I have traveled widely in Roanoke,
Virginia. I have thought a great deal about carnivorousness; I eat meat. These
things are not issues; they are mysteries.

Gentlemen of the city, what surprises you? That there is suffering here, or
that I know it?

We lay in the tent and talked. "If it had been my wife," one man said with
special vigor, amazed, "she wouldn't have cared *what* was going on; she would
have dropped *everything* right at that moment and gone in the village from here to
there to there, she would not have *stopped* until that animal was out of its
suffering one way or another. She couldn't *bear* to see a creature in agony like
that."

I nodded.

Now I am home. When I wake I comb my hair before the mirror above
my dresser. Every morning for the past two years I have seen in that mirror,
beside my sleep-softened face, the blackened face of a burnt man. It is a
wire-service photograph clipped from a newspaper and taped to my mirror. The
caption reads: "Alan McDonald in Miami hospital bed." All you can see in the
photograph is a smudged triangle of face from his eyelids to his lower lip; the rest
is bandages. You cannot see the expression in his eyes; the bandages shade them.

The story, headed MAN BURNED FOR SECOND TIME, begins:

"Why does God hate me?" Alan McDonald asked from his hospital bed.

"When the gunpowder went off, I couldn't believe it," he said. "I just
couldn't believe it. I said, 'No, God couldn't do this to me again.'"

He was in a burn ward in Miami, in serious condition. I do not even know
if he lived, I wrote him a letter at the time, cringing.

He had been burned before, thirteen years previously, by flaming gasoline.
For years he had been having his body restored and his face remade in dozens of
operations. He had been a boy, and then a burnt boy. He had already been
stunned by what could happen, by how life could veer.

Once I read that people who survive bad burns tend to go crazy; they have a very high suicide rate. Medicine cannot ease their pain; drugs just leak away, soaking the sheets, because there is no skin to hold them in. The people just lie there and weep. Later they kill themselves. They had not known, before they were burned, that the world included such suffering, that life could permit them personally such pain.

This time a bowl of gunpowder had exploded on McDonald.

"I didn't realize what had happened at first," he recounted. "And then I heard that sound from 13 years ago. I was burning. I rolled to put the fire out and I thought, 'Oh God, not again.'"

If my friend hadn't been there, I would have jumped into a canal with a rock around my neck."

His wife concludes the piece, "Man, it just isn't fair."

I read the whole clipping again every morning. This is the Big Time here, every minute of it. Will someone please explain to Alan McDonald in his dignity, to the deer at Providencia in his dignity, what is going on? And mail me the carbon.

When we walked by the deer at Providencia for the last time, I said to Pepe, with a pitying glance at the deer, "*Pobrecito*"—"poor little thing." But I was trying out Spanish. I knew at the time it was a ridiculous thing to say.

Critical Thinking

1.   What were your initial reactions to the story?

2.   How did the men in the story expect her to react?

3.   Why do you think she keeps the newspaper clipping? What are the parallel injustices she describes?

Writing Assignments

1. In the essay, the burn victim's wife says, "Life isn't fair." Do you agree? Why?

2. Do animals suffer pain as we do? In your opinion, does the juxtaposition of the deer and the suffering man trivialize the man's suffering? Explain.

3. Respond to Dillard's question at the end: "Will someone please explain to Alan McDonald in his dignity, to the deer at Providencia in his dignity, what is going on?"

RELATING THE AUTHORS' IDEAS

---

1. In what ways do any two of the authors look at the natural environment in relation to life? For example you might compare Woolf's "The Death of the Moth" to Eiseley's "The Brown Wasps." What are the messages they are trying to convey?

2. Look at how any two authors refer to the passage of time and memory. For example, you may want to compare Sanders' reflections at the lake to Eiseley's tree.

3. Write an essay examining the use of analogy in any two essays in this chapter.

4. Write about any of the relationships between father and son, or mother and daughter. How does the natural environment contribute to the story?

Chapter VII

Situating the Self:

Society and Politics

VII

Situating the Self:

Society and Politics

Introduction

We live in an ever-changing global society. As individuals, it is important to think about our place in society and politics.

The selections by William F. Buckley, Jr., Lance Morrow, Edward I. Koch, Peter Tomasino, and Martin Luther King, Jr. generate thought about political voice, the tragedy of September 11th, the death penalty, the assassination of President Kennedy, civil rights, freedom and peace.

When violence is committed and our rights are violated, we want justice. However, questions arise about what actions should be taken to ensure that justice is served. On September 11, 2001, the nation and world witnessed the tragedy of the World Trade Center. In "Rage and Retribution" Lance Morrow responds to the tragedy, boldly declaring "Let's have rage." What reactions are appropriate?

How does a society obtain justice? Should "the punishment match the offense" as Cicero declares. In "Death and Justice," Edward I. Koch outlines his defense of the death penalty. He believes, "If we create a society in which injustice is not tolerated, incidents of murder—the most flagrant form of injustice—will diminish."

What happens when the pursuit of justice and truth is thwarted and there are no clear answers and the questioning parties are not taken seriously? In "Who Killed President Kennedy" Peter Tomasino examines the mystery that still surrounds the death of President John F. Kennedy.

Lastly, essay "33" is written by Martin Luther King, Jr., one of the world's greatest leaders ever to live. Unfortunately, he, too, was assassinated in the prime of his life. In "Letter From Birmingham Jail," King responds to critics of his "work and ideas." He states, "We know through painful experience that freedom is never voluntarily given by the oppressor; it must be demanded by the oppressed." Clearly, Martin Luther King, Jr. is not one of the passive voices Buckley describes in "Why Don't We Complain."

Both King and Kennedy worked to improve the quality of life for all members of society. They were champions of freedom, peace, and civil rights. Their message is timeless.

*"When people cease to complain,
they cease to think."
--Napoleon I, Maxims (1804-15)*

"Why Don't We Complain?"[*]
William F. Buckley, Jr.

*William F. Buckley, Jr. is an outspoken, political writer, best
known for his conservative viewpoints. In 1955 he founded the
National Review. He is recognized for his syndicated column "On
the Right" and his television program "Firing Line." He has
published numerous essays, articles, and books.* [†]

It was the very last coach and the only empty seat on the entire train, so there was
no turning back. The problem was to breathe. Outside, the temperature was
below freezing. Inside the railroad car the temperature must have been about 85
degrees. I took off my overcoat, and a few minutes later my jacket, and noticed
that the car was flecked with the white shirts of the passengers. I soon found my
hand moving to loosen my tie. From one end of the car to the other, as we rattled
through Westchester County, we sweated; but we did not moan.

I watched the train conductor appear at the head of the car. "Tickets, all
tickets, please!" In a more virile age, I thought, the passengers would seize the
conductor and strap him down on a seat over the radiator to share the fate of his
patrons. He shuffled down the aisle, picking up tickets, punching commutation
cards. No one addressed a word to him. He approached my seat, and I drew a
deep breath of resolution. "Conductor," I began with a considerable edge to my
voice . . . . Instantly the doleful eyes of my seatmate turned tiredly from his
newspaper to fix me with a resentful stare: what question could be so important
as to justify my sibilant intrusion into his stupor? I was shaken by those eyes. I
am incapable of making a discreet fuss, so I mumbled a question about what time

---

[*] "Why Don't We Complain" by William F. Buckley, Jr. From *Rumbles Left and Right* by
William F. Buckley, Jr. Copyright © 1960, 1963. Used by permission of the Wallace Literary
Agency.
[†] Buckley, William F. *Contemporary Authors Online*. The Gale Group, 2001. 4 May, 2001.
January 26, 2002 <http://www.galenet.com/servlet/LitRC?c=1&ai=13997&ste=6&docNum= H1
000013566&bConts=15279&tab=1&vrsn=3&ca=1&tbst=arp&ST=Buckley%2C+William+F.&src
htp=athr&n=10&locID=nypl&OP=contains>.

were we due in Stamford (I didn't even ask whether it would be before or after dehydration could be expected to set in), got my reply, and went back to my newspaper and to wiping my brow.

The conductor had nonchalantly walked down the gauntlet of eighty sweating American freemen, and not one of them had asked him to explain why the passengers in that car had been consigned to suffer. There is nothing to be done when the temperature *outdoors* is 85 degrees, and *indoors* the air conditioner has broken down; obviously when that happens there is nothing to do, except perhaps curse the day that one was born. But when the temperature outdoors is below freezing, it takes a positive act of will on somebody's part to set the temperature indoors at 85. Somewhere a valve was turned too far, a furnace overstocked, a thermostat maladjusted: something that could easily be remedied by turning off the heat and allowing the great outdoors to come indoors. All this is so obvious. What is not obvious is what has happened to the American people.

It isn't just the commuters, whom we have come to visualize as a supine breed who have got on to the trick of suspending their sensory faculties twice a day while they submit to the creeping dissolution of the railroad industry. It isn't just they who have given up trying to rectify irrational vexations. It is the American peoples everywhere.

A few weeks ago at a large movie theater I turned to my wife and said, "The picture is out of focus." "Be quiet," she answered. I obeyed. But a few minutes later I raised the point again, with mounting impatience. "It will be all right in a minute," she said apprehensively. (She would rather lose her eyesight than be around when I make one of my infrequent scenes.) I waited. It was *just* out of focus-not glaringly out, but out. My vision is 20-20, and I assume that is the vision, adjusted, of most people in the movie house. So, after hectoring my wife throughout the first reel, I finally prevailed upon her to admit that it *was* off, and very annoying. We then settled down, coming to rest on the presumption that: (a) someone connected with the management of the theater must soon notice the blur and make the correction; or (b) that someone seated near the rear of the house would make the complaint in behalf of those of us up front; or (c) that— any minute now-the entire house would explode into catcalls and foot stamping, calling dramatic attention to the irksome distortion.

What happened was nothing. The movie ended, as it had begun, *just* out of focus, and as we trooped out, we stretched our faces in a variety of contortions to accustom the eye to the shock of normal focus.

I think it is safe to say that everybody suffered on that occasion. And I think it is safe to assume that everyone was expecting someone else to take the initiative in going back to speak to the manager. And it is probably true even that if we had supposed the movie would run right through the blurred image, someone surely would have summoned up the purposive indignation to get up out of his seat and file his complaint.

But notice that no one did. And the reason no one did is because we are all increasingly anxious in America to be unobtrusive, we are reluctant to make our voices heard, hesitant about claiming our rights; we are afraid that our cause is unjust, or that if it is not unjust, that it is ambiguous; or if not even that, that it is too trivial to justify the horrors of a confrontation with Authority; we still sit in an oven or endure a racking headache before undertaking a head-on, I'm—here—to-tell-you complaint. That tendency to passive compliance, to a heedless endurance, is something to keep one's eyes on—in sharp focus.

I myself can occasionally summon the courage to complain, but I cannot, as I have intimated, complain softly. My own instinct is so strong to let the thing ride, to forget about it—to expect that someone will take the matter up, when the grievance is collective, in my behalf—that it is only when the provocation is at a very special key, whose vibrations touch simultaneously a complex of nerves, allergies, and passions, that I catch fire and find the reserves of courage and assertiveness to speak up. When that happens, I get quite carried away. My blood gets hot, my brow wet, I become unbearably and unconscionably sarcastic and bellicose; I am girded for a total showdown.

Why should that be? Why could not I (or anyone else) on that railroad coach have said simply to the conductor, "Sir"—I take that back: that sounds sarcastic—"Conductor, would you be good enough to turn down the heat? I am extremely hot. In fact, I tend to get hot every time the temperature reaches 85 degr—" Strike that last sentence. Just end it with the simple statement that you are extremely hot, and let the conductor infer the cause.

Every New Year's Eve I resolve to do something about the Milquetoast in me and vow to speak up, calmly, for my rights, and for the betterment of our society, on every appropriate occasion. Entering last New Year's Eve, I was fortified in my resolve because that morning at breakfast I had had to ask the waitress three times for a glass of milk. She finally brought it—after I had finished my eggs, which is when I don't want it any more. I did not have the manliness to order her to take the milk back, but settled instead for a cowardly sulk, and ostentatiously refused to drink the milk—though I later paid for it—rather than state plainly to the hostess, as I should have, why I had not drunk it, and would not pay for it.

So by the time the New Year ushered out the Old, riding in on my morning's indignation and stimulated by the gastric juices of resolution that flow so faithfully on New Year's Eve, I rendered my vow. Henceforward I would conquer my shyness, my despicable disposition to supineness. I would speak out like a man against the unnecessary annoyances of our time.

Forty-eight hours later, I was standing in line at the ski repair 13 store in Pico Peak, Vermont. All I needed, to get on with my skiing, was the loan, for one minute, of a small screwdriver, to tighten a loose binding. Behind the counter in the workshop were two men. One was industriously engaged in servicing the complicated requirements of a young lady at the head of the line, and obviously he would be tied up for quite a while. The other— "Jiggs," his workmate called him-was a middle-aged man, who sat in a chair puffing a pipe, exchanging small talk with his working partner. My pulse began its telltale acceleration. The minutes ticked on. I stared at the idle shopkeeper, hoping to shame him into action, but he was impervious to my telepathic reproof and continued his small talk with his friend, brazenly insensitive to the nervous demands of six good men who were raring to ski.

Suddenly my New Year's Eve resolution struck me. It was now or never. I broke from my place in line and marched to the counter. I was going to control myself. I dug my nails into my palms. My effort was only partially successful:

"If you are not too busy." I said icily, "would you mind handing me a screwdriver?"

Work stopped and everyone turned his eyes on me, and I experienced that mortification I always feel when I am the center of centripetal shafts of curiosity, resentment, perplexity.

But the worst was yet to come. "I am sorry, sir," said Jiggs deferentially, moving the pipe from his mouth. "I am not supposed to move. I have just had a heart attack." That was the signal for a great whirring noise that descended from heaven. We looked, stricken, out the window, and it appeared as though a cyclone had suddenly focused on the snowy courtyard between the shop and the ski lift. Suddenly a gigantic army helicopter materialized, and hovered down to a landing. Two men jumped out of the plane carrying a stretcher, tore into the ski shop, and lifted the shopkeeper onto the stretcher. Jiggs bade his companion good-by, was whisked out the door, into the plane, up to the heavens, down—we learned—to a nearby army hospital. I looked up manfully—into a score of man-eating eyes. I put the experience down as a reversal.

As I write this, on an airplane, I have run out of paper and need to reach into my briefcase under my legs for more. I cannot do this until my empty lunch tray is removed from my lap. I arrested the stewardess as she passed empty-handed down the aisle on the way to the kitchen to fetch the lunch trays for the passengers up forward who haven't been served yet. "Would you please take my tray?" "Just a moment, sir!" she said, and marched on sternly. Shall I tell her that since she is headed for the kitchen anyway, it could not delay the feeding of the other passengers by more than two seconds necessary to stash away my empty tray? Or remind her that not fifteen minutes ago she spoke unctuously into the loudspeaker the words undoubtedly devised by the airline's highly paid public relations counselor: "If there is anything I or Miss French can do for you to make your trip more enjoyable, please let us—" I have run out of paper.

I think the observable reluctance of the majority of Americans to assert themselves in minor matters is related to our increased sense of helplessness in an age of technology and centralized political and economic power. For generations, Americans who were too hot, or too cold, got up and did something about it. Now we call the plumber, or the electrician, or the furnace man. The habit of looking after our own needs obviously had something to do with the assertiveness that characterized the American family familiar to readers of American literature. With the technification of life goes our direct responsibility for our material environment, and we are conditioned to adopt a position of helplessness not only as regards the broken air conditioner, but as regards the overheated train. It takes an expert to fix the former, but not the latter; yet these distinctions, as we withdraw into helplessness, tend to fade away.

Our notorious political apathy is a related phenomena. Every year, whether the Republican or the Democratic Party is in office, more and more power drains away from the individual to feed vast reservoirs in far-off place; and we have less and less say about the shape of events which shape our future. From this alienation of personal power comes the sense of resignation with which we accept the political dispensations of a powerful government whose hold upon us continues to increase.

An editor of a national weekly news magazine told me a few years ago that as few as a dozen letters of protest against an editorial stance of his magazine was enough to convene a plenipotentiary meeting of the board of editors to review policy. "So few people complain, or make their voices heard," he explained to me, "that we assume a dozen letters represent the inarticulated views of thousands of readers." In the past ten years, he said, the volume of mail has noticeably decreased, even though the circulation of his magazine has risen.

When our voices are finally mute, when we have finally suppressed the natural instinct to complain, whether the vexation is trivial or grave, we shall have become automatons, incapable of feeling. When Premier Khrushchev first came to this country late in 1959, he was primed, we are informed, to experience the bitter resentment of the American people against his tyranny, against his persecutions, against the movement which is responsible for the great number of American deaths in Korea, for billions in taxes every year, and for life everlasting on the brink of disaster; but Khrushchev was pleasantly surprised, and reported back to the Russian people that he had been met with overwhelming cordiality (read: apathy), except, to be sure, for "a few fascists who followed me around with their wretched posters, and should be horse-whipped."

I may be crazy, but I say there would have been lots more posters in a society where train temperatures in the dead of winter are not allowed to climb to 85 degrees without complaint.

Critical Thinking

1.   What is the author's main idea?

2.   Buckley uses several anecdotes to illustrate his point. List them, beginning with the railroad car. Which are most effective? Why? Which are the least effective? Explain.

3.   According to Buckley, what are the consequences of political apathy?

Writing Assignments

1.   Write a essay similar to Buckley's titled "Why Don't We_____." Fill in the blank.

2.   Do you agree with his statement that Americans are too reluctant to speak up? Explain why or why not.

3.   Place yourself in any of the various situations he describes. How would you react?

"By my physical constitution I am but an ordinary man . . . Yet some great events, some cutting expressions, some mean hypocrisies, have at times thrown this assemblage of sloth, sleep, and littleness into rage like a lion."

-- John Adams, <u>Diary</u>
(April 26, 1779)

"The Case for Rage and Retribution"[*]
Lance Morrow

Award winning journalist and essayist Lance Morrow received the <u>National Magazine</u> Award in 1981 for the body of his work in <u>Time</u> magazine. He has written numerous books and articles for various publications, including <u>Newsweek</u>, <u>The New York Times</u>, and the <u>Atlanta Journal-Constitution</u>. This article, "The Case for Rage and Retribution" appeared in <u>Time</u> magazine on September 14, 2001, just three days after the terrorist attack in New York.[†]

For once, let's have no "grief counselors" standing by with banal consolations, as if the purpose, in the midst of all this, were merely to make everyone feel better as quickly as possible. We shouldn't feel better.

For once, let's have no fatuous rhetoric about "healing." Healing is inappropriate now, and dangerous. There will be time later for the tears of sorrow.

A day cannot live in infamy without the nourishment of rage. Let's have rage.

What's needed is a unified, unifying, Pearl Harbor sort of purple American fury--a ruthless indignation that doesn't leak away in a week or two, wandering off into Prozac-induced forgetfulness or into the next media sensation (O.J. . . . Elian . . . Chandra . . .) or into a corruptly thoughtful relativism (as has happened in the recent past, when, for example, you might hear someone say, "Terrible what he did, of course, but, you know, the Unabomber does have a point, doesn't he, about modern technology?").

Let America explore the rich reciprocal possibilities of the fatwa. A policy of focused brutality does not come easily to a self-conscious, self-indulgent, contradictory, diverse, humane nation with a short attention span. America needs to relearn a lost discipline, self-confident relentlessness--and to relearn why human nature has equipped us all with a weapon (abhorred in decent peacetime societies) called hatred.

As the bodies are counted, into the thousands and thousands, hatred will not, I think, be a difficult emotion to summon. Is the medicine too strong? Call it, rather, a wholesome and intelligent enmity—the sort that impels even such a prosperous, messily tolerant organism as America to act. Anyone who does not loathe the people who did these things, and the people who cheer them on, is too philosophical for decent company.

It's a practical matter, anyway. In war, enemies are enemies. You find them and put them out of business, on the sound principle that that's what they are trying to do to you. If what happened on Tuesday does not give Americans the political will needed to exterminate men like Osama bin Laden and those who conspire with them in evil mischief, then nothing ever will and we are in for a procession of black Tuesdays.

This was terrorism brought to near perfection as a dramatic form. Never has the evil business had such production values. Normally, the audience sees only the smoking aftermath—the blown-up embassy, the ruined barracks, the ship with a blackened hole at the waterline. This time the first plane striking the first tower acted as a shill. It alerted the media, brought cameras to the scene so that they might be set up to record the vivid surreal bloom of the second strike ("Am I seeing this?") and then--could they be such engineering geniuses, so deft at demolition?--the catastrophic collapse of the two towers, one after the other, and a sequence of panic in the streets that might have been shot for a remake of The War of the Worlds or for Independence Day. Evil possesses an instinct for theater, which is why, in an era of gaudy and gifted media, evil may vastly magnify its damage by the power of horrific images.

It is important not to be transfixed. The police screamed to the people running from the towers, "Don't look back!"—a biblical warning against the power of the image. Terrorism is sometimes described (in a frustrated, oh-the-burdens-of-great-power tone of voice) as "asymmetrical warfare." So what? Most of history is a pageant of asymmetries. It is mostly the asymmetries that cause history to happen--an obscure Schickelgruber nearly destroys Europe; a mere atom, artfully diddled, incinerates a city. Elegant perplexity puts too much emphasis on the "asymmetrical" side of the phrase and not enough on the fact that it is, indeed, real warfare. Asymmetry is a concept. War is, as we see, blood and death.

It is not a bad idea to repeat a line from the 19th century French anarchist thinker Pierre-Joseph Proudhon: "The fecundity of the unexpected far exceeds the prudence of statesmen." America, in the spasms of a few hours, became a changed country. It turned the corner, at last, out of the 1990s. The menu of American priorities was rearranged. The presidency of George W. Bush begins now. What seemed important a few days ago (in the media, at least) became instantly trivial. If Gary Condit is mentioned once in the next six months on cable television, I will be astonished.

During World War II, John Kennedy wrote home to his parents from the Pacific. He remarked that Americans are at their best during very good times or very bad times; the in-between periods, he thought, cause them trouble. I'm not sure that is true. Good times sometimes have a tendency to make Americans squalid.

The worst times, as we see, separate the civilized of the world from the uncivilized. This is the moment of clarity. Let the civilized toughen up, and let the uncivilized take their chances in the game they started.

[September 14, 2001]

Critical Thinking

1. The dictionary defines rage as "violent, explosive anger."* How does Morrow define rage?

2. What arguments does Morrow present in support of his thesis?

3. How did you react to the last paragraph? Is it a rally to action? Explain.

Writing Assignments

1. Write a personal essay about your reaction(s) to the tragedy of September 11th.

2. What are the steps in the healing process? The article was written several days after the event. Do you think Morrow's article would have reflected a different attitude if he had written it a month later, six months later, or a year later?

3. Write an essay in the form of a letter to the editor responding to Morrow's piece.

---

* The American Heritage Dictionary of The English Language. Fourth Edition. NY: Houghton Mifflin Co, 2000.

"Let the punishment match the offense." ("Noxiae poena par esto.")

-- Marcus Tullius Cicero
<u>De Officiis</u> *(44 B.C.)*

"Death and Justice"[*]
Edward I. Koch

Former New York City Major (1978-89) Edward I. Koch has been a lifelong public servant. He has written numerous books, as well as articles for magazines and newspapers. In this essay, "Death and Justice," he outlines his keys arguments in support of the death penalty.[†]

Last December a man named Robert Lee Willie, who had been convicted of raping and murdering an 18-year-old woman, was executed in the Louisiana state prison. In a statement issued several minutes before his death, Mr. Willie said: "Killing people is wrong . . . . It makes no difference whether it's citizens, countries, or governments. Killing is wrong." Two weeks later in South Carolina, an admitted killer named Joseph Carl Shaw was put to death for murdering two teenagers. In an appeal to the governor for clemency, Mr. Shaw wrote: "Killing is wrong when I did it. Killing is wrong when you do it. I hope you have the courage and moral strength to stop the killing."

It is a curiosity of modern life that we find ourselves being lectured on morality by cold-blooded killers. Mr. Willie previously had been convicted of aggravated rape, aggravated kidnapping, and the murders of a Louisiana deputy and a man from Missouri. Mr. Shaw committed another murder a week before the two for which he was executed, and admitted mutilating the body of the 14-year-old girl he killed. I can't help wondering what prompted these murderers

---

[*] From *New Republic* 4/15/1985, Vol. 197, Issue 15, page 12 by Edward I. Koch. Copyright © 1985 by *New Republic*. Reprinted by permission.

[†] "Edward I. Koch,". *Contemporary Authors Online*. The Gale Group, 2001. 19 September 2001. January 26, 2002 < http://www.galenet.com/servlet/LitRC?c=1&ai=50234&ste=6&docNum =H1000055186&bConts=2191&tab=1&vrsn=3&ca=1&tbst=arp&ST=Koch+Edward+I%28rving %29&srchtp=athr&n=10&locID=nypl&OP=contains>.

to speak out against killing as they entered the death-house door. Did their newfound reverence for life stem from the realization that they were about to lose their own?   ⟶ Quote

Life is indeed precious, and I believe the death penalty helps to affirm this fact. Had the death penalty been a real possibility in the minds of these murderers, they might well have stayed their hand. They might have shown moral awareness before their victims died, and not after. Consider the tragic death of Rosa Velez, who happened to be home when a man named Luis Vera burglarized her apartment in Brooklyn. "Yeah, I shot her," Vera admitted. "She knew me, and I knew I wouldn't go to the chair."

During my 22 years in public service, I have heard the pros and cons of capital punishment expressed with special intensity. As a district leader, councilman, congressman, and mayor, I have represented constituencies generally thought of as liberal. Because I support the death penalty for heinous crimes of murder, I have sometimes been the subject of emotional and outraged attacks by voters who find my position reprehensible or worse. I have listened to their ideas. I have weighed their objections carefully. I still support the death penalty. The reasons I maintain my position can be best understood by examining the arguments most frequently heard in opposition.

(1) *The death penalty is "barbaric."* Sometimes opponents of capital punishment horrify with tales of lingering death on the gallows, of faulty electric chairs, or of agony in the gas chamber. Partly in response to such protests, several states such as North Carolina and Texas switched to execution by lethal injection. The condemned person is put to death painlessly, without ropes, voltage, bullets, or gas. Did this answer the objections of death penalty opponents? Of course not. On June 22, 1984, *The New York Times* published an editorial that sarcastically attacked the new "hygienic" method of death by injection, and stated that "execution can never be made humane through science." So it's not the method that really troubles opponents. It's the death itself they consider barbaric.

Admittedly, capital punishment is not a pleasant topic. However, one does not have to like the death penalty in order to support it any more than one must like radical surgery, radiation, or chemotherapy in order to find necessary these attempts at curing cancer. Ultimately we may learn how to cure cancer with a simple pill. Unfortunately, that day has not yet arrived. Today we are faced with the choice of letting the cancer spread or trying to cure it with the methods available, methods that one day will almost certainly be considered barbaric. But to give up and do nothing would be far more barbaric and would certainly delay the discovery of an eventual cure. The analogy between cancer and murder is imperfect, because murder is not the "disease" we are trying to cure. The disease is injustice. We may not like the death penalty, but it must be available to punish crimes of cold-blooded murder, cases in which any other form of punishment would be inadequate and, therefore, unjust. If we create a society in which injustice is not tolerated, incidents of murder—the most flagrant form of injustice—will diminish.

(2) *No other major democracy uses the death penalty.* No other major democracy—in fact, few other countries of any description—is plagued by a murder rate such as that in the United States. Fewer and fewer Americans can remember the days when unlocked doors were the norm and murder was a rare and terrible offense. In America the murder rate climbed 122 percent between 1963 and 1980. During that same period, the murder rate in New York City increased by almost 400 percent, and the statistics are even worse in many other cities. A study at M.I.T. showed that based on 1970 homicide rates a person who lived in a large American city ran a greater risk of being murdered than an American soldier in World War II ran of being killed in combat. It is not surprising that the laws of each country differ according to differing conditions and traditions. If other countries had our murder problem, the cry for capital punishment would be just as loud as it is here. And I daresay that any other major democracy where 75 percent of the people supported the death penalty would soon enact it into law.

(3) *An innocent person might be executed by mistake.* Consider the work of Adam Bedau, one of the most implacable foes of capital punishment in this country. According to Mr. Bedau, it is "false sentimentality to argue that the death penalty should be abolished because of the abstract possibility that an innocent person might be executed." He cites a study of the 7,000 executions in this country from 1893 to 1971, and concludes that the record fails to show that such cases occur. The main point, however, is this. If government functioned only when the possibility of error didn't exist, government wouldn't function at all. Human life deserves special protection, and one of the best ways to guarantee that protection is to assure that convicted murderers do not kill again. Only the death penalty can accomplish this end. In a recent case in New Jersey, a man

named Richard Biegenwald was freed from prison after serving 18 years for murder; since his release he has been convicted of committing four murders. A prisoner named Lemuel Smith, who, while serving four life sentences for murder (plus two life sentences for kidnapping and robbery) in New York's Green Haven Prison, lured a woman corrections officer into the chaplain's office and strangled her. He then mutilated and dismembered her body. An additional life sentence for Smith is meaningless. Because New York has no death penalty statute, Smith has effectively been given a license to kill.

But the problem of multiple murder is not confined to the nation's penitentiaries. In 1981, 91 police officers were killed in the line of duty in this country. Seven percent of those arrested in the cases that have been solved had a previous arrest for murder. In New York City in 1976 and 1977, 85 persons arrested for homicide had a previous arrest for murder. Six of these individuals had two previous arrests for murder, and one had four previous murder arrests. During those two years the New York police were arresting for murder persons with a previous arrest for murder on the average of one every 8.5 days. This is not surprising when we learn that in 1975, for example, the median time served in Massachusetts for homicide was less than two-and-a-half years. In 1976 a study sponsored by the Twentieth Century Fund found that the average time served in the United States for first-degree murder is ten years. The median time served may be considerably lower.

(4) *Capital punishment cheapens the value of human life.* On the contrary, it can be easily demonstrated that the death penalty strengthens the value of human life. If the penalty for rape were lowered, clearly it would signal a lessened regard for the victims' suffering, humiliation, and personal integrity. It would cheapen their horrible experience, and expose them to an increased danger of recurrence. When we lower the penalty for murder, it signals a lessened regard for the value of the victim's life. Some critics of capital punishment, such as columnist Jimmy Breslin, have suggested that a life sentence is actually a harsher penalty for murder than death. This is sophistic nonsense. A few killers may decide not to appeal a death sentence, but the overwhelming majority make every effort to stay alive. It is by exacting the highest penalty for the taking of human life that we affirm the highest value of human life.

(5) *The death penalty is applied in a discriminatory manner.* This factor no longer seems to be the problem it once was. The appeals process for a condemned prisoner is lengthy and painstaking. Every effort is made to see that

the verdict and sentence were fairly arrived at.   However, assertions of discrimination are not an argument for ending the death penalty but for extending it.   It is not justice to exclude everyone from the penalty of the law if a few are found to be so favored.   Justice requires that the law be applied equally to all.

(6)   *Thou Shalt Not Kill.*   The Bible is our greatest source of moral inspiration.   Opponents of the death penalty frequently cite the sixth of the Ten Commandments in an attempt to prove that capital punishment is divinely proscribed.   In the original Hebrew, however, the Sixth Commandment reads, "Thou Shalt Not Commit Murder," and the Torah specifies capital punishment for a variety of offenses.   The biblical viewpoint has been upheld by philosophers throughout history.   The greatest thinkers of the 19th century—Kant, Locke, Hobbes, Rousseau, Montesquieu, and Mill—agreed that natural law properly authorizes the sovereign to take life in order to vindicate justice.   Only Jeremy Bentham was ambivalent.   Washington, Jefferson, and Franklin endorsed it. Abraham Lincoln authorized executions for deserters in wartime.   Alexis de Tocqueville, who expressed profound respect for American institutions, believed that the death penalty was indispensable to the support of social order.   The United States Constitution, widely admired as one of the seminal achievements in the history of humanity, condemns cruel and inhuman punishment, but does not condemn capital punishment.

(7)   *The death penalty is state-sanctioned murder.*   This is the defense with which Messrs. Willie and Shaw hoped to soften the resolve of those who sentenced them to death.   By saying in effect, "You're no better than I am," the murderer seeks to bring his accusers down to his own level.   It is also a popular argument among opponents of capital punishment, but a transparently false one. Simply put, the state has rights that the private individual does not.   In a democracy, those rights are given to the state by the electorate.   The execution of a lawfully condemned killer is no more an act of murder than is legal imprisonment an act of kidnapping.   If an individual forces a neighbor to pay him money under threat of punishment, it's called extortion.   If the state does it, it's called taxation.   Rights and responsibilities surrendered by the individual are what give the state its power to govern.   This contract is the foundation of civilization itself.

Everyone wants his or her rights, and will defend them jealously.   Not everyone, however, wants responsibilities, especially the painful responsibilities that come with law enforcement. Twenty-one years ago a woman named Kitty Genovese was assaulted and murdered on a street in New York. Dozens of neighbors heard her cries for help but did nothing to assist her. They didn't even call the police. In such a climate the criminal understandably grows bolder. In the presence of moral cowardice, he lectures us on our supposed failings and tries to equate his crimes with our quest for justice.

The death of anyone—even a convicted killer—diminishes us all. But we are diminished even more by a justice system that fails to function. It is an illusion to let ourselves believe that doing away with capital punishment removes the murderer's deed from our conscience. The rights of society are paramount. When we protect guilty lives, we give up innocent lives in exchange. When opponents of capital punishment say to the state: "I will not let you kill in my name," they are also saying to murderers: "You can kill in your *own* name as long as I have an excuse for not getting involved."

It is hard to imagine anything worse than being murdered while neighbors do nothing. But something worse exists. When those same neighbors shrink back from justly punishing the murderer, the victim dies twice.

Critical Thinking

1. Locate Koch's thesis in the text.

2. What method does he use to present his argument?

3. Summarize his key ideas. In addition, indicate where and how he refutes the opposing point of view.

Writing Assignments

1. Conduct a brainstorming session on the issue of the death penalty. Regardless of where you stand on the issue, write down all the ideas that come to mind regarding both sides of the issue.

2.   Write an argumentation essay on the death penalty.   Use your brainstorming notes from the previous question. Conduct further research and cite sources to support your position.

3.   Rent the film *Dead Man Walking* and write an essay comparing the main idea of the film to Koch's ideas.

> *"Three may keep a secret, if two*
> *of them are dead."*
> *--Benjamin Franklin*

"Who Killed President Kennedy?"[*]
Peter Tomasino

Peter Tomasino has been researching the Kennedy assassination since 1989. He has one of the most comprehensive libraries on the subject. Famed attorney and author Mark Lane (Rush to Judgment and Plausible Denial) comments on the essay, "Peter Tomasino's excellent essay, almost four decades after the assassination, proves that the official version was a rush to judgment about a still unsolved murder."

On November 22, 1963 our country's 35th President, John Fitzgerald Kennedy, was murdered. He was cut down by gunfire on the streets of Dallas, Texas. As the secret service rushed the President to Parkland Memorial Hospital, where he would soon be pronounced dead, America asked–who killed our President? Thirty-eight years later we ask the same question.

Approximately ninety minutes after the President was shot, Lee Harvey Oswald, a twenty-four-year-old ex-marine, was arrested at the Texas Theater. Oswald would be charged with the murder of a Dallas police officer. Later, he would be charged with the killing of the President. However, before he was formally charged, reports filled the airwaves that he was the lone assassin. Oswald vehemently denied killing anyone. During a short filmed interview by the press he stated, "I am requesting that someone come forward to give me legal assistance" and when a reporter asked if he killed the President he responded, "No Sir, I didn't kill anyone". [1]

On Sunday, November 24th, the nation's media focused on the transfer of the alleged assassin from the Dallas Police Station to the Dallas Sheriff's Department. As Oswald was led by police, who were paid to protect him, he was shot and killed. Jack Ruby, a Dallas nightclub owner with underworld ties,

---

[*] Reprinted by permission of Peter Tomasino.

emerged from the crowd of reporters and shot Oswald. This nationally televised murder caused raised eyebrows throughout the land.

Rumors began to grow in Dallas that the murder was a plot. Several people claimed to have seen Oswald and Ruby together prior to the assassination. Many witnesses to the assassination claimed that shots were fired from behind a wooden fence—not the Texas School Book Depository where Oswald worked. Texas State Attorney General Waggoner Carr began a formal inquiry into the assassination and surrounding events. Curiously, the new President Lyndon Baines Johnson stopped all state inquiries by signing an Executive Order to form a Commission to report on the assassination.

The "President's Commission on the Assassination of President John F. Kennedy" would later become known as the Warren Commission, named after its chairman, Chief Justice Earl Warren. President Johnson selected each member. Joining Justice Warren were: Representative Gerald Ford, a future President; Senator Richard Russell; Representative Hale Boggs; Senator John Sherman Cooper; John J. McCloy, Chairman of Chase Manhattan Bank; and, Allen Dulles, former Director of the CIA. The Commission conducted the investigation in secret; all other inquiries were cut off, thus making the Warren Report the nation's official version of the tragedy.

The Warren Commission relied heavily on the evidence provided by the Federal Government. It is interesting to note that in 1963 there was no federal law in place for killing a President. However, J. Edgar Hoover, the Director of the FBI, seized control of the evidence and took control of the case. One of the most powerful men in the country and a close friend of President Johnson, Hoover made it clear from the start of the Commission's investigation that Oswald acted alone.[2] Johnson went along with Hoover's scenario. In addition, Johnson insisted on leaving Parkland Hospital with the body of President Kennedy, resulting in the autopsy being performed at Bethesda Naval Hospital. However, Dr. Earl Rose, the coroner of Dallas County protested. He reminded the Secret Service that Texas State law prevented the chain of evidence from being broken. This was a homicide in Dallas County and Rose insisted that he perform the autopsy at Parkland.[3] The situation intensified. Rose was physically pushed out of the way. Johnson's heavily armed secret service prevailed. The law was broken. Johnson flew to Washington with possession of the best evidence.

In 1964 the Warren Commission released its report.[4] It was concluded: that there was no conspiracy to kill the President; that Oswald acted alone; that Oswald alone fired three shots from the Texas School Book Depository, the building in which he was employed; all of the shots were fired from above and behind the President; that the only weapon used was an Italian made rifle, a 6.5 Mannlicher-Carcano. The Commission further concluded that approximately one hour after killing the President, Oswald killed police officer J.D. Tippet in the Oak Cliff section of Dallas. Finally, the Commission concluded that Ruby did not kill Oswald to silence him and that Tippet, Ruby, and Oswald did not know each other.

Through the years many private citizens found the report to be incomplete, inaccurate, and filled with omissions. A number of these citizens began to research the crime themselves and became known as assassination researchers. Leading the way was attorney Mark Lane who began with writing an article and went on to produce a number of best selling books and excellent documentaries on the subject. Mr. Lane openly called the report a "fraud." He interviewed many credible witnesses to the crime. Charles Brehm, S.M. Holland, Richard Dodd, Jesse Price, James Simmons, and Orville Nix, all of these witnesses stated that the shots were fired from behind the wooden fence.[5] The fence was in front of the President. This was a direct contrast to the Commission's conclusion that all the shots were fired from the rear.

The Commission explains the crime with a totally unbelievable explanation called "The Single Bullet Theory."[6] The theory is that the President's motorcade passed the Texas School Book Depository traveling about ten miles per hour. Three shots were fired from Oswald, who was perched behind an open window on the sixth floor of the infamous building. One shot missed the motorcade completely and injured bystander James Tague. The third shot, was the kill shot which struck the President in the head. That leaves one bullet to account for all of the remaining wounds to both Governor Connally and President Kennedy. The President was struck in the back, about five inches below the shoulder and in the throat. The Governor was stuck in the back, chest, wrist, and thigh. The theory is that the bullet fired downward from the sixth floor into the President's back and came out of his throat, hit the Governor in the back, broke his rib, exited his chest, went through his wrist breaking the radius bone and landed in his thigh. It is further alleged that once at Parkland Hospital the bullet fell from the Governor's thigh onto a stretcher. The Commission was very vague about the discovery of the bullet. Remarkably, the condition of the bullet was pristine. The Commission linked the bullet to Oswald and labeled the bullet "Commission Exhibit 399" – The Assassination researchers labeled it the "Magic Bullet."

With the passing of time, other evidence emerged which supported the many witnesses who claimed that the shots were fired from the front of the President. From Parkland Hospital, Nurse Audrey Bell described the President's throat wound as a wound of entry. In his book *Conspiracy of Silence,* Doctor Charles Crenshaw stated that the throat wound was one of entrance. He was later filmed standing by the wooden fence, stating that the President's head wound was consistent with a shot fired from the wooden fence, not the School Book Depository. He later wrote "I have wanted to shout to the world that the wounds to Kennedy's head and throat that I examined were caused by bullets that struck him from the front, not the back as the public has been led to believe."[7]

Although the Commission accounted for only one weapon, there is strong evidence that another rifle was found nearby. Dallas Deputy Sheriff Roger Craig claimed that he saw a 7.65 German Mauser rifle discovered on the sixth floor of the Texas School Book Depository on the day of the assassination. He spoke with certainty of his claim when he stated "stamped right on the barrel was seven, point, six, five, Mauser."[8] Craig stated that a gun expert, Deputy Constable Seymour Weitzman, was called over to identify the weapon. To corroborate Craig's statement is the affidavit of Weitzman. On November 23, 1963 Weitzman swore before Notary Public[9], Mary Rattan that the rifle found was a Mauser. The Commission never accounted for this weapon.

Although Craig was warned by Sheriff Bill Decker, "Tell them you didn't see or hear anything," he would openly speak his mind about the many facts that were being covered up. He spoke of another bullet found near the wooden fence by Deputy Buddy Walthers. He spoke of his encounter with Oswald, which contradicted the Commission's version of events. His courage to speak the truth became a burden. First, he was fired from the Dallas Sheriff's Department. Subsequently, many law enforcement officers from Dallas stopped speaking to him. In 1974 Lincoln Carle interviewed him.[10] Craig appeared very credible, when in chilling detail he spoke about the threats made on his life because he would not go along with the official version of the assassination. Soon after the interview, he was found dead from a bullet wound to the chest, fired from a rifle.

Death came to many witnesses of this tragic event.[11]   Walthers, who worked with Craig, was shot and killed.   Several men who met in Ruby's apartment the evening Ruby killed Oswald all died mysteriously after the meeting.   Lee Bowers, who worked in the Railroad Tower behind the wooden fence on the day of the assassination, said he saw a number of suspicious events. He gave an interview with Mark Lane – he was found dead! Dorothy Kilgallen, a newspaper columnist and star of the television game show "What's My Line?" was granted a rare interview with Ruby.   She claimed she was going to break the biggest story ever on the assassination—she was found dead.   Shortly after Kilgallen's death her best friend and confidant, Mrs. Earl Smith was killed. Many researchers believe that Smith had copies of Kilgallen's notes.[12]

There were those who were scared into silence or into changing their story. Aquilia Clemmons, stated she saw two men flee the crime scene of the J.D. Tippit murder and neither one looked like Oswald.[13]   However, after being told she "might get hurt" by a man who wore a gun, she stopped giving interviews. Warren Reynolds gave chase to a shooter at the Tippit murder scene. During a television interview he claimed the man he chased was not Oswald.   Warren Reynolds was a problem for the official version.   He was shot in the head.   He was lucky to survive and then promptly changed his mind and said Oswald was the man I followed.   Beverly Oliver, a dancer at Ruby's nightclub, stated years later that she did not want to become a "statistic." Many years later, she revealed that Ruby and Oswald knew each other.   She specifically stated that she was introduced to Oswald by Ruby.

The greatest evidence of a massive conspiracy emerges from the official autopsy.   Not only was the body of the President stolen from the proper authorities in Dallas, but there can be no plausible reason for the level in which the autopsy was botched! Dr. Thorton Boswell and Dr. James Humes worked at Bethesda Naval Center for the United States Navy.   They were called upon to perform the most important medical legal autopsy in history.   Unfortunately, it would become the most criticized autopsy in history.[14] The doctors claimed that they did not track the wounds to the President's back and throat. This is not only standard procedure, this is vital to finding the cause of death.   As a matter of fact they missed the throat wound completely.   Later, the doctors stated that the wound appeared to be a tracheotomy performed at Parkland Hospital.   However, the most important blunder was that the brain was not sectioned.   The President died of a bullet or bullets to the head; therefore, to identify the direction in which the shots were fired there is a standard procedure. The procedure was not performed. Although this is inexplicable there are many unexplainable results from this autopsy. Perhaps none more than the fact that Dr. Humes admitted to burning his original notes.

Dr. Cyril Wecht, a forensic pathologist, states in his book *Cause of Death* that the United States Army Pathologist, Dr. Pierre Fink, described the autopsy to him as "horrible." Fink further commented, " I only wish I could tell you about it".[15] There was an admiral and a general present during the autopsy. When the autopsy was completed, it was ordered that no personnel speak a word of it. If they did, they would be court-martialed. Years later this order was lifted. Paul O'Connor worked in the lab at Bethesda during the autopsy; he described the autopsy as a "massive cover-up." Petty officer Denis David, who was stationed at Bethesda, stated that he viewed the film of the autopsy. According to David an officer named William Bruce Pitzer allowed him to view the film. The film revealed that Kennedy was shot from the front—not from the back as the Warren Report concluded! David indicated that Pitzer might have had plans to air the film as soon as he retired from the service. Shortly before his retirement Pitzer was found dead, killed by a bullet to the head. The film has not surfaced. His death was ruled a suicide.

With such a large number of strange deaths happening to people involved in the assassination of President Kennedy, it is not reasonable to believe that they were all coincidental. It is much more likely they were killed as a method of silencing. Dead people do not testify. With so many witnesses who clearly stated, with no question, that there were shots fired from the wooden fence in front of the President, it is difficult to believe that Hoover, the FBI and the Warren Commission could not find any of them. The disappearance of the 7.65 Mauser Rifle indicates foul play. Doctor Humes and Dr. Boswell both overlooking a bullet wound in the throat when performing an autopsy on the President of the United States, not to mention they omitted several fundamental procedures that are essential in finding the cause of death. A magic bullet that defies any challenge to duplicate its alleged performance! Who would believe this? A study of this case clearly reveals that something very sinister happened to our nation and Democratic process on November 22, 1963. The American people were stripped of their President. A new President stood in his place, not as a result of an election–as a result of gunfire!

There was a contrast in the policy of the two Presidents. Shortly before he was killed, President Kennedy signed National Security Action Memorandum 263.[16] This act was to bring home one thousand United States military personnel each month from South East Asia, effectively ending our involvement in Vietnam. During an interview, Kennedy stated, "In the final analysis, it's their war, they have to win it or lose it." In short, Kennedy wanted out of Vietnam, the same way he wanted and obtained a peaceful solution to the Cuban Missile Crisis. With Johnson as President the war escalated to horrific stature. Young men were drafted and sent thousands of miles from home, in many cases to fight and die in a war that they did not believe in. There was an antiwar movement dividing our nation. In the end, America pulled our forces out. More than 56,000 Americans died in Vietnam after one President died in Dallas.

As for the question, *who killed President Kennedy?* . . . The truth may never be known, for the truth is buried with the dead witnesses.

Notes

1.   *The Plot to Kill JFK: Rush to Judgment*, a film by Emile de Antonio and Mark Lane, MPII Home Video, 1988.

2.   Lane, Mark. *A Citizen's Dissent: Mark Lane Replies*. (NY: Fawcett Crest, 1968) 234.

3.   David S. Lifton, *Best Evidence* (NY: Macmillan, 1980) 389.

4.   *President Commission on the Assassination of President Kennedy* (Washington, DC, U. S. Government Printing Office, 1964).

5.   *The Plot*.

6.   Robert J. Groden, *The Killing of a President* (NY: Penguin Group, 1993) 125.

7.   Charles A. Crenshaw, M.D. with Jens Hansen and Gary Shaw, *JFK: Conspiracy of Silence* (NY: Penguin Group, 1992) backpage.

8.   *Two Men in Dallas*, a film by Mark Lane, Tapeworm Video Distributors, 1987.

9.   Mark Lane, *Rush To Judgment* (NY: Thunder's Mouth P, 1992) 409 (Witzman Affidavit).

10.   *Two Men*. Carle interview.

11.   Craig Roberts and John Armstrong, *JFK: The Dead Witnesses* (NY: Consolidated P International, 1995 iii-vii.

12.   Roberts 33.

13.   *The Plot*, Aquilia Clemmons interview.

14.   Groden 73.

15.   Dr. Cyril Wecht, *Cause of Death* (NY: Penguin Group, 1994) 27.

16.   Groden 1.

Critical Thinking

1.   What information does the author use to support his main idea?

2.   What prompted private citizens to research the crime themselves?

3.   Is this written from a subjective or objective viewpoint?

Writing Assignments

1.   Write a comparison/contrast essay comparing what you learned in school about the Kennedy Assassination to the information presented by the author.

2.   Are there any official versions by the government of historical events that you question or disagree with? Respond in detail.

3.   Personal response. Write a response to the essay in the form of a letter to the editor.

"We hold these truths to be self-evident, that all men are created equal, that they are endowed by their creator with certain unalienable rights, that among these are life, liberty and the pursuit of happiness."

--Thomas Jefferson, Declaration of Independence (July 4, 1776)

"Letter from Birmingham Jail"[*]
Martin Luther King, Jr.

Martin Luther King, Jr., was a highly charismatic and recognized leader in the Civil Rights Movement. He received many honorary degrees and awards, including the Nobel Peace Prize in 1964. He was a champion for freedom, peace and brotherhood. In 1963, Time magazine named him Man of the Year. His "Letter from Birmingham Jail" is from The Autobiography of Martin Luther King, Jr. Unfortunately, he was assassinated on April 4, 1968.[†]

April 12, 1963—White Birmingham ministers write to King calling for end of demonstrations.

April 16—King writes letter of response.

I will never forget that one morning, I think the next morning after I was placed in the cell in solitary confinement, a newspaper was slipped in to me. I turned it over and found a kind of advertisement that had been placed there, taken out by eight clergyman of all of the major religious faiths in our nation. They

---

[*] Reprinted by arrangement with the Estate of Martin Luther King Jr., c/o Writers House as agent for the proprietor. Copyright Martin Luther King 1963, copyright renewed 1991 Coretta Scott King.
[†] "Martin Luther King, Jr.." Louisiana State University, Selected Reference Resources, no. 218, Mitchell Brown, Compiler. <http://www.lib.lsu.edu/hum.mlk/srs218.html>.

were criticizing our demonstrations. They were calling us extremists. They were calling us law breakers and believers in anarchy and all of these things. And when I read it, I became so concerned and even upset and at points so righteously indignant that I decided to answer the letter.

My response to the published statement by eight fellow clergymen from Alabama (Bishop C. C. J. Carpenter, Bishop Joseph A. Durick, Rabbi Milton L. Grafman, Bishop Paul Hardin, Bishop Nolan B. Harmon, the Reverend George M. Murray, the Reverend Edward V. Ramage, and the Reverend Earl Stallings) was composed under somewhat constricting circumstances. I didn't have anything at my disposal like a pad or writing paper. Begun on the margins of the newspaper in which the statement appeared, the letter was continued on scraps of writing paper supplied by a friendly Negro trusty, and concluded on a pad my attorneys were eventually permitted to leave me. I was able to slip it out of the jail to one of my assistants through the lawyer.

were not allowed to write

April 16, 1963

MY DEAR FELLOW CLERGYMEN: → _opposing view refers to them with respect._

While confined here in the Birmingham city jail, I came across your recent statement calling my present activities "unwise and untimely." Seldom do I pause to answer criticism of my work and ideas. If I sought to answer all the criticisms that cross my desk, my secretaries would have little time for anything other than such correspondence in the course of the day, and I would have no time for constructive work. But since I feel that you are men of genuine goodwill and that your criticisms are sincerely set forth, I want to try to answer your statements in what I hope will be patient and reasonable terms.

polite

I think I should indicate why I am here in Birmingham, since you have been influenced by the view which argues against "outsiders coming in." I have the honor of serving as president of the Southern Christian Leadership Conference, an organization operating in every Southern state, with headquarters in Atlanta, Georgia. We have some eighty-five affiliated organizations across the South, and one of them is the Alabama Christian Movement for Human Rights. Frequently we share staff, educational and financial resources with our affiliates. Several months ago the affiliate here in Birmingham asked us to be on call to engage in a nonviolent direct-action program if such were deemed necessary. We readily consented, and when the hour came we lived up to our promise. So I,

opposing view of "outsider"

re stands for what he believes

along with several members of my staff, am here because I was invited here. I am here because I have organizational ties here.

But more basically, I am in Birmingham because injustice is here. Just as the prophets of the eighth century B.C. left their villages and carried their "thus saith the Lord" far beyond the boundaries of their hometowns, and just as the Apostle Paul left his village of Tarsus and carried the gospel of Jesus Christ to the far corners of the Greco-Roman world, so am I compelled to carry the gospel of freedom beyond my own hometown. Like Paul, I must constantly respond to the Macedonian call for aid.

Moreover, I am cognizant of the interrelatedness of all communities and states. I cannot sit idly by in Atlanta and not be concerned about what happens in Birmingham. Injustice anywhere is a threat to justice everywhere. We are caught in an inescapable network of mutuality, tied in a single garment of destiny. Whatever affects one directly, affects all indirectly. Never again can we afford to live with the narrow, provincial "outside agitator" idea. Anyone who lives inside the United States can never be considered an outsider anywhere within its bounds.

You deplore the demonstrations taking place in Birmingham. But your statement, I am sorry to say, fails to express a similar concern for the conditions that brought about the demonstrations. I am sure that none of you would want to rest content with the superficial kind of social analysis that deals merely with effects and does not grapple with underlying causes. It is unfortunate that demonstrations are taking place in Birmingham, but it is even more unfortunate that the city's white power structure left the Negro community with no alternative.

In any nonviolent campaign there are four basic steps: collection of the facts to determine whether injustices exist; negotiation; self-purification; and direct action. We have gone through all these steps in Birmingham. There can be no gain saying the fact that racial injustice engulfs this community. Birmingham is probably the most thoroughly segregated city in the United States. Its ugly record of brutality is widely known. Negroes have experienced grossly unjust treatment in the courts. There have been more unsolved bombings of Negro homes and churches in Birmingham than in any other city in the nation. These are the hard, brutal facts of the case. On the basis of these conditions, Negro leaders sought to negotiate with the city fathers. But the latter consistently refused to engage in good-faith negotiation.

Then, last September, came the opportunity to talk with leaders of Birmingham's economic community. In the course of the negotiations, certain promises were made by the merchants—for example, to remove the stores' humiliating racial signs. On the basis of these promises, the Reverend Fred Shuttlesworth and the leaders of the Alabama Christian Movement for Human Rights agreed to a moratorium on all demonstrations. As the weeks and months went by, we realized that we were the victims of a broken promise. A few signs, briefly removed, returned; the others remained.

As in so many past experiences, our hopes had been blasted, and the shadow of deep disappointment settled upon us. We had no alternative except to prepare for direct action, whereby we would present our very bodies as a means of laying our case before the conscience of the local and the national community. Mindful of the difficulties involved, we decided to undertake a process of self-purification. We began a series of workshops on nonviolence, and we repeatedly asked ourselves: "Are you able to accept blows without retaliating?" "Are you able to endure the ordeal of jail?" We decided to schedule our direct-action program for the Easter season, realizing that except for Christmas, this is the main shopping period of the year. Knowing that a strong economic-withdrawal program would be the by-product of direct action, we felt that this would be the best time to bring pressure to bear on the merchants for the needed change.

Then it occurred to us that Birmingham's mayoralty election was coming up in March, and we speedily decided to postpone action until after election day. When we discovered that the commissioner of public safety, Eugene "Bull" Connor, had piled up enough votes to be in the run-off, we decided again to postpone action until the day after the run-off so that the demonstrations could not be used to cloud the issues. Like many others, we waited to see Mr. Connor defeated, and to this end we endured postponement after postponement. Having aided in this community need, we felt that our direct-action program could be delayed no longer.

You may well ask: "Why direct action? Why sit-ins, marches, and so forth? Isn't a negotiation a better path?" You are quite right in calling for negotiation. Indeed, this is the very purpose of direct action. Nonviolent direct action seeks to create such a crisis and foster such a tension that a community which has constantly refused to negotiate is forced to confront the issue. It seeks to dramatize the issue so that it can no longer be ignored. My citing the creation of tension as part of the work of the nonviolent resister may sound rather shocking. But I must confess that I am not afraid of the word "tension." I have earnestly opposed violent tension, but there is a type of constructive, nonviolent tension which is necessary for growth. Just as Socrates felt that it was necessary to create a tension in the mind so that individuals could rise from the bondage of myths and half-truths to the unfettered realm of creative analysis and objective appraisal, so must we see the need for nonviolent gadflies to create the kind of tension in society that will help men rise from the dark depths of prejudice and racism to the majestic heights of understanding and brotherhood.

The purpose of our direct-action program is to create a situation so crisis-packed that it will inevitably open the door to negotiation. I therefore concur with you in your call for negotiation. Too long has our beloved Southland been bogged down in a tragic effort to live in monologue rather than dialogue.

One of the basic points in your statement is that the action that I and my associates have taken in Birmingham is untimely. Some have asked: "Why didn't you give the new city administration time to act?" The only answer that I can give to this query is that the new Birmingham administration must be prodded about as much as the outgoing one, before it will act. We are sadly mistaken if we feel that the election of Albert Boutwell as mayor will bring the millennium to Birmingham. While Mr. Boutwell is a much more gentle person than Mr. Connor, they are both segregationists, dedicated to maintenance of the status quo. I have hope that Mr. Boutwell will be reasonable enough to see the futility of massive resistance to desegregation. But he will not see this without pressure from devotees of civil rights. My friends, I must say to you that we have not made a single gain in civil rights without determined legal and nonviolent pressure. Lamentably, it is an historical fact that privileged groups seldom give up their privileges voluntarily. Individuals may see the moral light and voluntarily give up their unjust posture; but, as Reinhold Neibuhr has reminded us, groups tend to be more immoral than individuals.

We know through painful experience that freedom is never voluntarily given by the oppressor; it must be demanded by the oppressed. Frankly, I have yet to engage in a direct-action campaign that was "well timed" in the view of those who have not suffered unduly from the disease of segregation. For years now I have heard the word "Wait!" It rings in the ear of every Negro with piercing familiarity. This "Wait" has almost always meant "Never." We must come to see, with one of our distinguished jurists, that "justice too long delayed is justice denied."

    We have waited for more than 340 years for our constitutional and God-given rights. The nations of Asia and Africa are moving with jet-like speed toward gaining political independence, but we still creep at horse-and-buggy pace toward gaining a cup of coffee at a lunch counter. Perhaps it is easy for those who have never felt the stinging darts of segregation to say, "Wait." But when you have seen vicious mobs lynch your mothers and fathers at will and drown your sisters and brothers at whim; when you have seen hate-filled policemen curse, kick, and even kill your black brothers and sisters; when you see the vast majority of your twenty million Negro brothers smothering in an airtight cage of poverty in the midst of an affluent society; when you suddenly find your tongue twisted and your speech stammering as you seek to explain to your six-year-old daughter why she can't go to the public amusement park that has just been advertised on television, and see tears welling up in her eyes when she is told that Funtown is closed to colored children, and see ominous clouds of inferiority beginning to form in her little mental sky, and see her beginning to distort her personality by developing an unconscious bitterness toward white people; when you have to concoct an answer for a five-year-old son who is asking: "Daddy, why do white people treat colored people so mean?"; when you take a cross-county drive and find it necessary to sleep night after night in the uncomfortable corners of your automobile because no motel will accept you; when you are humiliated day in and day out by nagging signs reading "white" and "colored"; when your first name becomes "nigger," your middle names becomes "boy" (however old you are), and your last name becomes "John," and your wife and mother are never given the respected title "Mrs."; when you are harried by day and haunted by night by the fact that you are a Negro, living constantly at tiptoe stance, never quite knowing what to expect next, and are plagued with inner fears and outer resentments; when you are forever fighting a degenerating sense of "nobodiness"—then you will understand why we find it difficult to wait. There comes a time when the cup of endurance runs over, and men are no longer willing to be plunged into the abyss of despair. I hope, sirs, you can understand our legitimate and unavoidable impatience.

    You express a great deal of anxiety over our willingness to break laws. This is certainly a legitimate concern. Since we so diligently urge people to obey the Supreme Court's decision of 1954 outlawing segregation in the public schools, at first glance it may seem rather paradoxical for us consciously to break laws. One may well ask: "How can you advocate breaking some laws and obeying others?" The answer lies in the fact that there are two types of laws: just and unjust. I would be the first to advocate obeying just laws. One has not only a legal but a moral responsibility to obey just laws. Conversely, one has a moral responsibility to disobey unjust laws. I would agree with St. Augustine that "an unjust law is no law at all."

Now, what is the difference between the two? How does one determine whether a law is just or unjust? A just law is a man-made code that squares with the moral law or the law of God. An unjust law is a code that is out of harmony with the moral law. To put it in the terms of Saint Thomas Aquinas: an unjust law is a human law that is not rooted in eternal and natural law. Any law that uplifts human personality is just. Any law that degrades human personality is unjust. All segregation statutes are unjust because segregation distorts the soul and damages the personality. It gives the segregator a false sense of superiority and the segregated a false sense of inferiority. Segregation, to use the terminology of the Jewish philosopher Martin Buber, substitutes an "I—it" relationship for an "I—thou" relationship and ends up relegating persons to the status of things. Hence segregation is not only politically, economically, and sociologically unsound, it is morally wrong and sinful. Paul Tillich has said that sin is separation. Is not segregation an existential expression of man's tragic separation, his awful estrangement, his terrible sinfulness? Thus it is that I can urge men to obey the 1954 decision of the Supreme Court, for it is morally right; and I can urge them to disobey segregation ordinances, for they are morally wrong.

Let us consider a more concrete example of just and unjust laws. An unjust law is a code that a numerical or power majority group compels a minority group to obey but does not make binding on itself. This is *difference* made legal. By the same token, a just law is a code that a majority compels a minority to follow that it is willing to follow itself. This is *sameness* made legal.

Let me give another explanation. A law is unjust if it is inflicted on a minority that, as a result of being denied the right to vote, had no part in enacting or devising the law. Who can say that the legislature of Alabama which set up that state's segregation laws was democratically elected? Throughout Alabama all sorts of devious methods are used to prevent Negroes from becoming registered voters, and there are some counties in which, even though Negroes constitute a majority of the population, not a single Negro is registered. Can any law enacted under such circumstances be considered democratically structured?

Sometimes a law is just on its face and unjust in its application. For instance, I have been arrested on a charge of parading without a permit. Now, there is nothing wrong in having an ordinance which requires a permit for a parade. But such an ordinance becomes unjust when it is used to maintain segregation and to deny citizens the First Amendment privilege of peaceful assembly and protest.

I hope you are able to see the distinction I am trying to point out. In no sense do I advocate evading or defying the law, as would the rabid segregationist. That would lead to anarchy. One who breaks an unjust law must do so openly, lovingly, and with a willingness to accept the penalty. I submit that an individual who breaks a law that conscience tells him is unjust, and who willingly accepts the penalty of imprisonment in order to arouse the conscience of the community over its injustice, is in reality expressing the highest respect for law.

Of course, there is nothing new about this kind of civil disobedience. It was evidenced sublimely in the refusal of Shadrach, Meshach, and Abednego to obey the laws of Nebuchadnezzar, on the ground that a higher moral law was at stake. It was practiced superbly by the early Christians, who were willing to face hungry lions and the excruciating pain of chopping blocks rather than submit to certain unjust laws of the Roman Empire. To a degree, academic freedom is a reality today because Socrates practiced civil disobedience. In our own nation, the Boston Tea Party represented a massive act of civil disobedience.

We should never forget that everything Adolf Hitler did in Germany was "legal" and everything the Hungarian freedom fighters did in Hungary was "illegal." It was "illegal" to aid and comfort a Jew in Hitler's Germany. Even so, I am sure that, had I lived in Germany at the time, I would have aided and comforted my Jewish brothers. If today I lived in a Communist country where certain principles dear to the Christian faith are suppressed, I would openly advocate disobeying that country's antireligious laws.

I must make two honest confessions to you, my Christian and Jewish brothers. First, I must confess that over the past few years I have been gravely disappointed with the white moderate. I have almost reached the regrettable conclusion that the Negro's great stumbling block in his stride toward freedom is not the White Citizen's Councilor or the Ku Klux Klanner, but the white moderate, who is more devoted to "order" than to justice; who prefers a negative peace which is the absence of tension to a positive peace which is the presence of justice; who constantly says: "I agree with you in the goal you seek, but I cannot agree with your methods of direct action"; who paternalistically believes he can set the timetable for another man's freedom; who lives by a mythical concept of time and who constantly advises the Negro to wait for a "more convenient season." Shallow understanding from people of good will is more frustrating than absolute misunderstanding from people of ill will. Lukewarm acceptance is much more bewildering than outright rejection.

I had hoped that the white moderate would understand that law and order exist for the purpose of establishing justice and that when they fail in this purpose they become the dangerously structured dams that block the flow of social progress. I had hoped that the white moderate would understand that the present tension in the South is a necessary phase of the transition from an obnoxious negative peace, in which the Negro passively accepted his unjust plight, to a substantive and positive peace, in which all men will respect the dignity and worth of human personality. Actually, we who engage in nonviolent direct action are not the creators of tension. We merely bring to the surface the hidden tension that is already alive. We bring it out in the open, where it can be seen and dealt with. Like a boil that can never be cured so long as it is covered up but must be opened with all its ugliness to the natural medicines of air and light, injustice must be exposed, with all the tension its exposure creates, to the light of human conscience and the air of national opinion before it can be cured.

In your statement you assert that our actions, even though peaceful, must be condemned because they precipitate violence. But is this a logical assertion? Isn't this like condemning a robbed man because his possession of money precipitated the evil act of robbery? Isn't this like condemning Socrates because his unswerving commitment to truth and his philosophical inquiries precipitated the act by the misguided populace in which they made him drink hemlock? Isn't this like condemning Jesus because his unique God-consciousness and never-ceasing devotion to God's will precipitated the evil act of crucifixion? We must come to see that, as the federal courts have consistently affirmed, it is wrong to urge an individual to cease his efforts to gain his basic constitutional rights because the quest may precipitate violence. Society must protect the robbed and punish the robber.

I had also hoped that the white moderate would reject the myth concerning time in relation to the struggle for freedom. I have just received a letter from a white brother in Texas. He writes: "All Christians know that the colored people will receive equal rights eventually, but it is possible that you are in too great a religious hurry. It has taken Christianity almost two thousand years to accomplish what it has. The teachings of Christ take time to come to earth." Such an attitude stems from a tragic misconception of time, from the strangely irrational notion that there is something in the very flow of time that will inevitably cure all ills. Actually, time itself is neutral; it can be used either destructively or constructively. More and more I feel that the people of ill will have used time much more effectively than have the people of good will. We will have to repent in this generation not merely for the hateful words and actions of the bad people but for the appalling silence of the good people. Human progress never rolls in on wheels of inevitability; it comes through the tireless efforts of men willing to be co-workers with God, and without this hard work, time itself becomes an ally of the forces of social stagnation. We must use time creatively, in the knowledge that the time is always ripe to do right. Now is the time to make real the promise of democracy and transform our pending national elegy into a creative psalm of brotherhood. Now is the time to lift our national policy from the quicksand of racial injustice to the solid rock of human dignity.

You speak of our activity in Birmingham as extreme. At first I was rather disappointed that fellow clergymen would see my nonviolent efforts as those of an extremist. I began thinking about the fact that I stand in the middle of two opposing forces in the Negro community. One is a force of complacency, made up in part of Negroes who, as a result of long years of oppression, are so drained of self-respect and a sense of "somebodiness" that they have adjusted to segregation; and in part of a few middle-class Negroes who, because of a degree of academic and economic security and because in some ways they profit by segregation, have become insensitive to the problems of the masses. The other force is one of bitterness and hatred, and it comes perilously close to advocating violence. It is expressed in the various black nationalist groups that are springing up across the nation, the largest and best known being Elijah Muhammed's Muslim movement. Nourished by the Negro's frustration over the continued existence of racial discrimination, this movement is made up of people who have lost faith in America, who have absolutely repudiated Christianity, and who have concluded that the white man is an incorrigible "devil."

I have tried to stand between these two forces, saying that we need emulate neither the "do-nothingism" of the complacent nor the hatred and despair of the black nationalist.   For there is the more excellent way of love and nonviolent protest. I am grateful to God that, through the influence of the Negro church, the way of nonviolence became an integral part of our struggle.

If this philosophy had not emerged, by now many streets of the South would, I am convinced, be flowing with blood. And I am further convinced that if our white brothers dismiss as "rabble-rousers" and "outside agitators" those of us who employ nonviolent direct action, and if they refuse to support our nonviolent efforts, millions of Negroes will, out of frustration and despair, seek solace and security in black nationalist ideologies—a development that would inevitably lead to a frightening racial nightmare.

Oppressed people cannot remain oppressed forever. The yearning for freedom eventually manifests itself, and that is what has happened to the American Negro.   Something within has reminded him of his birthright of freedom, and something without has reminded him that it can be gained. Consciously or unconsciously, he has been caught up by the Zeitgeist, and with his black brothers of Africa and his brown and yellow brothers of Asia, South America, and the Caribbean, the United States Negro is moving with a sense of great urgency toward the promised land of racial justice. If one recognizes this vital urge that has engulfed the Negro community, one should readily understand why public demonstrations are taking place.   The Negro has many pent-up resentments and latent frustrations, and he must release them. So let him march; let him make prayer pilgrimages to the city hall; let him go on freedom rides— and try to understand why he must do so. If his repressed emotions are not released in nonviolent ways, they will seek expression through violence; this is not a threat but a fact of history. So I have not said to my people: "Get rid of your discontent."   Rather, I have tried to say that this normal and healthy discontent can be channeled into the creative outlet of nonviolent direct action. And now this approach is being termed extremist.

But though I was initially disappointed at being categorized as an extremist, as I continued to think about the matter I gradually gained a measure of satisfaction from the label. Was not Jesus an extremist for love: "Love your enemies, bless them that curse you, do good to them that hate you, and pray for them which despitefully use you, and persecute you."   Was not Amos an extremist for justice: "Let justice roll down like waters and righteousness like an ever-flowing stream." Was not Paul an extremist for the Christian gospel: "I bear in my body the marks of the Lord Jesus." Was not Martin Luther an extremist: "Here I stand; I cannot do otherwise, so help me God." And John Bunyan: "I will stay in jail to the end of my days before I make a butchery of my conscience." And Abraham Lincoln: "This nation cannot survive half slave and half free." And Thomas Jefferson: "We hold these truths to be self-evident, that all men are created equal . . . "   So the question is not whether we will be extremists, but what kind of extremists we will be. Will we be extremists for hate or for love? Will we be extremists for the preservation of injustice or for the extension of justice? In that dramatic scene on Calvary's hill three men were crucified. We must never forget that all three were crucified for the same crime—the crime of extremism. Two were extremists for immorality, and thus fell below their environment. The other, Jesus Christ, was an extremist for love, truth, and goodness, and thereby rose above his environment. Perhaps, the South, the nation, and the world are in dire need of creative extremists.

I had hoped that the white moderate would see this need. Perhaps I was too optimistic; perhaps I expected too much. I suppose I should have realized that few members of the oppressor race can understand the deep groans and passionate yearnings of the oppressed race, and still fewer have the vision to see that injustice must be rooted out by strong, persistent, and determined action. I am thankful, however, that some of our white brothers in the South have grasped the meaning of this social revolution and committed themselves to it. They are still too few in quantity, but they are big in quality. Some—such as Ralph McGill, Lillian Smith, Harry Golden, James McBride Dabbs, Ann Braden, and Sarah Patten Boyle—have written about our struggle in eloquent and prophetic terms. Others have marched with us down nameless streets of the South. They have languished in filthy, roach-infested jails, suffering the abuse and brutality of policemen who view them as "dirty nigger lovers." Unlike so many of their moderate brothers and sisters, they have recognized the urgency of the moment and sensed the need for powerful "action" antidotes to combat the disease of segregation.

Let me take note of my other major disappointment. I have been so greatly disappointed with the white church and its leadership. Of course, there are some notable exceptions. I am not unmindful of the fact that each of you has taken some significant stands on this issue. I commend you, Reverend Stallings, for your Christian stand on this past Sunday, in welcoming Negroes to your worship service on a nonsegregated basis. I commend the Catholic leaders of this state for integrating Spring Hill College several years ago.

But despite these notable exceptions, I must honestly reiterate that I have been disappointed with the church. I do not say this as one of those negative critics who can always find something wrong with the church. I say this as a minister of the gospel, who loves the church; who was nurtured in its bosom; who has been sustained by its spiritual blessings and who will remain true to it as long as the cord of life shall lengthen.

When I was suddenly catapulted into the leadership of the bus protest in Montgomery, Alabama, a few years ago, I felt we would be supported by the white church. I felt that the white ministers, priests and rabbis of the South would be among our strongest allies. Instead, some have been outright opponents, refusing to understand the freedom movement and misrepresenting its leaders; all too many others have been more cautious than courageous and have remained silent behind the anesthetizing security of stained-glass windows.

In spite of my shattered dreams, I came to Birmingham with the hope that the white religious leadership of this community would see the justice of our cause and, with deep moral concern, would serve as the channel through which our just grievances could reach the power structure. I had hoped that each of you would understand. But again I have been disappointed.

I have heard numerous Southern religious leaders admonish their worshipers to comply with a desegregation decision because it is the law, but I have longed to hear white ministers declare: "Follow this decree because integration is morally right and because the Negro is your brother." In the midst of blatant injustices inflicted upon the Negro, I have watched white churchmen stand on the sideline and mouth pious irrelevancies and sanctimonious trivialities. In the midst of a mighty struggle to rid our nation of racial and economic injustice, I have heard many ministers say: "Those are social issues, with which the gospel has no real concern." And I have watched many churches commit themselves to a completely otherworldly religion which makes a strange, un-Biblical distinction between body and soul, between the sacred and the secular.

I have traveled the length and breadth of Alabama, Mississippi, and all the other Southern states. On sweltering summer days and crisp autumn mornings I have looked at the South's beautiful churches with their lofty spires pointing heavenward. I have beheld the impressive outlines of her massive religious-education buildings. Over and over I have found myself asking: "What kind of people worship here? Who is their God? Where were their voices when the lips of Governor Barnett dripped with words of interposition and nullification? Where were they when Governor Wallace gave a clarion call for defiance and hatred? Where were their voices of support when bruised and weary Negro men and women decided to rise from the dark dungeons of complacency to the bright hills of creative protest?"

Yes, these questions are still in my mind. In deep disappointment I have wept over the laxity of the church. But be assured that my tears have been tears of love. There can be no deep disappointment where there is not deep love. Yes, I love the church. How could I do otherwise? I am in the rather unique position of being the son, the grandson, and the great-grandson of preachers. Yes, I see the church as the body of Christ. But, oh! How we have blemished and scarred that body through social neglect and through fear of being nonconformists.

There was a time when the church was very powerful—in the time when the early Christians rejoiced at being deemed worthy to suffer for what they believed. In those days the church was not merely a thermometer that recorded the ideas and principles of popular opinion; it was a thermostat that transformed the mores of society. Whenever the early Christians entered a town, the people in power became disturbed and immediately sought to convict the Christians for being "disturbers of the peace" and "outside agitators." But the Christians pressed on, in the conviction that they were "a colony of heaven," called to obey God rather than man. Small in number, they were big in commitment. They were too God-intoxicated to be "astronomically intimidated." By their effort and example they brought an end to such ancient evils as infanticide and gladiatorial contests.

Things are different now. So often the contemporary church is a weak, ineffectual voice with an uncertain sound. So often it is an arch-defender of the status quo. Far from being disturbed by the presence of the church, the power structure of the average community is consoled by the church's silent—and often even vocal—sanction of things as they are.

But the judgment of God is upon the church as never before. If today's church does not recapture the sacrificial spirit of the early church, it will lose its authenticity, forfeit the loyalty of millions, and be dismissed as an irrelevant social club with no meaning for the twentieth century. Every day I meet young people whose disappointment with the church has turned into outright disgust.

Perhaps I have once again been too optimistic. Is organized religion too inextricably bound to the status quo to save our nation and the world? Perhaps I must turn my faith to the inner spiritual church, the church within the church, as the true ecclesia and the hope of the world. But again I am thankful to God that some noble souls from the ranks of organized religion have broken loose from the paralyzing chains of conformity and joined us as active partners in the struggle for freedom. They have left their secure congregations and walked the streets of Albany, Georgia, with us. They have gone down the highways of the South on tortuous rides for freedom. Yes, they have gone to jail with us. Some have been dismissed from their churches, have lost the support of their bishops and fellow ministers. But they have acted in the faith that right defeated is stronger than evil triumphant. Their witness has been the spiritual salt that has preserved the true meaning of the gospel in these troubled times. They have carved a tunnel of hope through the dark mountain of disappointment.

I hope the church as a whole will meet the challenge of this decisive hour. But even if the church does not come to the aid of justice, I have no despair about the future. I have no fear about the outcome of our struggle in Birmingham, even if our motives are at present misunderstood. We will reach the goal of freedom in Birmingham and all over the nation, because the goal of America is freedom. Abused and scorned though we may be, our destiny is tied up with America's destiny. Before the pilgrims landed at Plymouth, we were here. Before the pen of Jefferson etched the majestic words of the Declaration of Independence across the pages of history, we were here. For more than two centuries our forebears labored in this country without wages; they made cotton king; they built the homes of their masters while suffering gross injustice and shameful humiliation— and yet out of a bottomless vitality they continued to thrive and develop. If the inexpressible cruelties of slavery could not stop us, the opposition we now face will surely fail. We will win our freedom because the sacred heritage of our nation and the eternal will of God are embodied in our echoing demands.

Before closing I feel impelled to mention one other point in your statement that has troubled me profoundly. (You warmly commended the Birmingham police force for keeping "order" and "preventing violence." I doubt that you would have so warmly commended the police force if you had seen its dogs sinking their teeth into unarmed, nonviolent Negroes. I doubt that you would so quickly commend the policemen if you were to observe their ugly and inhumane treatment of Negroes here in the city jail; if you were to watch them push and curse old Negro women and young Negro girls; if you were to see them slap and kick old Negro men and young boys; if you were to observe them, as they did on two occasions, refuse to give us food because we wanted to sing our grace together. I cannot join you in your praise of the Birmingham police department.

It is true that the police have exercised a degree of discipline in handling the demonstrators.   In this sense they have conducted themselves rather "nonviolently" in public. But for what purpose? To preserve the evil system of segregation.   Over the past few years I have consistently preached that nonviolence demands that the means we use must be as pure as the ends we seek. I have tried to make clear that it is wrong to use immoral means to attain moral ends. But now I must affirm that it is just as wrong, or perhaps even more so, to use moral means to preserve immoral ends.   Perhaps Mr. Connor and his policemen have been rather nonviolent in public, as was Chief Pritchett in Albany, Georgia, but they have used the moral means of nonviolence to maintain the immoral end of racial injustice. As T. S. Eliot has said: "The last temptation is the greatest treason: To do the right deed for the wrong reason."

I wish you had commended the Negro sit-inners and demonstrators of Birmingham for their sublime courage, their willingness to suffer, and their amazing discipline in the midst of great provocation.   One day the South will recognize its real heroes. They will be the James Merediths, with the noble sense of purpose that enables them to face jeering and hostile mobs, and with the agonizing loneliness that characterizes the life of the pioneer. They will be old, oppressed, battered Negro women, symbolized in a seventy-two-year-old woman in Montgomery, Alabama, who rose up with a sense of dignity and with her people decided not to ride segregated buses, and who responded with ungrammatical profundity to one who inquired about her weariness: "My feets is tired, but my soul is at rest."   They will be the young high school and college students, the young ministers of the gospel and a host of their elders, courageously and nonviolently sitting in at lunch counters and willingly going to jail for conscience's sake.   One day the South will know that when these disinherited children of God sat down at lunch counters, they were in reality standing up for what is best in the American dream and for the most sacred values in our Judeo-Christian heritage, thereby bringing our nation back to those great wells of democracy which were dug deep by the founding fathers in their formulation of the Constitution and the Declaration of Independence.

Never before have I written so long a letter.   I'm afraid it is much too long to take your precious time.   I can assure you that it would have been much shorter if I had been writing from a comfortable desk, but what else can one do when he is alone in a narrow jail cell, other than write long letters, think long thoughts, and pray long prayers?

If I have said anything in this letter that overstates the truth and indicates an unreasonable impatience, I beg you to forgive me.   If I have said anything that understates the truth and indicates my having a patience that allows me to settle for anything less than brotherhood, I beg God to forgive me.

I hope this letter finds you strong in the faith.   I also hope that circumstances will soon make it possible for me to meet each of you, not as an integrationist or a civil rights leader but as a fellow clergyman and a Christian brother.   Let us all hope that the dark clouds of racial prejudice will soon pass away and the deep fog of misunderstanding will be lifted from our fear-drenched communities, and in some not too distant tomorrow the radiant stars of love and brotherhood will shine over our great nation with all their scintillating beauty.

Yours for the cause of Peace and Brotherhood,

Martin Luther King, Jr.

Critical Thinking

1.   What is Martin Luther King, Jr.'s purpose in writing this letter?   Consider to whom it is addressed.

2.   What are the allegations against King?   Where in the text does King respond to the allegations?   Write a brief outline of the key points King makes.   Is he persuasive?

3.   Explain King's statement, "Injustice anywhere is a threat to justice everywhere."

Writing Assignments

1.   Write an essay about the effectiveness or ineffectiveness of King's campaign.

2.   Go to the library or video store and rent a documentary on the life of Martin Luther King, Jr. Write a one page response.

3.   In what ways do the ideas in this essay apply to oppressed people around the world?

RELATING THE AUTHORS' IDEAS

1.   Write a comparison and/or contrast essay about the injustices in any two essays in this chapter.

2.   How do you think Martin Luther King, Jr. would respond to Buckley's essay?

3.   In what context does religion arise in the essays by Koch and King? Explore your reaction(s) to how religion is used. Generally, do you think it is best to avoid religious references in writing essays? Why or why not?

4.   President Kennedy and Martin Luther King, Jr. were great advocates for peace. What can we do, as members of the society, to create a future where we can all live in peace, safety, and brotherhood? Write an essay about your suggestions for creating a better future.

INDEX OF AUTHORS AND TITLES